"Dan Hill's book is a revelation. Marketers have clearly overemphasized the power of rational over emotional factors in their ads, packaging, product design, and sales presentations. We all know that emotions count but we lacked the vocabulary and tools for capturing and quantifying emotional appeals and impacts. Read this book so that your next marketing campaign creates high emotional buy-in."

—Philip Kotler, S.C. Johnson Distinguished Professor of International Marketing, Kellogg School of Management, Northwestern University

"*Emotionomics* leads the global business mindset into a new paradigm—one that demands and rewards sensory and emotional connections between the 21st century corporate entity and its consumers. Dan Hill's expertise guides business in securing the bonds of empathy that will drive commercial growth over the coming years."

—Martin Lindstrom, author of *BRAND sense* and *BRANDchild*

"This is not your dry business tome. Dan's written a modern book for a modern reader—well designed, great content, fascinating subject. It works on your bookshelf or your coffee table."

—Paco Underhill, author of *Why We Buy* and CEO of Envirosell Inc.

"Dan Hill's new book is the most penetrating and playful application of the latest research in the psychology of emotions, human interaction, neuroscience and endocrinology to sales and marketing. Read it—you'll never think about your brand the same again!"

—Professor Richard Boyatzis, Departments of Organizational Behavior and Psychology, Case Western Reserve University, co-author of *Primal Leadership* and *Resonant Leadership*

"Brand magnetism—the ability of a brand to attract and retain consumers in an emotional way—is the secret underlying today's most successful marketing. *Emotionomics* couldn't be more timely, because it forces all Chief Marketing Officers to face the importance of leveraging the "right-brain" marketing advantage: emotional connections with customers that are constantly recharged. Too many companies compete only on the basis of "left-brain" marketing, rationally selling product features. Successful marketing today, however, leverages the "right-brain," too. *Emotionomics* is essential reading for every CMO seeking to secure the sustained loyalty of their customers."

—Jim Schroer, President & CEO, Carlson Marketing Worldwide

"Dan Hill tantalizes us to the very end! He travels along familiar paths to what we are afraid to know and yet knew all along. *Emotionomics* compels us to rethink all old assumptions. It captures the heart of capitalism! We must blend our aspirations, business imagination with our heartfelt intentions to truly engage those we serve. This is a 'must read' for all great leaders and great followers!"

—Juli Ann Reynolds, President & CEO, Tom Peters Company

"*Emotionomics* is a powerful new work that pushes the limits of research into the emotional dynamics that connect brands with people. By using facial movements as an expression of the subconscious, *Emotionomics* captures powerful emotional responses and gives new insights into people's subconscious realities. This book is a must-read for marketers and designers, as it sheds a new light on the ways brands can better fulfill consumers' unspoken desires."

—Marc Gobé, author of *Emotional Branding* and *Brandjam*,
and Chairman and CEO, Desgrippes Gobé

"Dan Hill has cracked the code on how to get deep inside the hearts and minds of today's consumer. *Emotionomics* provides a "radical" approach to the holy grail of business: find out what the customer really wants. He deftly blends the best of the old (rational appeal) with the radically new (emotional connection) to offer businesses an effective way to reframe their products and their marketing. The book itself is visually exciting, simply presented, and well designed. Halleluiah! The heart can no longer be marginalized if you really want to connect to your customer."

—Robyn Waters, author of *The Trendmaster's Guide* and
The Hummer and the Mini: Navigating the Contradictions of the New Trend Landscape

"Every aspiring experience stager must understand how to manipulate—and I mean that in the nicest possible way!—the emotions of its customers. Read *Emotionomics* to learn how to do so in a way they will perceive as authentic. How you market to your customers will never be the same."

—B. Joseph Pine II, co-author of *The Experience Economy* and
Authenticity: What Consumers Really *Want*

"Emotions matter! Long gone are the days when it was enough to help your customers "understand" what you sell, or grasp rationally what it can do for them. On today's increasingly competitive playing field, marketers missing emotional savvy won't be able to keep up. How do you make your customers **care**? And how do you figure out what they really care **about**? Happily, Dan Hill's new science of facial coding can answer these questions; and his compelling examples show how the findings can predict the future **before** you commit your budget. If you're looking to build the success rate of your marketing, communication or hiring decisions—and who isn't?—cancel your meetings until you've read *Emotionomics* cover to cover!"

—Marti Barletta, author of *Marketing to Women*

"Consumers often answer 'yes' when the mean 'no.' *Emotionomics* will help you get emotionally and rationally integrated and finally understood."

—Michael J. Silverstein, author of *Treasure Hunt* and
Senior Vice President with The Boston Consulting Group

"This book is a valuable resource to any marketer who desires to achieve meaningful differentiation through insights their competitors are likely to ignore. Most research methodologies capture basic, surface-level insights. What makes Sensory Logic unique, as you will read in this book, is that they have a method for finding out what really makes people tick emotionally. And that is what drives behavior while people's knee-jerk opinions are the rationalizations. Dan is a rare breed in the research industry, and this book shows why. Reading it will permanently enlighten you to new and better ways of achieving a market-focused business strategy."

—Gregory M. Mather, market research consultant and former market research manager at McDonald's and former director of consumer insights for KPMG

"Hill has given us a clearly written, highly accessible, hands-on guide to how emotions and biology influence the critical relationship with customers."

—Richard Conniff, author of *The Ape in the Corner Office*

"*Emotionomics* is at least 50 years overdue. We now have more details about the emotional dimensions of behavior, but such marketing luminaries as David Ogilvy, Bill Bernbach and Leo Burnett knew over a half a century ago that emotions, not reason, drive consumer behavior. Dan Hill has now made that elephant in the living room unavoidably visible in *Emotionomics*—a marketing book of uncommon depth that is amazingly lucid and brilliantly illustrated."

—David B. Wolfe, co-author of *Firms of Endearment*, principle author of *Ageless Marketing* and president, Wolfe Resources Group

"At last there's a book that makes the connection between consumers' unconscious decision-making (the most important kind) and brands. A must read for enlightened marketers."

—Douglas Atkin, Chief Community Officer, Meetup Inc. and author of *The Culting of Brands: Turn Your Customers into True Believers*

"Dan Hill has created the ultimate resource for the modern business person. The integration of the managerial examples, scholarly research, and unique insights makes this book required reading for anyone wanting to gain an edge in business. The interplay of emotion and decision making is at the forefront of the latest research and theory in academia, and Dan Hill is the first to translate this approach into the realm of commerce and organizations. Everyone will find new ideas in this book and come away well-equipped to deal with the complexities and realities of business today.

—Kathleen D. Vohs, Ph.D., McKnight Land-Grant Professor, Department of Marketing, Carlson School of Management, University of Minnesota, editor of *Do Emotions Help or Hurt Decision Making? A Hedgefoxian Perspective*, and editor of *Self and Relationships: Connecting Intrapersonal and Interpersonal Processes*

"For too long businesses have been crunching numbers when they should have been processing emotions, applying calculators where they would be better served by conscientiousness. Dan Hill's *Emotionomics* cracks the code on the role of emotion in business, front to back, and shows us how to engage our whole brain in business endeavors."

—Mitch Anthony, author of *Selling with Emotional Intelligence* and
Making the Client Connection

"*Emotionomics* is an excellent handbook for academics and marketing practitioners. It equips the reader with tools to understand the complex role that emotions play in evaluation. Notably, it draws on advances in neuroscience and psychology to refresh the reader familiar with these areas, to inform the novice and to persuade the skeptic…overall a book for everyone interested in the fascinating area of emotions. I found the book highly accessible, user-friendly and engaging. It is one of those rare books in which tough concepts have been made accessible to the reader through vivid visuals and lively examples."

—Vanessa Patrick, Ph.D., Professor of Marketing, University of Georgia

"Women drive today's economy, and for them—*everything* about a brand or purchase matters. *Emotionomics* provides the background, research, and insights to help businesses realize that emotional intelligence is a necessity (not a luxury) in our world of abundant choice. Dan Hill knows his stuff."

—Andrea Learned, President of Learned on Women and
co-author of *Don't Think Pink: What Really Makes Women Buy—
and How to Increase Your Share of this Crucial Market*

"Dan Hill has written a book that will be very useful to business practitioners as an introduction to the topic of emotional responses in business situations. Borrowing from a diverse field of subjects such as psychology, neuroscience, behavioral economics, anthropology, etc., Dan has presented a colorful background to the topic of emotional behavior and its consequences in various business applications like branding, advertising, customer service, sales, employee management and customer satisfaction. Researchers will also benefit from reading his treatment of facial coding which holds promise for suitable applications in many business contexts. This is an enjoyable book."

—Arjun Chaudhuri, Rev. Thomas R. Fitzgerald, S.J. Professor of Marketing Chair of the
Marketing Department Charles F. Dolan School of Business, Fairfield University

A profound, practical guide to navigating the emotional dynamics that determine a company's sales and productivity

Step closer to customers and employees, step ahead of competitors. How? First, by acknowledging the say/feel gap: the frequent disconnect between what people say versus how they feel and what they will actually do. Then by adopting a new approach to measure and manage emotions in order to achieve success by ensuring that one's efforts avoid the say/feel gap into which most of the business world falls.

In the tradition of *Blink* and *Emotional Intelligence*, Dan Hill takes a concise, incisive look at how breakthroughs in brain science have mind-opening implications for how companies should be conducting business in the 21st century. Gone is the old consumer and worker model in which appeals to utilitarian benefits alone will carry the day. Instead, making a sensory-emotional connection through superior creativity and empathy becomes the key to winning over those on whom profitability depends.

What can bridge the say/feel gap, exposing the self-justifying rationalizations (intellectual alibis) that often mask people's true, intuitive gut reaction? It's facial coding, a research tool so powerful that both the CIA and FBI rely on it and so universal that, as Charles Darwin first realized, even a person born blind signals feelings to others using the same facial muscle movements.

As the originator and decade-long veteran of applying facial coding to business issues, Hill is uniquely qualified to quantify the extent of the say/feel gap and instruct companies on ways to maximize emotional buy-in. To help readers survive and thrive in today's extraordinarily competitive environment, where advantage now depends on mastering the emotional dynamics that actually drive results, *Emotionomics* comes complete with:

- Emotional strategies for success, using the Emotionomics Matrix™ as a guide

- Specific, tactical action plans ready to be enacted

- Real-life examples from leading companies

- A top-line introduction of how to read faces

- A vast supply of helpful, provocative and, at times, amusing insights about human nature.

EMOTIONOMICS™

EMOTIONOMICS™

DAN HILL

WINNING HEARTS AND MINDS

Adams Business & Professional

ISBN 13: 978-1-59298-182-3
ISBN 10: 1-59298-182-8

Library of Congress Catalog Number: 2007901602

Printed in Canada

First Printing: September 2007

11 10 09 08 07   5 4 3 2 1

Adams Business & Professional is an imprint of the Beaver's Pond Group
7104 Ohms Lane, Suite 216
Edina, MN 55439-2129
(952) 829-8818
www.BeaversPondGroup.com

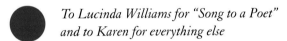 *To Lucinda Williams for "Song to a Poet"
and to Karen for everything else*

contents

For far too long, emotions have been concealed behind closed doors and ignored in favor of rationality and efficiency. But as businesses are forced to forge emotional connections in this age of commoditization, emotions are now front-and-center.

Emotionomics opens this long locked door and shows the importance of leveraging emotions in business.

Breakthroughs in brain science have revealed that people are primarily emotional decision-makers. To help readers capitalize on those scientific findings, this book is two-fold in nature. At a strategic level, the key point is that emotions matter. Emotions are central, not peripheral, to both marketplace and workplace behavior. As a result, companies able to identify, quantify and thereby act on achieving emotional buy-in or acceptance from consumers and employees alike will enjoy a tremendous competitive advantage.

Meanwhile, at a tactical level this book showcases facial coding—the research tool highlighted in Malcolm Gladwell's bestseller, *Blink*—as a means of scientifically gauging emotional response. It's a powerful tool my company, Sensory Logic, Inc., first brought to business applications a decade ago.

Taken together, both the theory and practice of combining psychology, biology and commerce, as shown in this book, can benefit three distinct groups of readers:

- The first group consists of business leaders, creatives (including notably those at advertising agencies and design firms) as well as anybody else in business who has long advocated for the importance of emotional buy-in in achieving business results. For them, this book is meant not only as affirmation or supporting evidence for their views, but also as a source of additional insights.

Gladwell's *Blink* has brought to popular attention the degree to which people make quick, intuitive decisions and how facial coding can be used to reveal them.

- Second, the book is meant to serve those readers who have been noticing the accelerating wealth of brain science and emotion-related articles in mainstream publications. For them, this book represents an opportunity to get up to speed on a topic they find interesting and sense is vital, but haven't had the time to investigate on their own.

- Last but not least, this book is also meant to serve those already in business or about to enter the business world who are looking for that extra edge. In marketplaces where differentiation is ever more crucial and yet harder to achieve, leveraging the centrality of emotions offers a new, largely untapped wealth of information. At the same time, in workplaces, using emotional intelligence to improve the company culture and interactive dynamics can provide a cost-free way to lift productivity.

Facing the Rational/Emotional Split

What's most obviously left to be explained is the title of this book. The first part, *Emotionomics*, is a term I've coined to signal the role of emotions in economics. Its underlying significance, however, is to signal to the business community that measuring and managing emotions is the new strategic playing field on which companies must play well. After all, cost-cutting measures can only go so far. And technological advances will almost inevitably be me-too'ed over time. That leaves making a stronger emotional connection with customers and employees as the key to long-term, sustainable success.

Meanwhile, the subtitle, *Winning Hearts and Minds,* reinforces the fact that achieving a competitive advantage depends on both rational and emotional endorsement from the target market—and that the two are by no means synonymous. If they were, then perhaps words alone would be enough. But because people spin, deflect, hint or hold back from others and even from themselves, everybody's a facial coder. We all intuitively study faces to understand whether the rational explanation being given confirms or is at odds with the emotional response being communicated in any dialogue, presentation, or speech.

> *"A man makes a decision for two reasons—the good reason*
> *and the real reason."*
>
> —J.P. Morgan

In that sense, this book is moreover about lifting what is common, casual practice into a carefully honed business process. Facial coding is essential because ascertaining the truth can be difficult given that J.P. Morgan was right: the *deeper* reasons for our choices aren't the good, rational, defensible ones. In other words, there's a rational/emotional split in all of us, which we're often not consciously aware of, and which makes getting to emotions crucial. The book's familiar subtitle, *Winning Hearts and Minds,* reflects a core reality: without knowing what the other party really feels, it's hard to make progress.

The dilemma posed by the rational/emotional split J.P. Morgan noted is personal. Who among us doesn't want to appear more logical than we actually are? The effort to put up an appearance creates a huge gap between what we feel and what we say, and between what we say and what we actually do. If putting up appearances becomes a habit, we may even create a disconnect between what we think and what we feel.

The dilemma is also corporate wide. Company after company espouses the ruling orthodoxy that feelings are messy, dangerous, inferior and perhaps even irrelevant to day-to-day business. So to one degree or another we end up downplaying the fact that emotions are central to life, and our business planning and outcomes suffer accordingly.

4

This book aims to help readers to understand emotions in terms of business opportunities. Not only do actions speak louder than words, emotions and the motivations linked to them drive those actions. Fortunately, there are ways to navigate and leverage feelings in order to enhance any company's effectiveness and ability to succeed.

Part One of this book will establish the scientific basis for the relevance of emotions and explain how they can now be measured to ensure optimal results. But to start laying the groundwork for why the business world should take emotions seriously, consider a couple of statistics, one from the marketplace and one from the workplace:

- A *Journal of Advertising Research* study, involving 23,000 U.S. consumers, thirteen categories of goods and 240 advertising messages, concluded that "emotions are twice as important as 'facts' in the process by which people make buying decisions" (Morris).

- *Time* magazine's cover story linking emotions and productivity involved a round-up of expert opinion, including the estimate that the emotional happiness present in employees can account for 10% to 25% higher job performance (Thottam).

The Paradigm Shift Awaiting Business

Given statistics like these, one would think the business world would place emotions at the center of decision making. It seems so obvious. What is business if not providing services or products by and for emotionally-driven people? And yet emotional literacy is viewed as mystical, a force few companies have explored and even fewer have constructively managed to interject into their cultures.

Perhaps the root of this bias against emotion can be attributed to a seventeenth-century, French philosopher. In 1667, Rene Descartes famously uttered, "I think, therefore I am." With those brief words the western world's love affair with rationality began.

The results are often nothing but static.

As we'll discuss in Chapter 1, the rational and emotional parts of the brain are distinct separate entities. So think-your-feelings research questions run the risk of being like trying to find an FM station using the AM dial.

Given this cultural legacy, we shouldn't be surprised that business is very adept at, and comfortable with, rational, utilitarian functionality. After all, that basis for evaluation can be measured. By contrast, emotions often go unacknowledged. Or if they are taken into account, emotions are typically accessed through what might be called "think-your-feelings" survey methods that rely on people being able—and willing—to rationally assess and accurately report their emotional responses. In reality, however, people are frequently unable to do so.

From a business point of view, the reason for ignoring emotions has been that, according to the popular view, emotions can't be quantified, segmented and put into a spreadsheet. If emotions can't be measured, they can't be managed. If they can't be managed, they can't be planned for and have no viable role to play in commerce.

In human terms, however, we avoid emotions because we're uncomfortable with them. To evade personal conflict, people bypass talking about sadness, anger and frustration. It's easier to discuss financial yardsticks like returns-on-investment and to simply *be* sad, angry or frustrated. Even more simple is to avoid acknowledging the existence of feelings altogether.

At the root of this behavior lies what French psychologist Claude Rapaille calls the rational or "intellectual alibi." In other words, we invoke the supporting "good reason" J.P. Morgan cited to defend our responses. Thus we rationalize the emotion-based decisions we've already made in our hearts.

Without a method of learning how customers and employees are actually feeling, perhaps the business world has always had a valid point in ignoring emotions. The reluctance of business leaders to deal in a non-measurable medium makes some sense in that, without an accurate measuring tool, emotions can't be strategically anticipated or tactically handled well.

Nevertheless, companies ignore the role of emotions in business at their own peril. After all, emotions affect awareness, consideration, persuasion, recall and loyalty in the marketplace. They also apply to management issues such as performance and retention. The bottom line? It's impossible to escape the role emotional buy-in plays in achieving success.

In *One Size Fits One*, Heil, Parker and Stephens look at why a variety of business initiatives launched during the last two decades didn't achieve all that they might have. In the section "Putting a Face on the Faceless Customer," they observe that companies simply tend:

> to overlook the essential fact that, at its heart, business is a human endeavor where individuals meet, talk, work, and otherwise try to help and benefit one another and that emotions were and are at least as much the currency of exchange, satisfaction, and loyalty as dollars. Messy, elusive, irrational, and difficult to quantify, the emotional component of the value equation has been ignored—and often for these very reasons.

A Scientific Solution

Fortunately, there is now a viable, actionable way to measure emotional responses. This scientific method is known as facial coding. Its roots lie in the observational work of Charles Darwin and it has become well known due to Malcolm Gladwell's extensive account of it in his previously mentioned best-seller *Blink: The Power of Thinking Without Thinking*.

Facial coding enhances traditional research by ensuring the reliability of what subjects are reporting. Facial coding captures a person's emotional buy-in, while verbal input, including verbal responses and ratings, best reflects the person's rationalized intellectual alibi.

When used together to gauge the degree of any target market's buy-in to a product or service, the combination will, if in sync and positive, confirm that the target market is on-board. But if the two sets of data conflict, then a business leader is always wiser to make decisions based on the results of emotional responses because the rational "facts" are malleable, unlike people's emotional gut-reactions.

From its start in 1998, Sensory Logic has led the way in measuring emotional buy-in through the analysis of facial muscle activity. While we'll discuss facial coding in detail in Chapter 2, here's a teaser: the human tendency to express feelings through facial expressions is so stable, ubiquitous and uniform that even a person born blind has the same innate facial expressions as those who can see.

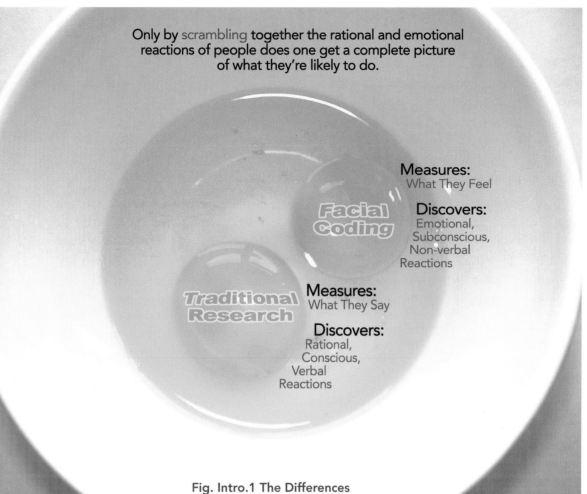

Only by scrambling together the rational and emotional reactions of people does one get a complete picture of what they're likely to do.

Facial Coding

Measures:
What They Feel

Discovers:
Emotional,
Subconscious,
Non-verbal
Reactions

Traditional Research

Measures:
What They Say

Discovers:
Rational,
Conscious,
Verbal
Reactions

Fig. Intro.1 The Differences Between Traditional Research and Facial Coding

The danger of traditional research is that people try to look smart by engaging in intellectual filtering. By adding facial coding to the usual verbal input, companies can learn how people are responding on a more gut-level basis through the correlation of facial expressions and relevant emotions, thereby being better positioned for success.

Two Studies with Different Outcomes

Case #1: Bad Luck

A major cell-phone company creates a humorous TV spot in which an architect demolishes his scale model during a post-presentation meltdown. Unbeknownst to him, his current phone service causes him to miss a call telling him the clients have changed their minds; they now like the building. He finds out, but too late. It's a funny mishap of events. The ad agency's client found the concept amusing and approved production. Filming and editing were completed.

Then the events of September 11th, 2001 happened.

Enter Sensory Logic to conduct the field testing research, the last step necessary before the spot launched. The charts in Figure Intro.2 depict the results of that research. The pie chart on the left shows the positive/negative breakdown of the verbal-rating responses given by subjects participating in the test. Obviously, most people said they liked the commercial.

In contrast, the pie chart on the right reveals the results of research using facial coding. Based on the coding of individual emotional responses, the commercial was in serious trouble.

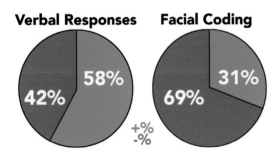

Verbal Responses **Facial Coding**

58% 42% 31% 69%

+%
-%

Fig. Intro.2 Introducing the Say/Feel Gap

Even though over half the subjects gave a positive verbal response to the TV spot involving the architect, less than a third of the emotional response was positive—a nearly 50% drop.

Only a third of the subjects' emotional responses were positive. Most people said they liked the commercial, but our research revealed a large gap between what subjects said about the TV spot and what their facial expressions revealed about how they felt about it. Subjects claimed to like the commercial, but their emotional reactions told us they didn't.

Given the contrasting data, the question becomes: which set of scores makes more sense? Is it the verbal ratings signaling acceptance or the emotional responses indicating resistance to a post 9/11 commercial involving the stylized, violent destruction of a building?

Case #2: Triumph

As Cargill prepared to launch its consulting practice, Sensory Logic was asked to test the campaign's TV spots to gauge their strengths and identify any opportunities for improvement. In this case, the facial coding response was almost twice as positive as it was for the architecture spot—and in range of the strongest responses we've ever measured.

As a result, our role consisted of recommending that already strong commercials could benefit from slightly slower pacing and a little less imagery. In essence, we gave the client and its agency guidance on how to make winners even better. What was the outcome? For the best spot in the campaign, Cargill and its advertising agency, Martin/Williams, won the Creative Excellence in Business Advertising (CEBA) award.

This Book's Theme & Scope

The key concept of this book is that rational reasons alone don't win people over. It's not enough for companies and their leaders to be on-message. In addition, they must be on-emotion, which means being able to connect with consumers and employees by knowing which emotions matter, how they matter and also when exactly they're being invoked.

In the end, a company's profitability depends on how the targeted market internalizes its emotional response to whatever experiences it has regarding that company. Consequently, a company's long-term viability depends on how it shapes, gauges and responds to people's feelings.

Besides sharing cutting-edge research about how, when and why people experience emotions, this book will share insights from a decade of tests involving almost every customer touch point—from products and services to branding and retail environments—as well as about workplace issues. It draws on Sensory Logic's database of over 40,000 comparisons of verbal and nonverbal responses.

"The success of our strategy depends on knowing the rational and emotional drivers that build customer loyalty for a brand."

—Jeff Fettig,
CEO of Whirlpool

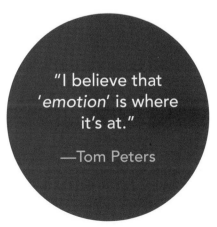

"I believe that 'emotion' is where it's at."

—Tom Peters

10

Part One: Why Emotions Matter—Chapters 1–3

Breakthroughs in brain science show us that emotions drive outcomes. Readers will develop an understanding of of why and how the core emotions deciphered through facial coding are related to the core motivational drivers that lead to action. And they will learn how to incorporate this knowledge into projects through a strategic model: the Emotionomics Matrix.

Part Two: Marketplace Applications—Chapters 4–8

Branding is primarily emotional because it is primarily about trust. But branding is not the only arena in which emotional buy-in generates revenue. Readers will see that from designing an offer to promotion, sales, shopping sites and customer service, it's actually more important (and lucrative) to be on-emotion than on-message alone.

Part Three: Workplace Applications—Chapters 9–10

Given that only 29% of employees report being engaged by their jobs, and 16% are actively disengaged ("Feeling"), it's imperative to create greater emotional as well as intellectual commitment. Employees' feelings will inevitably impact the bottom line. These chapters cover the best means of bringing employees emotionally on-board to lift productivity and increase retention.

Remember the pair of eggs a few pages back?, Well, let's continue that analogy here. *Emotionomics* has three eggs in its basket: 1) Why Emotions Matter, 2) Marketplace Applications and 3) Workplace Applications. By the time readers are finished with all three, they will have acquired the insights necessary to make emotionally informed decisions in all aspects of the business world.

reader's guide & terminology

A fair amount of information will be new to many readers of this book. So I have decided to provide my sources of information both as a form of validation and for people eager to do additional, follow-up study. Those sources appear in parentheses in-text, with a complete listing to be found in the Works Cited section.

Moreover, this book uses terminology readers may not be familiar with or may be seen in a new and different light. Some of it is a result of how my company, Sensory Logic, uniquely approaches business issues. At other times, it may be because of the science and psychology involved. To help get readers oriented, here are some of the key terms present in *Emotionomics*:

Appeal: The degree of positive or negative emotional response (based on facial coding).

Bridge of Consideration: The gap a salesperson tries to get a prospect to cross, using both emotional and rational influence factors to convince the prospect that buying the offer is a safe, smart move.

Commodity Trap: The problem of having the offer regarded by consumers as undistinguished, interchangeable or vulnerable to price pressures. The solution lies in being able to differentiate a product or service in terms of what it does for consumers on a sensory-emotional level, driven at times by superior functionality.

Emotional Response Rate: The measure of response or no response to a given stimulus. Lack of response indicates failure to break through the clutter.

Emotionomics Matrix: An actionable model used in broadening strategic business planning to include not only rational but also the often neglected human factors of emotions and motivations. The model serves as a guide for connecting with the target market so that it cares and buys into the offer or course of action being proposed.

Facial Coding: The analysis of people's emotional response to stimuli, including questions, which is achieved by studying the movement of facial muscles using the system developed by Dr. Paul Ekman.

Feature-itis: A company's tendancy to over-think and over-execute the design of a product, service or experience by including too many, extraneous features.

Fiction: The strongest version of brand equity, which exists in the hearts of consumers based on a brand story they believe in so strongly that it drives preference without regard to utilitarian "facts." In contrast, nonfiction refers to marginal brand equity that relies—not on how the brand makes consumers feel—but on what the branded offer does for them in more limited, functional terms.

Great Chain of Buying: Everything for sale has a chain of longer or shorter length, based on the purchase cycle frequency, and heavier or lighter weight based on the emotional interest or significance with which the purchase is imbued.

Intellectual Alibi: Rational thoughts that are used to justify gut reaction after completion of the decision-making process.

Impact: The degree of intensity or enthusiasm in people's emotional response (based on facial coding).

Message-itis: A company's tendency to attempt to persuade consumers by loading up its advertising with extra, rationally-oriented messages that overly-complicate the execution.

Me-Story: The recited story that spells out the consumer's underlying emotional reasons for seeking vindication through a customer service redress of a problem.

Offer: A product, service or experience deliberately created for the customer.

On-Emotion: Generating an emotional response in the target market that's appropriate to support one's business goal. Being on-emotion is at least as important as being on-message or on-strategy, both of which often fail to engage the heart and win people over.

Say/Feel Gap: The disconnect that frequently occurs between what people say versus their actual feelings.

Script: The meaning behind every code-able emotion.

Sensory Bandwidth: The ability to engage consumers with stimuli that play to their five senses of sight, sound, touch, taste and smell.

PART**ONE**

why**emotionsmatter**

1

the new mental model

In an increasingly interdisciplinary world, breakthroughs in brain science have first challenged psychology, then economics, to rethink old assumptions underestimating the role of emotions.

1986
Joseph LeDoux
discovers the role
of the amygdala, the brain's "hot button"

Science

1990
President
Bush declares
1990s the
"Decade of
the Brain"

1995
Daniel
Goleman's
Emotional Intelligence
sells almost
five million
copies

Psychology

1998 Dr. Martin Seligman
launches the
positive
psychology
movement

Economics

2002 Daniel Kahneman wins a Nobel Prize
for his work in behavioral economics

2005 Malcolm Gladwell's *Blink*
challenges the
traditional
consumer
decision-making
model

OVERVIEW

In business, we've traditionally been told to think with our heads and not with our hearts. Break-throughs in brain science have now shown that this is impossible. Rather than being cast aside and hidden, emotions have begun to move from the margins to the center of discourse in many fields. As illustrated by the puzzle-piece diagram, this chapter will focus on three key, interlocking developments:

- **Science:** The old mental model in which conscious, rational, verbally-oriented thought was predominant has given way. Technology like fMRI brain scans has instead affirmed a new model in which our three-part brain (sensory, emotional and rational) is most influenced by the two oldest, non-rational parts. As a result, people's decision-making process is primarily quick, emotional and subconscious; in a word, it's intuitive. The bottom line is that people feel before they think. The implication for business? Looking for commitment from customers and employees based on rational messages alone won't be nearly as effective as communication that emphasizes emotional benefits.

- **Psychology:** The news that people's psyches have been "hardwired" through evolution, linking us to cave men and women, could lead to the assumption that everything in human nature is set in stone and can't be changed. But psychologists are balancing that reality with a second neurological reality: as shown by the creation of new neurons throughout life (neurogenesis) and the existence of empathetically-oriented brain receptors (mirror neurons), people have the ability to grow and adapt. The implication for business? The type of marketplace and workplace experiences people have may re-wire the brain, meaning that the concept of building brand equity—accruing positive feelings—now extends to every company/customer interaction and outcome as well as to manager/employee relationships.

- **Economics:** Long the preserve of rationality, this field is also experiencing a transition. As Nobel Laureate Daniel McFadden has said, the new movement of "behavioral economics is where gravity is pulling the field." What's the impetus? It's again the influence of brain science, which has undermined the old notion that people make logical choices. The implication for business? Value gets assigned emotionally, not rationally. Failure to account for emotions will lead to assumptions that could be seriously off-base regarding everything from pricing to productivity.

Now let's look more closely at developments in each of these three fields, starting with brain science.

Science:
the meaning of a three-part brain

Synopsis: This section opens by detailing the order in which the three brains developed. Then it provides the general followed by the specific implications of that order in terms of how our three-part brain works and what its processing patterns mean to business.

Key take-aways:
- Emotion drives reason more than reason drives emotion.
- The brain's hardwiring makes us more primitive than we might think.
- Feelings happen before thought, and they happen with great speed.
- Conscious thought is only a small portion of mental activity.
- Visual imagery and other non-verbal forms of communication predominate.

Our Three Brains
Emotion drives reason more than reason drives emotion.

Let's get the facts down first. Until the Victorian Era, people thought we only had one brain. Then in the 1860s, French scientist Paul Broca became famous for his studies on the two hemispheres of the brain. It is now common knowledge that left-brain people are "logical" thinkers, while right-brain people are more "emotional." Fair enough, but it's actually a little more complex than that.

After World War II, the U.S. government funded extensive brain research in an effort to aid the large number of G.I.s who had suffered head wounds. As a result, in 1949 Paul MacLean discovered that human beings really have a three-part brain whose complexity developed sequentially over time (Howard 2000).

What is known as the original brain supports our senses. In fact, this part of the brain began as a small clump of tissue atop the spinal column, facilitating smell, which is still the most robust of people's five senses (Ackerman). Reptile brains didn't make it past this developmental point. In humans, this part of the brain is notable for engaging in pattern matching, automatically benchmarking current experience against previous encounters. This ability allows us to orient and gauge levels of safety and comfort.

The second part of the brain, the limbic system, is our emotional center and evolved with the first mammals. It turns sensory perceptions into emotional and physical responses. It also interfaces with the newest brain, the rational brain, which forms the third part of the modern human brain. Thus one could say that the limbic system serves as our Grand Integrator, linking the sensory, emotional and rational parts of the brain. Its key activity is to assign gut-level value to the situations we encounter.

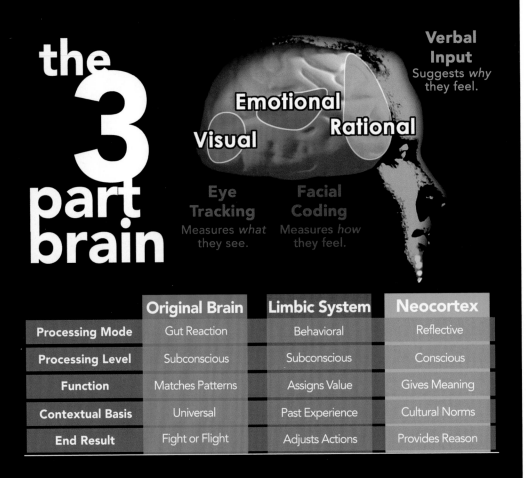

the 3 part brain

Visual **Emotional** **Rational**

Verbal Input
Suggests *why*
they feel.

Eye Tracking
Measures *what*
they see.

Facial Coding
Measures *how*
they feel.

	Original Brain	**Limbic System**	**Neocortex**
Processing Mode	Gut Reaction	Behavioral	Reflective
Processing Level	Subconscious	Subconscious	Conscious
Function	Matches Patterns	Assigns Value	Gives Meaning
Contextual Basis	Universal	Past Experience	Cultural Norms
End Result	Fight or Flight	Adjusts Actions	Provides Reason

Fig. 1.1 The Three Parts and Their Functions. This illustration provides an overview of the location of each of the three parts of the brain. The evolutionary function chart below it compares the parts to give a more in-depth understanding of how each part processes, utilizes and responds to stimuli (Ortony 2003). The original brain has been estimated to be 500 million years old, the limbic system 200 million years old, and the neocortex 100,000 years old (Postma).

The neocortex was the last part of the brain to develop. As the rational part, it often gets called the "mind." Its frontal lobes are the executive center of the brain, where complex data is processed. Social mammals evolved this part of the brain. The size of the neocortex is directly proportional to the size of the group they live in (Baker) because having to track more relationships requires more brain power. Given our complex societal ties, humans have the largest neocortex on the planet.

That's the progression of development over the millennia. But calling it a progression may incorrectly cause people to assume that since the rational part of the brain came into existence last, its being new and capable of more complex processing also means it dominates. In other words, that rationality *wins*.

But in truth we aren't supremely rational creatures like Mr. Spock or Data from *Star Trek*. To clarify matters, let's turn to prominent neuroscientist Joseph LeDoux. He notes that, "emotions can flood consciousness. . . because the wiring of the brain at this point in our evolutionary history is such that connections from the emotional systems to the cognitive systems are stronger than connections from the cognitive systems to the emotional systems" (2003).

To reiterate: emotion drives reason more than reason drives emotion.

Or here's another take on human nature from the individual *Ad Age* named the most influential person of the century. To quote the legendary Bill Bernbach, whose agency gave us groundbreaking advertising for accounts like Volkswagen and Alka-Seltzer: "It took millions of years for man's instincts to develop. It will take millions more for them to even vary. A communicator must be concerned with unchanging man, with his obsessive drive to survive, to be admired, to succeed, to love, and to take care of his own."

General Implications of Having a Three-Part Brain
The brain's hardwiring makes us more primitive than we might think.

In general terms, the fact that people have a hardwired, three-part brain has two major implications. The first major implication has already been introduced by LeDoux. It's that the older, sensory and emotional brains dominate our decision-making process. Emotions are central, not peripheral, because they drive reason more than vice versa. In other words, we're not nearly as rational as we would like to think we are.

The second major implication is that we're much more similar to our ancient ancestors than to the sophisticated consumers and workers we would like to think we are. As Bernbach is alerting us, businesspeople who make their plans based on complex, intellectual assumptions about how targeted consumers or affected employees will behave are missing an opportunity to leverage recent breakthroughs in brain science. Our neuron-biological legacy means that emotions enjoy pre-emptive, first-mover advantage in every decision process.

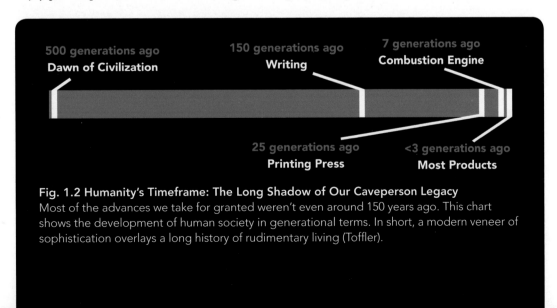

Fig. 1.2 Humanity's Timeframe: The Long Shadow of Our Caveperson Legacy
Most of the advances we take for granted weren't even around 150 years ago. This chart shows the development of human society in generational terms. In short, a modern veneer of sophistication overlays a long history of rudimentary living (Toffler).

As a result, futurist Alvin Toffler is correct in observing that our long, generally slow evolutionary history makes it hard for us to absorb all of the changes now hurtling our way (Fig. 1.2). How basic is basic human nature? The answer is that human nature is in some ways downright primitive. For starters, it's true that we're still 99% genetically identical to chimpanzees (Conniff). Moreover, it's been estimated that as much as two-thirds of the human brain has been "hard-wired" to reflect what our early ancestors learned about survival (Pinker).

The bottom line is that we're not very far removed from our cave-dwelling ancestors who—driven by the fight-or-flight impulse—were more concerned with escaping wild animal attacks than activities such as viewing abstract art, enjoying nouvelle cuisine, shopping or showering.

Rob Beckman's long-running show, *Defending the Caveman*, humorously reveals just how little we've actually progressed.

Specific Implications of Having a Three-Part Brain

So far, we've addressed the two big general implications of having a three-part brain: emotions dominate and our ancient, hardwired nature casts a long shadow. Along with those general implications, however, there are also specific ones we're now ready to detail so that you can have a firmer grasp of how people's decision-making process really operates.

Feelings happen before thought and happen with great speed.

Feelings come first. Feelings precede conscious thought. Since it's true that in evolutionary terms the rational brain literally grew out of the emotional brain and remains intricately tied to it, this order of influence makes sense. Indeed, the emotional part of the brain is larger than the rational part and so the entire brain processes more emotive than cognitive activity (Baker). Moreover, the degree to which signals run from the emotional brain to the rational brain outnumber those running the opposite direction by a ratio of ten to one (Hawkins).

To emphasize the extent to which the rational brain isn't at the center of determining what happens in life, consider the fact that only the sensory and emotional brain centers direct our muscle activity (Ortony 2003). Thus by analogy the rational brain is a little bit like a logic lobbyist who tries to get the other two duly authorized parts of the brain to actually vote for his bill on the floor of Congress.

We take the low road, not the high one. The brain has both high-road and low-road response mechanisms (Goleman 1995) and, as in most aspects of life, the low road dominates. (People may tell you that they watch PBS, but *American Idol* gets the ratings.) For example, the low road is the path we take in making impulse purchases as input gets filtered straight to the amygdala (the brain's hot button). In contrast, the high road takes longer to travel and isn't nearly as sovereign as it may seem to be. In other words, our rational responses get colored by the low road's quicker emotional responses. Moreover, guess where the high road ends? Back at the amygdala to "sign the check" we've already emotionally spent.

> "The essential difference between emotion and reason is that emotion leads to action while reason leads to conclusions."
>
> —Dr. Donald Calne

Recall is emotion-based. Let's start by introducing the parts of the brain that bring us recall. First, there's the hippocampus, our memory device. Next, the amygdala is not only the part of the brain associated with feelings of fear and aggression, for it also plays a role in visual learning and memory. Not by chance, the hippocampus and the amygdala are both located in the emotional brain and in close proximity to one another because memory formation happens in only two ways (LeDoux 1994).

- A new memory can be established when a stimulus hits the amygdala and makes an emotional connection.

- Secondly, another similar stimulus may hit the amygdala and be easily assimilated since it resembles the previously established connection.

What results is a network of recalled associations that gets started by an actual hot-button stimulus or even the memory of a hot-button stimulus. So everything we retain owes that outcome to its having gained an emotional toehold in our brain.

We have gut reactions in three seconds or less. Think of our instinctual response to stimuli as the equivalent of a quarterback's "hut-hut-hike" cadence, which leads to the snap of the football. In other words, our gut reactions happen very quickly (Gladwell 2005). In fact, emotions process sensory input in only one-fifth the time our conscious, cognitive brain takes to assimilate that same input (Marcus). Quick emotional processing also happens with cascading impact. Just as the quarterback says "hike" more emphatically, so does our emotional reaction to a stimulus resound more loudly in our brain than does our rational response, triggering the action to follow.

To put the long-term implications of this action in straight, scientific terms: neurons that fire together wire together (Banich). The experiences we have rewire the brain by fusing together neural networks. As a result, what we've already seen will predispose us to what we can see the next time around. That incumbent advantage makes the next "hut-hut-hike" more intuitive and quicker to unfold because it leverages a network already in existence.

Conscious thought is only a small portion of mental activity.

Conscious thought is the tip of the iceberg. Both the sensory and emotional brains operate subconsciously. In all, less than .0005% of our mental activity qualifies as fully conscious. According to the latest estimates, the brain takes in 400 billion bytes of information per second, but only consciously processes 2,000 (Vincente). The implication? We are much less aware than we prefer to believe. Likewise, the eye picks up 10,000,000 bytes of visual information per second but only 40 bytes per second become mental images; that's a ratio of 250,000 to one (Zimmerman; "Bandwidth").

Visual imagery and other non-verbal forms of communication predominate.

"A picture is worth a thousand words." Cliché, but true. In fact, it's a cliché *because* it's true. A battle between pictures and words is like one between Mike Tyson and Tiny Tim: the picture throws the bigger punch. Consider these illuminating facts:

- Two-thirds of the stimuli reaching the brain are visual (Zaltman 1996).

- Over 50% of the brain is devoted to processing visual images (Cleese).

- As a result, 80% of learning is visually-based (American).

Business people, take note. Humans are extremely visual: we think largely in images, not words. What consumers and employees can't actually see, or at the very least mentally envision based on how a topic gets explained, is most likely going to be lost on them.

Most communication is nonverbal in ambiguous situations. Every day, we find ourselves in situations where the other party's words and body language strikes us as either ambiguous or conflicting. In those cases, what do we do? We tend to rely more on the non-verbals to evaluate the emotional state of the person speaking. Here are the exact statistics (Mahrabian):

- 55% of communication comes through facial expressions.
- 38% of communication gets accomplished by tone of voice.
- Only 7% of communication relies on verbal exchange.

For anyone who wants to "get back to basics," remember that nothing is more basic than non-verbal communication. Human beings have existed for over 500,000 years, but we've had the benefit of language for less than a quarter of that time (Dunbar). Moreover, because the rational and sensory parts of the brain aren't adjacent neighbors, we're not very good at describing verbally the details our senses detect. Ironically, that's true despite the fact that our initial, gut-level perceptions are largely based on sensory impressions.

In summary, here's what we've just covered: 1) we feel first and last in the decision-making process, asking the amygdala to sign the check, 2) we feel more quickly than we think, 3) even the formation of memories is emotionally-based, 4) most of our mental activity also happens beyond our awareness, subconsciously, and 5) mental activity is often initiated by visual, sensory impressions that lead to emotional responses that we mostly communicate non-verbally.

"Who are you going to believe, me or your own eyes?"

—Groucho Marx

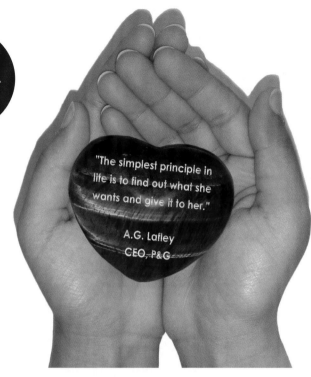

"The simplest principle in life is to find out what she wants and give it to her."

A.G. Lafley
CEO, P&G

The business implications of all of this will be explored in depth in Chapters 4 through 10. But for now, remember that looking for commitment from consumers and employees based on rational messages alone won't be nearly as effective as communication that emphasizes emotional benefits. A case in point is Procter and Gamble, a company that by its own admission used to market based on the technical features of its offers. The company's performance since its CEO began to emphasize a less technical, more emotional, female-centric strategy is an impressive 17% rise in annual earnings (Ellison).

Psychology:
balancing blind instinct with growth

Synopsis: As mental healthcare workers, psychologists parallel companies in seeking to make the people they serve happier. In doing so, they balance two aspects of human nature that also have broad relevance to business. The first applies especially to the marketplace, where people's "blind" instincts influence how perceptions are emotionally evaluated. The second applies especially to the workplace, where the goal of working more effectively with staff can benefit from new brain science insights about people's capacity for growth.

Key take-aways:

- We perceive matters in ways that emotionally protect and enhance our self-image.
- Two open-loop mental capacities facilitate our use of emotional intelligence in pursuit of happiness.

Emotions Color Perceptions and Inhibit Change
We perceive matters in ways that emotionally protect and enhance our self-image.

First, let's tackle the bad news: unbiased perception is not one of humanity's strong suits. The processing of "facts" is, in essence, as much about the processing of one's emotions as it is the processing of whatever external dynamics a person happens to be experiencing. After all, genetically we're designed for self-preservation. Goals high on the list for human beings are feeling good about ourselves and accruing allies and partners drawn by our vitality (Wright).

As Robert Zajonc and other psychologists have noted, the perceptual process, and the reactions and judgments that flow from it, are emotionally encoded ("Preferences"). Feelings provide us with information. We usually ask ourselves, "How do I feel about such and such?" Feelings also influence how we process information.

For instance, how do we "choose" which brands to notice? Well, the first step in the perceptual process is that of screening, which often occurs subconsciously. We tend to screen out the unfamiliar (since paying attention to unfamiliar stimuli requires effort). Instead, we prefer to focus on what we already know and can relate to more easily. Then when looking at a TV commercial or the store shelf in front of us, for example, we classify and interpret brand choices based on perceptual reactions—or biases—that again are rooted in emotion.

Yes, at times people will analyze the "facts" vigorously. But emotions are basic and more dominant. Remember: we feel before we think, and those reactions are subconscious, immediate and inescapable. That's why our reactions are often hard to verbalize. Our language skills reside in the rational brain, which may not get invoked because automatic reactions are primarily emotional in nature. As Zajonc notes, to say "I decided in favor of X" often means nothing more or less than "I liked X"—and that's good enough.

Why is instinctive preference good enough in life in general as well as in business specifically? The reason is that emotional judgments tend to be irrevocable because they implicate the self, revealing our biases. In terms of our basic emotional reactions, we're never wrong about what we like or dislike. So it's important for companies not just to sell objectively or to appeal to consumers only rationally. As Zajonc again notes, the factual reality of "The cat is black" pales in contrast to the more intimate emotional reality of "I don't like black cats."

> "I don't like spinach, and I'm glad I don't, because if I liked it, I'd eat it, and I just hate it."
>
> —Clarence Darrow

What's the last stage in perception? It's retrieval, which is mediated by our emotions yet again. We tend to store and recall more readily those experiences that fit most comfortably into our existing mental frameworks. In other words, memory is driven by preferences rooted in being at ease with our choice. Consumers and employees alike often defend their choices or actions based on details they previously deemed rationally irrelevant. Why? The explanation is that emotions are self-justifying and, therefore, emotional reactions can become totally separated from content.

The net result is that there's no business advantage in going against such items from the brain's functional rulebook as feelings come first, we take the low road not the high road, and recall is emotion-based.

In other words, remember that what we've already seen will predispose us to what we can see the next time around because of our emotional investment in what's familiar to us. This incumbent advantage has implications for branding (Chapter 4), offer design (Chapter 5) and advertising (Chapter 6) in particular. While a company may believe it has a technically or functionally superior offer, consumers' evaluations are in essence emotionally-based. Objectivity doesn't exist because everything gets filtered and colored by emotional responses. The bottom line is there's almost always more commercial gain to be made by going with, rather than against, what people have already emotionally internalized and accepted.

How Emotions Feed the Brain and Aid Growth
Two open-loop mental capacities facilitate our use of emotional intelligence in pursuit of happiness.

If people's innate tendency to control, even distort, perceptions to fit their emotionally-encoded pre-conceptions constitutes the bad news (or at least a reality business needs to acknowledge and plan for accordingly), what's the good news? It would have to be that people also have the capacity to learn, grow, adopt and adapt. While as much as two-thirds of the brain may be hardwired to reflect ancient survival lessons, that leaves at least a third open and receptive to discovery.

For a long time, psychology has been oriented to erasing pain: treating neuroses, and in the process focusing on negative emotions. But as we're now about to see, in recent years the field has begun to shift—aided by two specific brain science discoveries and a growing respect for the power of positive feelings (as well as thinking).

The first of those two discoveries is neurogenesis (Lehrer; Boyatzis 2006). That term refers to the creation of new neurons throughout life. It means we're not set for life; we have an ability to change. We have the means to achieve mental flexibility and thereby enhance our lives. Emotion plays a direct role here because the natural brain chemistry that gets those neurons to fire and wire together is, as mentioned earlier, a function of emotional responses that resound more loudly in our brain than do our rational responses. In effect, we get new mental building blocks to utilize throughout life—and it's up to us to make the most of that opportunity to refresh ourselves.

Our ability not to simply repeat past behavior is supported by the second recent discovery: the existence of mirror neurons (Goldberg). These neurons enable us to imitate and empathize with other people, thus reinforcing the importance of using our emotions to gather information in interpersonal situations.

Combined with neurogenesis, the crucial benefit of mirror neurons is that there then exists a pair of open-loop mental capacities that have helped carry psychology into a new, more upbeat and emotionally-enriched era, past earlier movements such as behaviorism and cognitive psychology. Gone is the hyper-rational view of humans evolving into *Star Trek's* Mr. Spock. An emphasis on emotions has emerged instead. Backed by the breakthroughs in brain science, psychology now recognizes two evaluation systems. The slower, thinking system is dominated by the faster, intuitive feeling system that must finally be given due respect.

Born of emotion's new-found prominence is the Positive Psychology movement. Its founder is Dr. Martin Seligman, who—like Walt Disney did—focuses on nothing less than creating happiness. His key formula is H = S + C + V (Happiness equals our genetic **S**et point, plus our

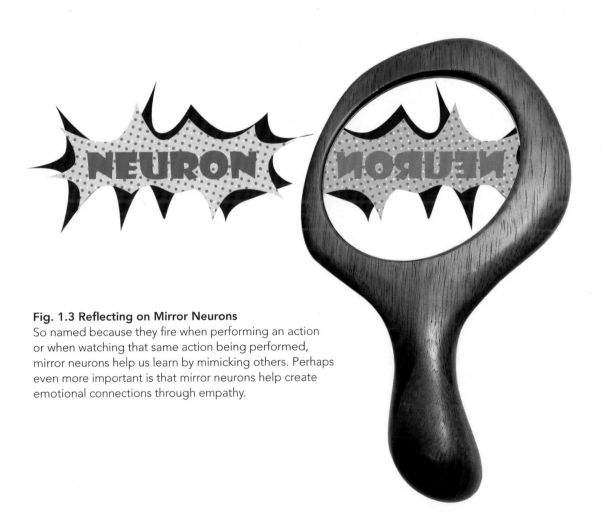

Fig. 1.3 Reflecting on Mirror Neurons
So named because they fire when performing an action or when watching that same action being performed, mirror neurons help us learn by mimicking others. Perhaps even more important is that mirror neurons help create emotional connections through empathy.

Circumstances, plus what we **V**oluntarily change). How can we change our feelings? By changing external stimuli or by learning to perceive them differently, we're able to alter the left side of the equation.

Moreover, Positive Psychology in league with neurogenesis and mirror neurons points to the importance of another term, which Daniel Goleman made famous: emotional intelligence. In essence, emotional intelligence as practiced by consumers, executives, managers and employees entails being in touch with one's feelings (not thinking them). It also means being able to understand them, deal with them, and profit by letting them inform and work in harmony with more rationally-oriented insights.

The reason why the two brain science discoveries and the concepts of Positive Psychology and emotional intelligence all fit together is quite simple: people and companies in general can change their performance for the better. After all, the new neural networks that neurogenesis enables can be more constructive, more beneficial, by virtue of using mirror neurons and emotional intelligence to pick up on improvements we want to incorporate. Positive Psychology, in turn, provides the impetus by encouraging us in the belief that greater happiness is possible.

$$\frac{\mathbf{S}\text{et point} + \mathbf{C}\text{ircumstances} + \mathbf{V}\text{oluntary change}}{\mathbf{H}\text{appiness}}$$

Fig. 1.4 The Formula for Happiness
What's the formula for happiness? **H**appiness equals our genetic **S**et point, plus our **C**ircumstances, plus what we **V**oluntarily change.

The underlying key, however, remains emotions. In the fact that emotions drive us internally and are externally so contagiously shared between people lies the basis for why the brain's dual open-loop capacity can be put to work as an engine for growth. Without the spark of feelings, progress is drawing on limited, merely rational mental resources.

All of this—neurogenesis, mirror neurons, Positive Psychology and emotional intelligence—has tremendous implications for business. Let's start with the marketplace. As we'll discuss in Chapter 4, branding is in essence purely emotional and psychological in that it pertains to beliefs and to the mental models or neural networks by which we form our associations about a company. Therefore, the type of marketplace experiences consumers have is crucial because they may re-wire the brain, meaning that the concept of brand equity—accruing positive feelings—now extends to every company/customer interaction and outcome.

In other words, the connections and the conclusions we intuitively form regarding a company will follow from how our old and new neurons and mirror neurons all get encoded. From brand icons to advertising, offer design to retail and e-tail sites—and especially customer service—the sensory-emotional impressions and experiences that consumers take away from encountering a company will dictate whether the inherently emotional barometer of brand equity rises or falls.

Meanwhile, the implications of all of this for the workplace is, if anything, even stronger. As will be discussed in Chapters 9 and 10, the basis for success is getting employees emotionally engaged in their jobs. Neurogenesis is important in that regard because it means people don't have a fixed or even depleting mental capacity. Instead, they have the resources for growth and positive change. But that's true only so long as the mirror neurons that practice continuous monitoring detect signals within the workplace environment—including notably from leaders and managers—that give cause for the hope enshrined in the Positive Psychology movement.

As a result, the type of workplace experiences employees have may re-wire the brain, meaning that the concept of brand equity—accruing positive feelings—also extends to creating constructive interactions and outcomes among co-workers. If faithfully followed, the concepts of emotional intelligence and Positive Psychology promise to create a whole new way to handle workplace practices like hiring, training and providing feedback. The bottom-line is that by nurturing employees' well-being and fulfilling on their desire for meaning, companies can establish a self-reinforcing cycle that will lead to higher productivity through genuine employee satisfaction.

Economics:
plugging emotions into the equation

Synopsis: Like psychology, the field of economics has also been profoundly influenced by the breakthroughs in brain science. As a result, emotions—not logic alone—have become the focus point of the new emerging practice of behavioral economics. As will be discussed here, the influence of emotions can be found in areas that range from big issues like achieving offer differentiation and value in a hyper-competitive global economy to everyday practices like the way in which people react to prices.

Key take-aways:
- The best way to predict outcomes is to fully account for the vagaries of human nature.
- Delivering a unique emotional value proposition is the key to success.
- How consumers respond to price points is profoundly influenced by their emotions.

What Behavioral Economics Can Teach Us

The best way to predict outcomes is to fully account for the vagaries of human nature.

In 2002, Princeton University's Daniel Kahneman won the Nobel Prize in economics. His work is part of the emerging field of behavioral economics. Supported by neurobiology's recent findings, this new brand of economics is challenging the rationally oriented economic theories of yesteryear. After all, its basic premise is that people aren't very logical decision makers. Like others exploring this field, Dr. Kahneman knows people are fallibly human and don't necessarily make very rational choices. Instead, forces like altruism, greed and revenge are likely to tip the decision balance as much as anything else.

Professor Daniel Kahneman is a Nobel Prize winner and a pioneer in the field of behavioral economics.

Emerging from observations of human behavior instead of from abstract theory, behavioral economics involves a handful of essential concepts. For the purposes of simplifying the discussion here, those concepts have been put into one of two realms: either categorization or loss aversion (Kahneman; Wahrman).

The first set of concepts has to do with the categorization tricks we engage in for emotional reasons. Besides taking mental shortcuts by labeling things so they fit easily into preconceived categories, we also get caught up in:

- **Framing**—making a choice more attractive by deliberately comparing it to inferior options.

- **Mental Accounting**—placing artificial limits on the amounts we're willing to spend in certain categories.

- **Prospect Theory**—judging pleasure based on a change in condition rather than on how happy we are.

- **Anchoring**—evaluating new information strictly in terms of what our baseline of knowledge happens to be.

- **Recency**—giving undue weight to recent experiences.

The second set of concepts has to do with loss aversion. As neurologist LeDoux has concluded from his research, "Negative emotions are linked to survival—and are much stronger" (LeDoux 2003). It's not surprising then that people feel more pain from loss than pleasure from

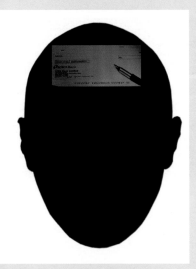

Mental accounting is based on the idea that consumers have a mental "check" made out for how much they're willing to spend on an item.

profit. The result is loss aversion behavior, for people will take more risks to avoid losses than they will to realize gains. Aspects of loss aversion include:

- **Familiarity**—having a bias toward the status quo.
- **New-risk Premium**—inflating the cost of accepting new risks while casually discounting familiar risks.
- **Fear of Regret**—suffering from having to admit a mistake.
- **Decision Paralysis**—failing to make a decision when faced with lots of choices for fear of making the wrong one.

More obviously so than brain science or psychology, behavioral economics also has huge implications for business. What are they? From a marketplace perspective, companies have already taken into account *framing* (by using a good-better-best format), and they have used *recency* as the rationale for engaging in heavy bouts of advertising around major holidays (most notably the Christmas season).

Companies have not been nearly as good at coming to terms with *mental accounting*, which would require repositioning categories so that consumers lift artificially imposed expenditure limits. Nor have most companies made the effort to really understand the baseline knowledge people have of an offer in order to make *anchoring* work in their favor. But the most clear-cut shortcoming of almost all companies is the way in which their confusing product line extensions have ignored the lesson of *decision paralysis*.

As for the workplace, all leaders know they must grapple with the preference for *familiarity* in trying to get employees to accept change. Meanwhile, leaders and managers alike struggle with the *fear of regret*—but may not always recognize the extent of the influence it's likely to have on worker motivation and behavior.

Finally, the other two remaining concepts introduced here can also be relevant to the workplace. For instance, leaders can cope with the *new-risk premium* by reminding employees of the dangers of staying with the status quo. Meanwhile, efforts must also be made to lessen the corrosive effect of the *prospect theory*. Employees given to jealousy based on their relative status within the company not only negate the happiness they can enjoy from their own success, they also plant the seeds for discord among colleagues.

The Top Rung of the Hierarchy of Value
Delivering a unique emotional value proposition is the key to success.

As brain science has shown, and as behavioral economics is reflecting, people often don't make logical choices. Instead, they go with their gut reactions and justify them afterwards using intellectual alibis. Now companies may find that kind of decision-making process confusing, frustrating, even objectionable. To protest against the hardwired nature of human nature isn't a productive business strategy. Far better is to acknowledge human nature and work with it accordingly.

To that end, consider Maslow's famous hierarchy of needs: the one in which basic needs like food and shelter must be met before higher needs ranging from the social to the spiritual kick in. Well, a similar hierarchy of value also exists—based on the scientific fact that value gets assigned emotionally, not rationally, given the role the emotional, middle brain plays in people's decision-making process.

At the lowest rung, you'll find a desire for security. The next step up is comfort. Finally, at the top rung is the pleasure consumers will pay the most for. Throughout this hierarchy of emotional value, rationality is a factor. After all, security comes in part from the offer working properly, and comfort can involve the social utility of being able to defend the purchase to friends and family. But rationality is never the decisive factor and it disappears almost entirely at the top rung.

Pleasure

Comfort

Security

Here's how the ladder of value stacks up when looked at from an emotional vantage point. At the bottom is the basic need for security. At the top is the desire for pleasure and the beauty and indulgence that comes with it.

There the game changes. Atop the highest rung—the place of sensory indulgence, thrilling aesthetic beauty and the sweet joy of being intimately immersed in an experience afforded by an offer—is where greater profitability, differentiation, even business survival increasingly reside nowadays. Let's explore why.

How come plugging emotions into the value equation, throughout the hierarchy but especially at the top rung, is so important to the performance of companies? To focus just on selling to consumers for the moment, the reason is that the best way to avoid having a commoditized offer in a world of product parity is by adding emotional value. It's no longer enough to have a unique selling proposition. Companies must develop a unique emotional proposition to get out of the commodity trap, which is easier than it may sound.

Consumers evaluate an offer—by which is meant a product, service or experience deliberately created for the customer—by internalizing it and assigning it emotional value. So add the right emotional cues to trigger a positive consumer encounter. Then consumers will intuitively form a strong connection to the offer deep in their emotional brain. Better yet, it will be a connection customized by their feelings about the offer and in which they will have invested emotionally, thereby creating a resilient barrier against entry by the competition.

Good designers are the new "rock stars" of the business world, in part because of the way they infuse their work with emotional charge. As Richard Florida notes in *The Rise of the Creative Class,* about 30% of American workers are already engaged in feeling-fueled creative endeavors.

Their development of innovative new technology and other intellectual property causes a kind of organic growth that forklifts and computers alone can't produce.

Whether a company's focus is on the marketplace or workplace, adding emotion into its strategic planning and tactical executions adds value. Moreover, recognizing emotions reaps rewards. The way to maximize sales is to get consumers more emotionally devoted to what a company offers. The way to maximize productivity is to get employees and business partners more emotionally committed to delivering exceptional offers and support. But to do either one, a company must know how to identify the emotions of others, customers and co-workers alike.

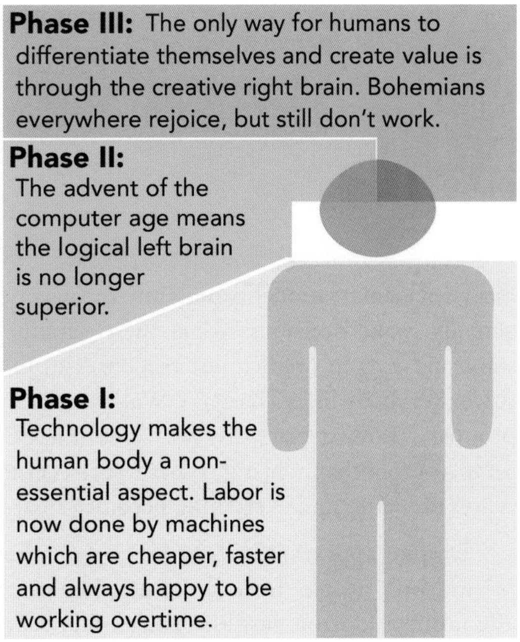

The point being made in Figure 1.5 is that the creative class authors like Florida and Daniel Pink have heralded constitutes the leading edge, the tip of the iceberg. Its

Phase III: The only way for humans to differentiate themselves and create value is through the creative right brain. Bohemians everywhere rejoice, but still don't work.

Phase II: The advent of the computer age means the logical left brain is no longer superior.

Phase I: Technology makes the human body a non-essential aspect. Labor is now done by machines which are cheaper, faster and always happy to be working overtime.

Fig. 1.5 The Phasing Out of Humans

substantial and growing presence points to where all companies in America and the world at large must increasingly go over time to fortify their offers and survive against the lowest-cost providers, regardless of whatever country those providers locate in at the moment—China today, somewhere else tomorrow.

In short, being strategic about plugging emotions into the mix is no longer optional. For companies that want to be winners, it's imperative—as Chapters 4 through 10 will discuss in depth.

The Cost of Emotions
How consumers respond to price points is profoundly influenced by their emotions.

Granted, for the cautious or even skeptical reader not easily convinced that emotions truly affect what happens in business, everything that's been said so far might seem rather abstract or theoretical in nature. If you're that kind of person, you may be saying to yourself: "Okay" or "So what? Show me the money. Prove relevance." For you, it isn't enough that the physical arrangement of the brain makes feelings both the starting point and end point in the transformation of responses into actions.

So in concluding this opening chapter of *Emotionomics*, let's go straight to the intersection of money and emotions. After all, in addressing logic, value and feelings, the assertion being made here is that failure to account for emotions will lead to assumptions that could be seriously off-base regarding everything from pricing to productivity.

Now it's time for some tangible evidence.

As behavioral economists have observed, there's an awful lot of irrationality built into the way people actually make decisions. What then remains constant and easy to predict: our responses to pricing, since everybody likes a bargain. Wal-Mart's famous promise, "Lowest price always," would appear to serve as proof that, when it comes to price, emotion ceases to matter and everything becomes clear-cut.

Despite appearances, however, responding to pricing isn't simple. Instead, it's another perceptually influenced issue, just like every other aspect of business, because the value we assign to a potential purchase is so emotional. Consider a study, for example, that found that since prices ending in the number nine suggest bargains, a company was able to increase the price of its dresses from \$34 to \$39 while also *increasing* sales volume (Anderson).

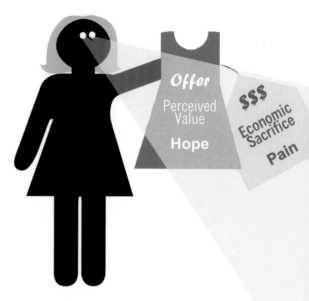

Fig. 1.6 Pleasure vs. Pain and Perception of Product.
When considering an offer, we intuitively make emotional judgments. Does the value received outweigh the economic sacrifice? Does the hope of future happiness gained in acquisition outweigh the pain of purchase?

As Sensory Logic confirmed in work for a manufacturer contemplating three different price points for a new product, the lowest price doesn't always win with consumers. Figure 1.7 shows a case in which people emotionally opted for the middle price. Why? The reason is that the subjects felt good about accepting a slightly higher price because they believed it meant the offer must be superior to cheaper alternatives.

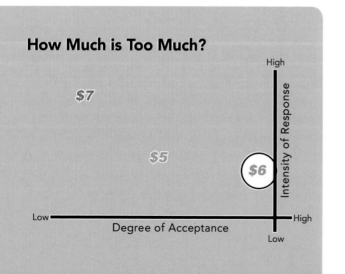

Fig. 1.7 Price and Quality Implications
Like the story of Goldilocks and her porridge, people found the middle price to be just right. It was high enough to denote quality but not overpricing. And it was low enough to be affordable without giving off an air of shoddiness.

Even more striking, consider the results of a study investigating the impact that sadness and disgust have on people's willingness to buy and sell at different prices (Lerner; Begley). After watching a movie clip designed to induce either sadness or disgust, the subjects were asked to considering buying or selling a highlighter pen.

As Figure 1.8 shows, members of the control group, who were not shown any movie clips, were, not surprisingly, given to selling high and buying low. In contrast, the subjects induced to feel disgust were eager to sell low and hesitant to pay anything to purchase something new because they expected to find it unacceptable. Meanwhile, those feeling sad were also inclined to sell low. But unlike their disgusted colleagues, those feeling sad were eager to improve their circumstances and paid by far the highest price for the pen.

The take-away here is that emotional states clearly create behavior contrary to rational thought. To understand how the world at large truly functions, and business within it, understanding how emotions operate is crucial to realizing success. To gain a practical, real-life window into emotions, let's move on to Chapter 2, which discusses the facial coding tool that brings this discussion of emotions into a measurable, manageable realm.

Fig. 1.8 Talk About Price Sensitivity
For anyone who thinks emotions don't effect actions, look at the results from a study that induced emotional states in subjects and then had them make financial decisions. Isn't it astounding (and somewhat intuitive) that how people feel affects what they do? People who were made sad were much more likely to sell—or get rid of—an item they associated with sadness.

2

the science of facial coding

While many companies still struggle to acknowledge, let alone reliably take emotions into account in their everyday business practices, others have secured insights and business advantages through the science of facial coding.

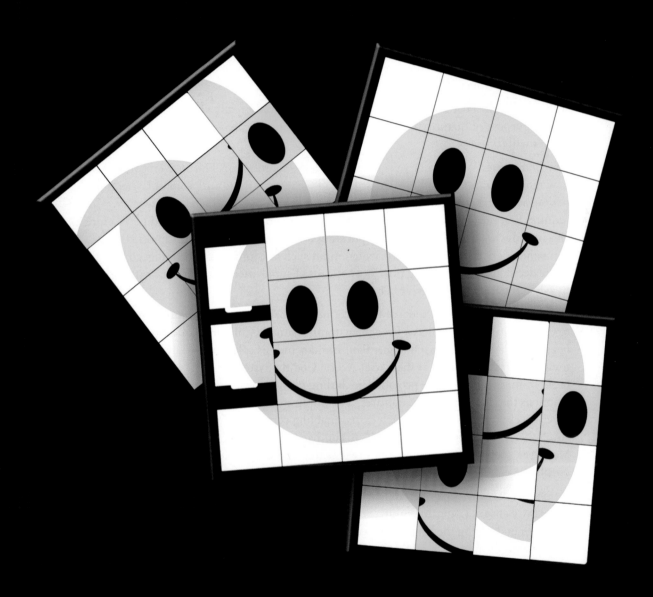

OVERVIEW

The primary goal of Chapter 1 was to establish how central emotions are to business. From a scientific perspective, however, it's equally important to note how important it is to move beyond a think-your-feelings to a feel-your-feelings approach to capturing emotional responses. That's because conscious, cognitively-based verbal input alone is unlikely to be true to the quick, largely subconscious nature of emotions.

In Chapter 2, the goal is to explain facial coding—the only really viable tool currently available for the purpose of quantifying the impact specific emotions have on business. In particular, this chapter will focus on:

- **The Challenge:** What problem is facial coding the solution to? The answer is that as the new model of a three-part brain made clear in Chapter 1, there are profound, scientific reasons why verbal input alone is inadequate. To overcome the challenge, however, requires first recognizing the extent of the problem, which gets summarized here before also introducing the solution. The implication for business? At present, almost all companies depend on rationally-oriented input such as comments and ratings to help them make decisions. Facial coding provides a means of supplementing that data with insights based on the feelings that drive behavior.

- **Origins and Scope:** The roots of facial coding go back more than a century, most notably to Charles Darwin as well as a French anatomist named Guillaume Duchenne. Then, beginning in the 1960s, psychologist Paul Ekman and his colleague Wally Freisen codified their additional learnings as the Facial Action Coding System (FACS). A summary of facial coding's scope will be provided, including its biological basis and the seven core emotions that it gauges across cultures. The implication for business? Finally, a thorough, precise feel-your-feelings approach exists, enabling companies to know consumers' and employees' actual emotional responses to company initiatives and to plan accordingly. Moreover, computer vision research suggests that automated facial coding may soon be possible. Automation promises to allow faster coding and quicker results.

- **Deliverables:** Since first bringing facial coding into the business realm a decade ago, my company, Sensory Logic, has built a set of unique deliverables. These charts (and the processes underlying them) make it possible to extract the maximum degree of utility from facial coding as a research tool. Deliverable formats will be shown, along with a pair of mini case studies that illustrate the tool's validity. The implication for business? Not only is facial coding a repeatable, actionable methodology, it's also true that companies can use it to gain a more complete picture of people's responses across a wide range of applications, from offer design and advertising to personnel issues as well as other opportunities.

Now let's look more closely at the competitive advantage facial coding offers, starting with why it's needed in the first place.

The Challenge:
when words alone fail us

Synopsis: New scientific insights about human nature and how our decision-making process actually works require new research tools to quantify these new insights. Where the current set of tools reach its inherent limits will be summarized first, followed by a more personal history of how people, including myself, have come to know about and use facial coding for their own purposes.

> **Key take-aways:**
> - To access emotions requires going beyond rationally-filtered verbal input.
> - Facial coding is incredibly versatile in terms of applications.

Limitations Confronting Traditional Methods
To access emotions requires going beyond rationally-filtered verbal input.

The degree to which people *can't or won't* indicate their preferences should be abundantly obvious based on the brain science, psychology and behavioral economics material covered in Chapter 1. But now let's bring it home to how research gets conducted. As Gerald Zaltman has noted in *How Consumers Think*: "A great mismatch exists between the way consumers experience and think about their world and the methods marketers use to collect this information."

Indeed, for every company the difficulty involved in trying to ascertain people's commitment levels to brands, offers, advertising and employers is great. The following few paragraphs show some reasons why the difficulty exists. Then the discussion will turn to how facial coding provides a solution by using an activity-oriented, scientific approach that isn't invasive and yet is able to capture the subtle responses that indicate people's true inclinations in real-time.

Sometimes we simply can't, or won't, say what we really feel.

Here then are some key limitations confronting traditional research:

Words won't suffice. In many ways we live in a post-literate society. Book reading is down while television watching stays sky high. One urban myth is that teenagers' vocabularies are shrinking with each new generation. While that might not be true, a credible report from an Oxford University professor estimates that up to 20% of adults in the Western world are functionally illiterate (O'Shaughnessy). These are people who will have money to spend but are unlikely to give very articulate responses to questions about their choices. What's the other big factor limiting the effectiveness of words? It's the difficulty of crossing language barriers—an issue that continues to grow given both globalized marketing as well as greater mobility, leading to countries with increasingly diverse ethnic groups within their own borders.

Subjects may be going through the motions. Do marketing research recruiters really call on recurring, "professional subjects" when they can't meet quotas? Yes, despite screeners meant to avoid that problem (Leitch; Bernthal). These professional subjects may prove to be the most articulate, helpful subjects. But in receiving incentives as an on-going revenue source, these subjects run the risk of being overly polite and given to saying "yes" whether they mean it or not. Moreover, there's an additional segment of subjects who, despite the best efforts of good moderators or hosts, succumb to routine by giving indifferent, essentially unvarying answers or ratings to survey questions or don't even finish the surveys. Coverage in *Quirk's Marketing Research Review* (Mullet; Sack; Lauer) indicates that as much as 50% to 70% of some online surveys are left incomplete, and that too often someone else steps in for the original subject part way through the test (a daughter taking over while the mother starts dinner, for example).

Subjects have a tendency to fall in line. A study quoted in *Advertising & The Mind of the Consumer* (Sutherland) found that 75% of people in a given situation are willing to go against their own perceptions and give the responses they know or think others will give. This limitation often arises in focus groups, where people are sitting around with twelve strangers but are

Darwin noted that there was no specific body language that denoted emotional response. To help prove his point, consider this graphic. Can you correctly identify the emotional state of each model? Neither can I. While body language undoubtedly helps us read the feelings of those around us, only facial expressions provide the precision necessary to truly uncover what's going on behind the mask.

somehow expected to be "open." A skilled moderator can help some, but games will be played. An alpha male or female group member may, in effect, take over the discussion. Another big problem related to this limitation is that people will give answers that make them look smart. Rational, defensible answers are great—but not if they're unrelated to people's true feelings or motivations.

The answers aren't in real time. People's rational reactions aren't likely to be given in real time. In large part that's because of the pervasive influence of our subconscious, which we can't access but is likely to drive our reactions more quickly than we can report verbally. There are other problems, too. In focus groups, people can sit back and wait for the consensus to form before safely joining in. In response dial testing, subjects may move a hand-held dial to indicate a positive or negative reaction before they really intend to, not move it often enough to reflect shifts in response, or go too slowly as they rationalize their responses. Finally, in fMRI brain scan testing that tracks blood flow, people's responses tend to peak around eight seconds *after* exposure to the stimulus (Banich).

Emotions aren't being adequately accessed. While brain scans can capture the physiology of specific emotional responses, they're likely to remain expensive and invasive. Verbal input suffers from all the limitations cited above. In contrast, ethnography is good because it can tell you what people are doing. But it can't access how they're internalizing their emotional response, so as to show how they *feel* about what they're doing. That leaves facial coding and its originator Charles Darwin, who notes that "Emotions are shown primarily in the face, not in the body. The body instead shows how people are coping with emotion. There is no specific body movement pattern that always signals anger or fear, but there are facial patterns specific to each emotion."

In summary, what researchers, analysts, consultants, strategic planners and anybody else in the business world trying to understand how consumers and employees are feeling needs to recognize—and address—is that quite often our responses are cast in a *silent language*. Most of us still aren't always comfortable honestly discussing them out loud, especially with strangers. And for those who are, it is sometimes impossible to accurately describe how we truly feel, which is where facial coding enters the picture as a viable solution.

And Now. . . Facial Coding
Facial coding is incredibly versatile in terms of applications.

For readers who know nothing of facial coding and may be inclined to consider it a fairly esoteric topic, please think again. Not only has the tool received some surprisingly mainstream press coverage in recent years, it also has a way of showing up in the most unexpected places.

Consider one of my own experiences:

A few years ago I was in Beijing to give a speech at the American Chamber of Commerce. It was the Sunday beforehand, during a visit to the Great Wall, when a fellow tour group member asked me what I did for a living. When I said consumer research, his eyes glazed over. So I tried to peak his interest by adding, "But we do it somewhat differently. Rather than just depend on what people say, my company also studies people's facial expressions to learn how much they're really buying-in *emotionally*."

"Oh, micro-expressions," he replied, referring to brief expressions that typically flit across the face in less than $1/_5$ of a second.

Startled, I couldn't help but lean in toward him and ask with an inquisitive smile, "Yeah. How do you know about them?" After all, micro-expression isn't exactly a household term.

It turned out he had just ended a fifteen-year stint in the Middle East, where he used facial coding for surveillance and general counter-intelligence purposes.

Alarmed? Don't be. The applications to be covered in this book are much more benign than interrogation. But beyond business uses for the tool, yes, it's true that the CIA, FBI and the Pentagon (including the defense contractor my fellow traveler had been working for) have turned to facial coding for the same reason any company might: to gain a competitive edge by learning more than people may be willing or able to communicate through words alone. As a result, everything from national security to police forces rely on facial coding to be of assistance.

Just how versatile is facial coding? Listed below are various ways in which Sensory Logic uses it to gain emotional insight where traditional market research methods aren't able to do so.

Copy Testing

TV Spots
Print Ads
Direct Mail
Outdoor
Radio
Casting

Usability

Products & Packaging
Web Sites
Customer Experience
Customer Satisfaction

Strategy

Offer Design & Positioning
Segmentation
Price Elasticity
Brand Equity
Brand Icons & Characters

Personnel

Sales Force Training
Hiring
Media Coaching
Negotiation Training
Morale & Retention
Change Management

At the same time, however, facial coding also has a far *softer* side to it in terms of possible applications. For example, my first brush with facial coding was in an academic text devoted to psychology that I happened to read in 1998. So imagine my surprise when the tool first hit the mainstream in 2001. That's the year John Cleese, of Monty Python fame, produced and starred in *The Human Face*, a five-part series for the BBC. Part psychology, part biology, with lots of interjected humor, the series was ultimately about how central the face is to communication, mating and other types of social activities.

Coverage in *Esquire* (Torday) and Oprah Winfrey's *O* magazine ("Professor") soon followed, emphasizing the tool's benefit in daily interactions with a loved one. Then a year later Malcolm Gladwell wrote an essay on facial coding for *The New Yorker* (2002). That publicity led, in turn, to a front-page article in *The Wall Street Journal (*Davis*)*. Capping it all off was the eventual publication of Gladwell's international bestseller *Blink: The Power of Thinking Without Thinking* in 2005.

So facial coding has obviously received a fair amount of popular attention. But how accurate is it?

In *Blink*, Gladwell cites the success of the "Love Lab" at the University of Washington. There, psychologist John Gottman has spent well over a decade studying couples talking to each other. Using only an hour of video footage, his ability to predict whether a couple will be married fifteen years later is 95% accurate. By viewing only 15 minutes of videotape, his success rate is still around 90%. Gottman's tool of choice: facial coding.

The marriage counseling Gottman practices is of course highly emotional in nature, a territory few companies have investigated and even fewer have staked out effectively. As stated earlier, business is already very knowledgeable about and comfortable with rationality. Criteria related to it can be measured using verbal input. But now through facial coding, it's also possible to tackle business issues involving emotions—as we're about to see. Daniel Goleman is right to note that "Just as the mode of the rational mind is words, the mode of the emotions is non-verbal." The bottom line? While at present, almost all companies rely on rationally-oriented input such as comments and ratings to help them make decisions, facial coding provides a means to extract emotional data with insight on the feelings that drive behavior.

Origins and Scope:
why and how facial coding works

Synopsis: This section details the origins and refinement of facial coding, including an explanation of its biological basis. But the heart of the section involves profiles of the seven core emotions that facial coding can universally gauge, as well as how deceit is most likely to reveal itself.

Key take-aways:
- The founders of facial coding worked from careful physiological observations.
- Facial coding is robust because of the face's unique properties.
- Every code-able emotion has its own meaning or "script," but there is no specific muscle movement that betrays a liar.
- Computer assisted coding will enable quicker, less expensive results.

As DNA has shown, we are quite genetically similar to apes. Darwin made a discovery about emotions while observing an orangutan and comparing its facial expressions to his children's.

Discovery and Development of Facial Coding
*The founders of facial coding worked from
careful physiological observations.*

Facial expressions are uniform and universal. Indeed, even a person born blind, who could not possibly learn expressions through imitation, has the same facial expressions as everyone else. Moreover, as discussed in the afterword, a team of Israeli scientists has recently gone even farther. Their conclusion? People born blind exhibit characteristic expressions nearly identical to those displayed by their families and close relatives.

Charles Darwin first discovered this amazing truth about the innate, hard-wired nature of facial expressions. As a father, he was eager to know what his young children were feeling before they could talk. So as a scientist, Darwin began to observe them carefully. What he found stunned him. Their facial expressions were very similar to those of an orangutan named Jenny also under his observation on a regular basis, albeit at the London Zoo.

After an extensive amount of research, Darwin published *The Expression of the Emotions in Man and Animals* in 1872. The *Blink* of its day, it quickly became a bestseller. In his book, Darwin provided evidence that the facial expressions of humans correlate to those of other primates. He went on to note that the face is the primary vehicle used to communicate emotions to others.

From an evolutionary perspective, the key to Darwin's pioneering research was that we have universal facial expressions because communicating emotions in this way is an adaptive advantage. Long before we could speak, humans communicated with each other primarily via what their faces "said." But from a business perspective, Darwin was laying the groundwork for a scientifically valid means of measuring emotions in order to manage outcomes more successfully.

Unfortunately, it took until the mid-1960s before modern science picked up

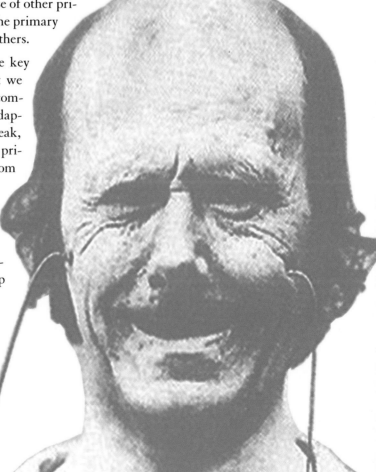

A contemporary of Darwin with whom he corresponded, the French anatomist, Duchenne, used electric shocks to force patients to show the facial expressions he wanted to study because emotion can trigger muscle movement in the face without control. What facial coding terms a true smile is also known as a Duchenne smile.

Paul Ekman and his colleague Wally Friesen spent over seven years scientifically decoding the muscle movements of every type of facial expression. Their end product: the Facial Action Coding System (FACS).

where Darwin had left off. It was then that Dr. Paul Ekman, a professor at the University of California San Francisco, received a grant to confirm or disprove Darwin's theory regarding the universality of facial expressions.

Eventually, Ekman traveled to Papua, New Guinea, to study a tribe that lacked a written language and had lived in virtual cultural isolation from the Western world. There he told stories and asked tribal members to select among photographs of various facial expressions the one that best fit each given story. Except for some problems distinguishing between fear and surprise, the native people clearly recognized the other core emotions, providing evidence that Darwin's theory was correct (Ekman 2003).

Armed with these findings, Ekman and colleague Wally Friesen from the San Francisco School of Medicine proceeded to spend over seven years systematically studying a large pool of facial expressions. Their goal: to precisely document the movements of people's facial muscles.

When they were done, Ekman and Friesen had created the Facial Action Coding System (FACS) which categorizes the activity of forty-three facial muscles. These muscles moving in various combinations form twenty-three Action Units (AUs), which serve as the basic building blocks of all facial expressions. Finally, Ekman and Friesen documented the AUs in terms of which core emotions they express.

Darwin's discovery of the powerful universality of facial expressions had originated in comparing his children to a primate. Now his discovery had become a sophisticated system for deciphering human feelings. Thanks to FACS, it has become possible to quantify emotions by systematically reading other people's faces. As a result, a thorough, precise feel-your-feelings approach exists, enabling companies to know consumers' and employees' actual emotional responses to company initiatives and to plan accordingly.

When I learned about the Darwin-to-Ekman connection, the business applications intrigued me. Nearly three decades after Ekman first traveled to New Guinea, I would arrive at his office in San Francisco eager to learn how best to bring this astounding capacity to the business world.

It was my belief that the old joke "Half of my advertising is wasted; I just don't know which half" reflected a crucial truth.

The purpose was clear: FACS's scaleable, repeatable method of gauging emotional effectiveness could be used to find out what was working, what wasn't and how companies could improve on their best options.

The Brain-to-Face Connection
Facial coding is robust because of the face's unique properties.

When Ekman and Friesen created their facial coding system, they relied on two facts that make it a natural and highly effective tool. The first is that human beings have more facial muscles than any other species on the planet. This fact alone makes analyzing the face a "gold mine" of data. Second, the face is the one and only place on the body where our muscles attach directly to the skin. As a result, the face is highly mobile—with skin that shapes itself quickly in response to impulses from the brain (McNeill). Thus the face provides a spontaneous window into people's feelings.

The expressiveness of our facial muscles provides the basis and the rationale for facial coding. Whenever the brain generates emotionally-encoded impulses, these impulses are delivered to the face via a single facial nerve that controls all our facial muscles and resulting facial expressions.

Much as an ocean wave forms, builds and dissolves, facial expressions have an onset, a peak and a fade. The duration of expressions will typically range from half a second to four seconds. Meanwhile, the length of time and the type and degree of movement all combine to serve as barometers by which to gauge the intensity of the underlying causal emotion.

Seven Core Emotions

Positive: happiness

Neutral: surprise

Negative: fear, anger, sadness, disgust, contempt

As good as the dinner was, it never makes doing the dishes fun. The reason that negative emotions predominate is because humans respond more quickly to bad news than good news as a matter of survival.

The Seven Core Emotions

Every code-able emotion has its own meaning or "script," but there is no specific muscle movement that betrays a liar.

To help get a better grasp on facial coding as a method of determining the *true* emotional response of consumers and employees, let's look at its basic elements. What exactly emerges? Regardless of race, ethnicity, age or gender, people's faces reveal seven core emotions. One is essentially neutral: surprise. Five are negative: fear, anger, sadness, disgust and contempt. The other is positive: happiness. Moreover, happiness can be divided based on two different kinds of smiles, true smiles and social smiles. The latter involves only the mouth and may indicate deceit.

As shown in Chapter 3, this core set of emotions can be expanded through gradations and mixtures. But these are the essential emotions, of which, yes, only one involves upbeat feelings.

In evolutionary terms, a ratio favoring the negative can be explained by the fact that life is kind of like making dinner. We have to go buy the groceries and do the cooking. Eating the food is fabulous fun. But it only takes a few minutes, after which the dishes sit waiting to be washed. In other words, survival instincts dictate being more alert to hearing bad news than good news—and our core emotions reflect that reality.

Now that my readers have been forewarned about the negative tilt, let's review the core emotions. In each case, an emotion's meaning or script will be explained. (Script refers to what typically causes the emotion and what kind of physical response and behavior happen as a result of it.)

Please note that the following photographs of yours truly were staged and may be a little exaggerated, like caricatures, to make studying them easier. Furthermore, note that references to the early age at which these emotions appear on the face is to reinforce the point that facial expressions are universal and innate (McNeill).

Surprise

Our ability to express surprise appears at birth. Uniquely, surprise is neither inherently positive nor negative. Its valence all depends on what we perceive after the surprise has passed. In the basic surprise script, we're confronting a "mystery" we haven't faced before, one that's yet to be solved. We don't know whether pleasure or pain awaits us, and we tend to freeze until we know the outcome.

A surprised face expands upward and downward, north and south, and has much in common with one expressing fear. Here's how the face may show surprise:

- eyes go big
- eyebrows fly high
- mouth falls open

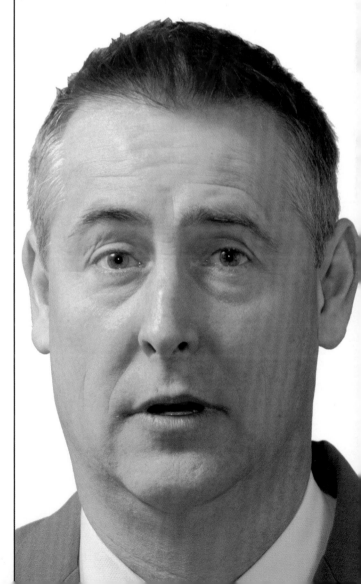

Fear

This is the single most important emotion. Prominent in presidential campaign messages—from John F. Kennedy's "missile gap" to George W. Bush's "War on Terror"—its use is also a mainstay of business. Fear is constantly monitored by consumers in the marketplace. After all, an offer's safety is the first item on people's intuitive checklist—the equivalent of looking both ways before crossing the street. No wonder fear rips through companies when employees hear the latest reorganization rumor. In short, fear cuts through the clutter like nothing else and is used to sell everything from snow tires to toothpaste.

In fear's basic script, we seek to escape some perceived danger in order to protect ourselves. The loss aversion concept, emphasized by behavioral economists, fits right in here.

The ability to express fear appears about five to nine months after birth. Fear opens the face, which will blanch and, in extreme cases, tremble. Here's how the face may show fear:

- eyebrows lift up and in
- eyes widen
- chin pulls wider
- lips stretch back horizontally
- jaw drops open

Anger

Talk to people who work customer service and they'll probably suggest that anger, not fear, is the single most prominent emotion! What they witness is anger's reactionary nature. It involves a lashing out. It's the fight part of our fight-or-flight instinct and arises whenever our expectations are violated. In anger's basic script, people seek to remove or otherwise attack a barrier they believe is *unfairly* blocking progress or undermining their personal identity and sense of self-worth. A secondary script related to desiring progress is that anger arises in response to experiencing a loss of control.

The ability to show anger appears three to seven months after birth. The angry face contracts—like a snake coiling to strike—and its appearance becomes more concentrated and intense. When a person becomes red-faced or "boiling mad," blood floods the face's capillaries. Here's how the face may show anger:

- eyebrows lower and knit together
- eyes narrow into "snake-eyes"
- lips will tighten or form a funnel

Sadness

In business, sadness as expressed in the marketplace is usually about buyer's regret. In the workplace, the despondency created by alienation, stress and fatigue robs a company of its most vital resource: an engaged employee. When we're sad, we slow way, way down. Withdrawal, listlessness and general avoidance behavior become typical. "Always sell hope" is a valid motivational mantra because sadness means feeling helpless. With respect to employees, companies can defuse feelings of rejection and irrevocable loss by offering the prospect of feasible rewards instead of threats of further reprimand.

Sadness appears between birth and three months. Generally speaking, sadness makes the face sag, giving a person a "long face" frown. Here's how the face may show sadness:

- wrinkles form a mid-forehead "puddle"
- eyebrows drop, but inner corners rise slightly
- corners of eyes crease in a wince
- "trench" running between corners of nostrils and upper mouth corners will deepen
- lip corners sag or form an "upside-down" smile

Disgust

Disgust is an adverse reaction shown when we attempt to distance ourselves from an offensive source. It's our way of showing that an object, person, place or even an idea "stinks." Not surprisingly, disgust manifests itself in an upturned nose and curling lips and can be seen as the equivalent of having a foul taste in one's mouth. Unfortunately for those offers lacking spice, a mild form of disgust—*boredom*—which signifies *no taste* for what is being offered is very prevalent.

Disgust appears between birth and three months. It involves a lifting up and away, like a gag reflex, as we try to protect ourselves from "poison." Here's how the face may show disgust:

- nose turns up and wrinkles
- upper lip rises, sometimes as part of an "upside down smile"
- lower lip pulls down and away

Contempt

Less physical and more attitudinal—one might say *moral*—in orientation than disgust, customer contempt in response to feeling deceived, for instance, can be fatal for companies. After all, Dr. Gottman's "Love Lab" research has shown that nothing predicts the collapse of a couple's relationship better than the settling in of contempt. And what's bad for marital bliss surely isn't going to be healthy for company/customer or manager/employee relationships, either.

This emotion reflects deep disdain: a belief that the other party in the deal is beneath you. It's an emotion hard to recover from. Watch out for contempt in others, because it means one's offer, promotional efforts or managerial style has become repugnant to that audience.

Contempt is expressed in subtler but more profound ways than is disgust. The old cartoon character Snidely Whiplash is contempt personified. When feeling this emotion, people's lips will tighten and lift on one side of the face, forming a little pocket or cavity in the cheek like the eye of a hurricane. Here's how the face will show contempt:

- a unilateral expression (the left side of the face is generally more expressive than the right side), with one upper corner of the mouth curling into a sneer
- upper lip rises
- eyes may partly close and turn away

And The Winner Is. . .

As mentioned earlier, there is only one truly positive emotion in Ekman's set of core emotions: happiness. That's because in evolutionary terms survival is job #1, and we don't need happiness to survive. Once we move past meeting basic survival needs, we grant happiness more and more importance.

In therapeutic terms, and based on measures of finding authentic meaning in life, the Positive Psychology movement classifies happiness in levels ranging from fleeting pleasure to deep, sustained contentment. Meanwhile, recognize the reality that people are willing to pay more for their dream-like wants than needs. So making happiness possible can be handsomely rewarded. The happiness script is fairly stable: we've experienced a gain or success and are now making what we deem to be reasonable progress toward a goal.

> *"Happiness makes up in height*
> *what it lacks in length."*
> *—Robert Frost*

The True Smile or Duchenne Smile

Like surprise, our unique capacity for expressing true smiles is present from birth. Maybe that's why the front of breakfast cereal boxes are always full of cartoon characters like a smiling Tony the Tiger, who is meant to coax children into pulling at the heartstrings and billfolds of parents worldwide.

A true smile's signature features are eyes that twinkle or gleam because the muscles surrounding them are animated. Ekman calls a true smile a Duchenne smile in honor of the French anatomist whose photographs of people's expressions aided Darwin's work. Here's how a true smile looks:

- skin near the outer corner of the eye pinches together into "crow's feet"
- the upper eyelid slightly droops and skin under the eye may gather upward
- the corners of the mouth move up and out, the cheeks lift upwards

a **TRUE** smile

The Social Smile

If there are *true* smiles, there must also be false smiles, right? Correct. Human beings have more ability to manipulate the muscles around the mouth (we like to eat, after all) than we do those around the eyes. It's why we have sayings like "the eyes never lie" and "the eyes are the window to the soul." Just think of the "grip and grin" photos present in numerous print ads, television commercials and public relations events. What they have in common is that viewers can intuitively tell that the smiles on the people's faces are "phony" or at least less substantial.

Social smiles appear at one and a half to three months after birth. In other words, toddlers quickly pick up this skill (a revelation that caused a department store researcher I once met with to remark, "I *knew* my kid was manipulating me!"). While there is only one true smile, Ekman has cataloged a score of slightly different social smiles. In essence:

- the face becomes rounder as the corners of the mouth move up and out and the cheeks lift upwards
- missing, however, is the activity around the eyes that would cause them to *twinkle* or *gleam*, thereby indicating the presence of a true smile

a **SOCIAL** smile

Lying Smiles and Other Signs of Deception

The presence of a social smile may simply reveal a degree of enjoyment that falls short of spirited, joyful happiness. Consumers or employees who are pleased with what they've received may nevertheless not experience an exalted happiness because while their expectations were met they were not exceeded.

How they then respond to being satisfied, but not thrilled, could involve the exhibiting of a social smile. But if there's pressure to be happy about the raise a boss has just given you, for example, the employee may gamely put a happy face on the situation. Or a prospect put off by a salesperson's overly aggressive style may exhibit a social smile to hide the fact that the deal is headed south.

In those cases, a degree of deception is involved. And later on, the manager or salesperson may wish he or she had been able to tell from the other party's facial expressions that the end was near. But alas, there is no one muscle movement that categorically reveals deception.

What better example for deceit than the classic clown face?

Painted to look like it's always full of smiles, one glance beneath the makeup can dispel the myth of continuous merriment.

Facial coding does much the same thing by gleaning true, unfiltered, positive or negative emotional reactions.

Instead, bear in mind that while Adolf Hitler practiced his speeches in front of a mirror to test his accompanying expressions, most of us aren't that deliberate. All of us can adequately guard against "two-faced" people whose smiles aren't the real thing by being alert to a few, basic situations or patterns.

In particular, be alert to a polite, masking smile in situations where:

- **It doesn't involve the whole face.** The cheeks will lie flat and still and the eyes don't narrow as they do during a genuine smile.

- **It lingers too long.** A true smile tends to fade around the four-second mark. A false smile may run from five to ten seconds.

- **It has odd timing.** A deceitful smile tends to start or end too abruptly or arrive too early or late. A smile may also be deceitful if what the person is saying and the expression are out of sync.

- **It's asymmetrical** and much more pronounced on just one side of the face. That happens because the smile is likely to have been consciously delivered.

- Finally, watch out for smiles given when the person's face hints of other, darker emotions at or near the same time. In a case of **mixed signals** like happiness and anger, be careful not to discount the anger on display.

That last description of a deceitful smile involves what Ekman calls "leakage" (1992). Basically, it amounts to unintended, fleeting glimpses of what the person is really feeling and involves the kind of brief, micro-expressions referred to by the fellow traveler I met at the Great Wall in China. On a related note, a micro-expression may happen because of "squelches." These occur when a person interrupts his or her natural expression, usually to cover up a negative feeling with a smile. The squelch is something skilled politicians the world over attempt to master.

Data Capture and Analysis
Computer assisted coding will enable quicker,
less expensive results.

In practice, facial coding begins by capturing video. While it can be done by placing cameras in store environments, for instance, Sensory Logic most often tests by running individual interviews with webcams mounted on a laptop computer. Those tests can be administered in focus group facilities, mall facilities, and over the internet, among other settings. The tests are pre-programmed so that the intervals when the webcam will turn on to record video and audio of subjects looking at stimuli and/or answering questions is timed and includes the option of rotating the order in which stimuli are shown.

A webcam atop a laptop screen captures digital video of all responses to computer programmed tests in which the individually tested subjects may look at stimuli as well as answer questions and provide ratings.

How can this help? Consider the prevalence of internet surveys. Cheap and relatively easy to do, they run the risk of being garbage in, garbage out. On the next page are frames captured from webcam recordings. The woman on the left is letting out her dog while "watching" the TV spot she went on to comment about. The woman to the right is talking to her boyfriend the whole way through the spot she also went on to critique. The value of a webcam starts, but doesn't end, with knowing whether the subjects are really paying attention or, in other cases, even fit the screening criteria.

Once the video is captured, it is then manually reviewed at intervals as precise as $1/30^{th}$ of a second, looking for signs of the action units that serve as the building blocks of Ekman's facial coding system. Just prior to completion of this book, however, Sensory Logic entered into an exclusive agreement with the computer-engineering firm, Reallaer. Steps are now under way to automate the coding of the action units, creating the opportunity for greater scale, time efficiencies and reduced costs.

As revealed by webcam footage, both of these subjects went on to critique a TV spot they didn't watch (in favor of letting out the dog and talking to a boyfriend instead).

Using Reallaer's FACtory approach, video is presently coded using software that facilitates the manual coding of facial images by optimizing the review and entry process. Action unit onset, peak and offset are identified by the coder. Additional details such as intensity and laterality are optional. The noted action units can occur individually or in combinations.

In the near future, the FACtory system will provide computer assisted coding whereby the software aids the coder in identifying action units. With computer assisted coding, computer algorithms used by Reallaer and made available for Sensory Logic's exclusive use in the market research realm will enable the automated analysis of data, subject to quality control checks. Using the internet, video files can be submitted for centralized processing and analyzed in relatively turn-key operation. This process will move, to an increasing degree, toward fully automated identification of AUs provided in near real time.

With the aid of the computer-engineering firm Reallaer, facial coding will become an increasingly automated process. Shown here is how the data gets analyzed for tabulation purposes.

Deliverables:
facial coding in practice

Synopsis: Until now emotions have been hard to quantify and, therefore, even harder to plan for. Facial coding changes all that, providing precise metrics that companies can use in plotting strategies and handling tactical executions. To that end, this section shows sample result formats and a couple of case studies. Then it concludes by summarizing Sensory Logic's findings about the extent of the gap between what people say versus what they feel in response to marketing efforts.

Key take-aways:
- Each emotional data set provides its own unique insights.
- Being on-emotion is more important than being on-message.
- There is verbal "grade" inflation in people's responses.

What the Results Look Like
Each emotional data set provides its own unique insights.

As is true when learning to play chess or acquiring any new skill, one can learn some of the basics of facial coding within a short time, but it takes countless hours of practice to master all of the intricacies, let alone decide how best to tabulate the results. Serving as a consultant to Sensory Logic during its start-up phase, Ekman provided my company with not only training materials, but also with advice and feedback as we learned our way.

What Ekman did not have, however, was a scoring system that would enable facial coding to realize its potential as a scientific, cross-cultural tool for quantifying emotional responses. To bring it to scale globally and access a platform of applications, Ekman's FACS system would have to be given additional rigor. In utilizing facial coding on a daily basis in a business context, I, and my company, Sensory Logic, are uniquely qualified because we've added a scoring system, norms and deliverables suitable to business practice. As protected through U.S. patents, granted and pending, our scoring and reporting methods had to be developed and refined over a decade of on-going work in order to fulfill on facial coding's ability to guide companies forward.

The following topline review of a few key charts shows how the data derived from facial coding can be presented. Six charts will be shown:

- Emotional Response Rate (Fig. 2.2)
- Percentage of Positive/Negative Emotional Response (Fig. 2.3)
- Specific Emotional Spectrum (Fig. 2.4)
- Quadrant Chart (Fig. 2.5)
- Second-by-Second Chart (Fig. 2.6)
- Eye Tracking and Concurrent Emotions (Fig. 2.7)

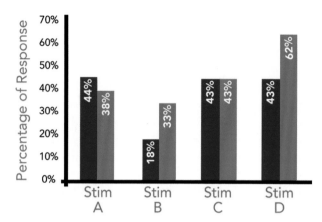

Fig. 2.2 Emotional Response Rate Levels
This chart compares the Emotional Response Rates of four components of two different campaigns. Note the variance in response rates for different components. The blue campaign has an average response of 37% and the green has an average response of 44%. Keep in mind that Emotional Response Rate doesn't measure like or dislike but, rather, whether or not subjects get emotionally engaged by what they're experiencing.

The first decisive measure is whether anybody notices or cares. A company can't win people over if it hasn't awakened them by causing an emotional reaction. At Sensory Logic, we track Emotional Response Rate by discerning the exact percentage of subjects who show at least one action unit (AU), or "hit," on their faces (Fig. 2.2) in reaction to experiencing a stimulus and/or while answering a question.

Once a company knows whether it's engaging people, next is learning the general type of response. From facial coding, a company can also determine which is more prevalent: the percentage of positive or negative emotions shown on people's faces, on average, across the sample population (Fig. 2.3). Remember, however, that negative emotions don't always correlate to bad outcomes. In a problem/solution TV spot, for example, it's vital to establish the problem as real and relevant in order to sell the branded solution. So negative emotions early in the commercial will be an indication that a credible connection is being made.

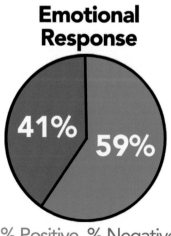

Fig. 2.3 Percentage of Positive and Negative Emotional Response

Then there is also the matter of identifying the specific emotion expressed by subjects (Fig. 2.4). As we know by now, each emotion has its own "script" or meaning. It can be helpful to understand the amount each specific emotion contributes to the overall response of a group.

For our purposes Sensory Logic has divided social smiles into three categories (robust, weak and micro smiles shown briefly on only one side of the face). Surprise is categorized as a slight positive here because of the urgency of obtaining attention in a crowded marketplace. Meanwhile, among the negative emotions skepticism refers to a social smile used to mask or soften a negative comment. Dislike encompasses disgust and contempt. Frustration and anxiety correspond to anger and fear, respectively.

Next up is a quadrant chart (Fig. 2.5), whose importance resides in the fact that each of the emotions shown on people's faces will vary in terms of the Impact and Appeal values of those emotions. To illustrate, there are about five primary ways in which people may exhibit anger on their faces. Those ways vary from outright, blood-curdling rage to far more mild annoyance. Based on the facial muscle activity or AUs, the emotional outcome must take into account the degree of Impact or intensity of those AUs and the degree to which the Appeal being exhibited is positive or negative in orientation. As a result, a quadrant chart maps data reflecting the *emotional temperature* of those AUs we've detected.

Next, in regard to examples like TV commercials, offer usage or customer service experience, people's emotional response unfolds over time. In those cases, a second-by-second chart is in order (Fig. 2.6).

These five charts account for the primary ways in which Sensory Logic shows results, with each version providing a slightly different insight. Due to the fact that people have such a hard time accurately articulating responses to

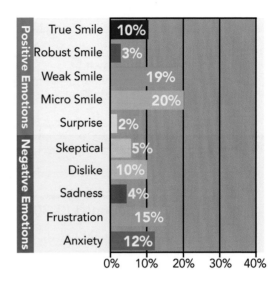

Fig. 2.4 Specific Emotional Spectrum

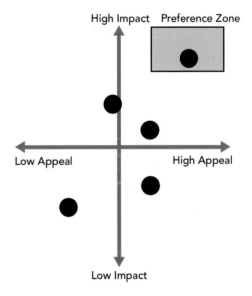

Fig. 2.5 Quadrant Chart
Quadrant charts graphically represent the Impact (intensity of emotional response) and Appeal (degree of positive or negative response) of stimuli. Especially when it comes to purchase intent, the ideal result is in the top, right quadrant—an indication that the target market is enthusiastically positive.

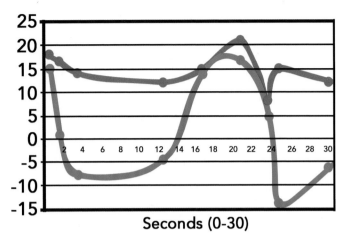

25
20
15
10
5
0
-5
-10
-15

2 4 6 8 10 12 14 16 18 20 22 24 26 28 30

Seconds (0-30)

Fig. 2.6 Second-By-Second Chart
The second-by-second chart provides a way to correlate Impact and Appeal scores to specific details in, for example, a TV commercial. The green line represents Appeal and the red line shows Impact. Remember that Impact can by definition never be negative, so it always looks higher on average.

stimuli (whether visual or word-based), there is also one more relevant measure that we use. To specifically link emotional responses to what is causing them, it's helpful to be able to determine *exactly* what people are looking at.

That's where eye tracking enters the picture. Eye tracking is the recording of where people look and what they focus on. When tied to facial coding, the results indicate the precise amount of gaze activity (where people looked) and specific emotional response to elements of a stimulus (how people feel about what they see). This synchronization of emotional response and visual focus provides a reliable method for understanding what is driving subject reactions (Fig. 2.7).

In effect, the combination of eye tracking and facial coding provides a one-two punch based on people's actual behavior. The eye tracking correlates to awareness: does one get noticed? Meanwhile, the facial coding correlates to consideration. Yes, they noticed but is the company winning them over?

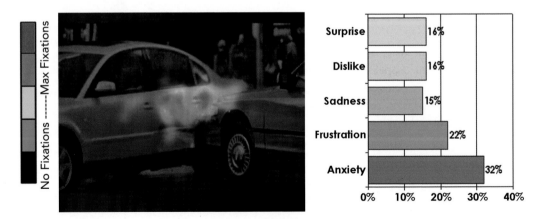

Fig. 2.7 Eye Tracking Hot Spots and Concurrent Emotions
This photo and bar chart represent the ability of eye tracking and facial coding to provide specific insight into the emotional effect of stimuli. Based on the advanced eye trackers available from the Swedish company Tobii, the photo shows the results of eye tracking relative to a scene in a TV spot. As is evident, the main focus of people's gaze fixations is where the collision has occurred. The chart above shows the specific emotional responses present during the viewing of the scene. Together they determine how people feel and what is causing those responses.

Granted, it's an array of charts and formats. But don't worry. Nobody is being asked to memorize them. At the same time, however, familiarity will help because they will appear throughout the chapters that follow to illustrate the results from numerous projects. So readers can use the material just covered as a resource to orient themselves, as a review option, during the pages ahead.

The Power of Being On-Emotion
Being on-emotion is more important than being on-message.

The ultimate, big-picture story being conveyed here is that, yes, it's important to be rationally on-message. But it's even more imperative to be on-emotion. A company's message will only be successful if it attracts interest *and* emotionally appeals to the receiver enough to commit to the proposition being promoted.

As the examples of deliverable formats illustrate, facial coding is a repeatable, actionable methodology. Moreover, companies can also use it to gain a more complete picture of people's responses across a wide range of applications from offer design and advertising to personnel issues as well as other opportunities.

> *"Rational motives are merely a cover-up of unconscious, archaic motive complexes."*
> —Ernest Dicher

So now that we've seen how significant emotions are, how they are measured and how to understand the information they can provide, let's look at a pair of real-world examples that will combine these elements and demonstrate the importance of being on-emotion.

Case #1:
Direct Mail Pieces in the Financial Sector

We tested almost 30 direct mail pieces for a financial services company. (Note that unless permission was granted, the names of clients and examples of their work won't be shown in this book in order to protect their confidentiality.) Of those mailings, eight qualified as part of what might be called a "hell" strategy.

In general terms, that means the company attempted to use fear to motivate consumers into opening a mailing by creating enough concern over the mailing's contents that recipients would be afraid of throwing it into the trash without looking at it. In order to succeed, the "hell" strategy needed to generate a strongly negative emotional reaction.

As shown in Figure 2.8, in four of the five instances where facial coding detected a very negative emotional reaction, the in-market response rate to the mailing was high. In other words, the mailers were on-emotion and elicited the negative response necessary to convince people that the mailers were important and that not opening them could have negative consequences.

In contrast, when the facial coding Emotional Response result was positive—and therefore off-emotion—the response rates for the "hell" mailings were abysmally low.

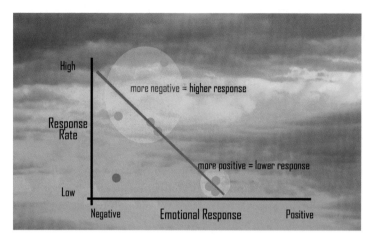

Fig. 2.8 Hell Strategy
88% of fear-based direct mail offers demonstrated strong correlation between increasing negative emotional response and market response. The more negative the emotional response, the higher the market response proved to be in accordance with this strategy for breaking through the clutter.

The "heaven" strategy reveals similar results (Fig. 2.9) in regard to the importance of being on-emotion. Seven of the eleven "heaven" mailers were off-emotion. They failed to have strong positive Emotional Responses because they didn't emotionally convince the recipients that they would find good news inside an envelope promising either an attractive interest rate or other generous terms. In every case, those seven off-emotion "heaven" mailers had low in-market response rates.

As for the other four "heaven" mailers, they were 50% accurate. Half the time, a high response rate was the result of generating a very positive Appeal reaction. But the other half of the in-market wins came from "heaven" mailers that didn't generate favorable emotional reactions. As a result, the predictive power for a "heaven" strategy proved to be slightly less robust.

Overall, however, Sensory Logic correctly predicted the in-market effectiveness of 16 of 19 mailers and proved the power of being on-emotion. What does generating the desired emotional reaction accomplish? It enables success in a fickle medium like direct mail, where the average response rate per piece hovers around 2% (DMA).

In this case, our ability to gauge which "hell" and "heaven" strategy executions would work reached:

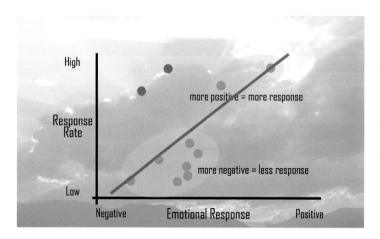

Fig. 2.9 Heaven Strategy
82% of hope-based direct mail offers demonstrated strong correlation between increasing positive Emotional Response and market response. The more negative and off-emotion the response was, the lower the odds that it generated a strong market response.

- 88% for "hell" mailings—seven of eight right (Fig. 2.8) —based on knowing that highly negative reactions were the key for this strategy to pay off.

- 82% for "heaven" mailings—nine of eleven correct (Fig. 2.9)—based on knowing that the mailers meant to be positively received but unlikely to generate that kind of response were likely to fail.

In other words, plucking the correct emotional heartstrings was the key to determining which direct mail pieces were worth sending out the door.

Finally, it is important to note that the overall percentage of direct mail pieces leading to the preferred response rate was higher among "hell" mailings, proving that "going negative" does pay off. Half of the "hell" executions—four of eight (Fig. 2.8)—were successful, while approximately 35% of the "heaven" strategy—four of eleven (Fig. 2.9)—were successful. So it would appear that mailers meant to sell hope but failing to generate positive emotional responses—i.e., landing in *purgatory*—fall flatter in market than do mailers pushing people's fear buttons.

Case #2:
Designing the Next Big Pickup Truck

For a major motor vehicle company, we looked at various design options for a forthcoming pickup truck model. In Case #1, the degree of positive or negative Appeal was the key measure in detecting what would work. This time around, the key proved to be the Impact or intensity level of the emotional responses we saw in the subjects. In short, weak positive support—lacking enthusiasm—proved insufficient to be a winner in the marketplace.

Here's what happened:

As shown in Figure 2.10, there were six design options the company was considering for final production. Of the six, two blew away the competition based on subjects' positive verbal responses. In fact, the two designs were the only ones to receive positive rational responses. And this duo also received positive Appeal results based on the emotional facial coding—although the Impact results were worrisome. They were dishearteningly low.

Our concern was that subjects said and showed that they liked both options; however, their smiles were tepid. They lacked the fire of conviction. Wouldn't this lack of enthusiasm prove fatal in a sector where price tags are high, competition fierce and innovation so constant that a company risks looking dated by the time its design hits the streets?

We thought so. And as the eventual sales results show, the marketplace unfortunately proved us right. Our advice was to go back to the drawing board. Instead, the client opted for one of the rational "winners" and put it on showroom floors. As the right side of Figure 2.10 shows, the 2004 sales (the year the design was put into production) dropped by 1%.

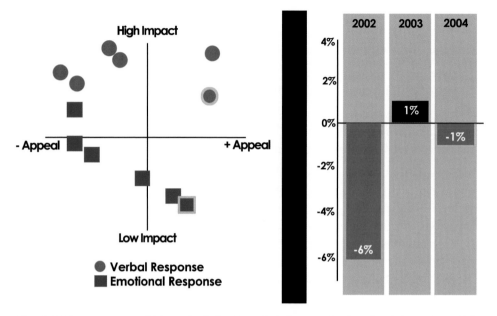

Fig. 2.10 Responses to Pickup Truck Designs & Sales Results for the Selected Model
The chart on the left shows the emotional and verbal response of subjects to proposed pickup truck designs for a 2004 release. On the right are preceding sales figures and the outcome for the year of the model's release. Though emotional Appeal was strong for the chosen design (outlined in orange), Impact was low—reflecting a lack of enthusiasm. As is evident based on the 2004 sales results, the design's lack of emotional Impact during testing proved to be an accurate prediction of eventual marketplace response.

Exploring the Say/Feel Gap
There is verbal "grade" inflation in people's responses.

With years of projects and thousands of examples behind us, Sensory Logic is in the unique position of being able to quantify the extent of the gap that can exist between what people say and how they actually feel. So in the closing section of this chapter, let's examine the gap—knowing that actions really do speak louder than words. Thus it makes sense that Ekman refers to the various types of facial muscle activity as *action* units (AUs). Though miniature in scale, what people show on their faces is still behavior. As a result, facial expressions are reliable guides to how people are likely to respond as consumers or employees.

The key question is, "To what extent do people's verbal and facial coding responses conflict with one another?" To answer it, Sensory Logic has engaged in extensive reviews of our database. Here are some general guidelines as to what we have found true over the years:

- **Grade inflation exists.** As a rule of thumb, the percentage of positive verbal results often exceeds the percentage of positive facial coding activity by at least 10%. At times, the gap gets as large as 20% to 30% either way—more negative or positive—depending on whether people feel comfortable disclosing what they like. Overall, the track record suggests that people tend to say they like something more than their actual feelings merit.

- **There are racial differences.** We often get asked about differences between races and cultures, especially whether the Japanese reveal their emotions enough to do facial coding. The answer is, yes. Playing videotape on a split-second basis and freeze-framing it for further review helps. The Japanese may be more subtle and reserved in their facial movements but, as fellow human beings, they show their emotions using the exact same facial muscles moving in identical patterns. The difference is something Ekman calls display rules, i.e. the degree to which emotions are easily evident or else get "squelched." Suffice it to say, the ability to detect micro-expressions is crucial in doing work in Japan given that cultural differences favor the discreet. In contrast, we've seen some fairly profound differences here in America regarding the size of the say/feel gap. Caucasians and Hispanics are in one group. They typically have a fairly large gap, tilted toward positive exaggeration. In the other camp are African-Americans, who are much more forward about saying exactly what's on their minds (and in their hearts).

- **There are really two tribes: men and women.** Is there a gender gap related to the say/feel gap? Yes, we've found one. For men, the say/feel gap is smaller than it is for women for two reasons. First, men tend to have a lower percentage of positive verbal response than women. In other words, they're less inclined to "make nice." Second, men tend to have a higher percentage of positive facial coding activity than women. In other words, they're more emotionally promiscuous—less choosy than their more discriminating female colleagues.

Now that we have established how facial coding works, both in theory and practice, it's time to move on to Chapter 3 and build the rest of the analytical model that will form the basis for the application chapters to follow.

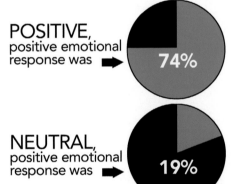

When survey ratings were...

POSITIVE, positive emotional response was ➡ 74%

NEUTRAL, positive emotional response was ➡ 19%

NEGATIVE, positive emotional response was ➡ 4%

Fig. 2.11 A Say/Feel Gap Discrepancy
Using statistics Sensory Logic has calculated from two major projects, this chart demonstrates the fact that *people don't always know how they really feel, even if they think they do.* The top pie chart shows that when our subjects said they had a positive reaction, it was emotionally positive only 3/4th of the time. When they stated a neutral reaction, they actually responded in an emotionally positive manner 1/5th of the time. And when they voiced negative feelings, they had a positive reaction unbeknownst to them 1/20th of the time.

3

emotions and motivations

Like meshed gears that transfer power
to an engine, emotions and motivations
are the source behind all human action.

How can companies anticipate and
leverage this essential knowledge?

Read on.

OVERVIEW

To explore, not ignore, the role that emotions play in how people respond to circumstances is vital. Only then can companies secure insights that lead to success by being better able to decide among options that aren't being viewed through only a rational perspective. At the same time, however, the motivations that compel people to act are also important. Without taking motivations into account, it's as if those emotions supposedly arose without cause or reason for being. In this chapter we'll take a deeper look at emotions while linking them to motivations. More specifically, we will focus on:

- **Contextualizing Emotions**—In Chapter 2, the seven core emotions were briefly profiled. Now in this section, we will establish a deeper understanding of emotions. That requires, first, defining what emotions are. Next, the secondary emotions that arise from blends of the primary or core emotions will be identified. From there, those secondary emotions will be subdivided into internally-oriented versus externally-oriented emotions. Finally, how the core emotions correspond to specific action tendencies will also be identified. The implication for business? When executives understand emotions and the context in which they are experienced, businesses can plan for and better manage the behavior linked to them.

- **Motivations**—Numerous business models exist in which industry sector and offer-specific needs have been identified to aid a company in its strategic planning. But how about the basic, underlying needs that exist across cultures and relate to the basic human condition? Fortunately, a pair of Harvard professors have identified four core motivations or needs that drive human behavior and will be profiled here. The implication for business? To create and communicate initiatives that will engender long-term commitment from consumers and employees alike, companies must link those initiatives to motivations that are essential and eternally relevant.

- **The Emotionomics Matrix**—What is the Emotionomics Matrix? It's an actionable model that companies can use in broadening their strategic business planning to include not only rational elements but also the intimately related, though often neglected human factors of emotions and motivations. Think of the Matrix as an architect's blueprint. It tells us what the underlying structure is. The implication for business? Creating these matrices as, for instance, a platform for an advertising campaign or how to introduce a new initiative to employees will enable companies to anticipate the feelings and needs that will most compel the audience to care and buy-in.

Now let's look more closely at how companies can engage in more incisive business planning, starting with a fuller understanding of emotions.

Contextualizing Emotions:
how feelings fuel behavior

Synopsis: This section lays the groundwork for being able to gain a richer, working knowledge of what emotions are and how the core emotions often blend to create secondary emotions. In addition, this section will describe the meaning or "script" of those secondary emotions before finally looking at correlations between feelings and the actions that typically result from them.

Key take-aways:

- Unlike rational thoughts, emotions are action-oriented.
- It's possible to expand the set of core emotions to anticipate more situations.
- Some emotions we effect, while others reflect external forces dominating us.
- Specific emotions signal that specific behavioral outcomes are likely.

Defining What Emotions Actually Are
Unlike rational thoughts, emotions are action-oriented.

Not only are emotions messy, but so are the discussions involving them. Look closely at the business writings and research or strategic planning models that attempt to address emotions and what will one find? Confusion. People rarely know what they're talking about when they refer to emotions. Too often, the discourse gets cloudy with terms that aren't emotions at all but, rather, business objectives masking as feelings. For instance, *relevant* isn't an emotion. Nor is *warm*. Nor is *familiar*. And yet these words appear as emotions that businesses are attempting to generate in target markets.

People rarely know what they're talking about when they discuss emotions.

To begin, let's define what an emotion is and, therefore, what it isn't. Thankfully, real experts have already looked at this issue and provided us all (me included) with some answers.

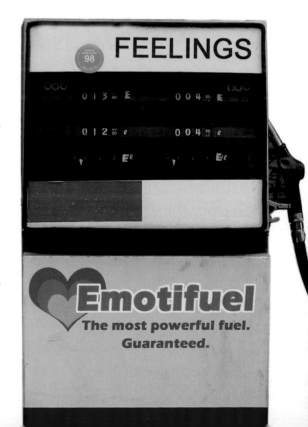

In sifting through the various expert opinions available on this matter (Cornelius), a psycho-physiological (mind/body) consensus emerges. These are the three universal qualities that characterize emotions:

- A **feeling** component—physical sensations, including chemical changes in the brain
- A **thinking** component—conscious or intuitive "thought" appraisals
- An **action** component—expressive reactions (like smiles or scowls), as well as coping behaviors (think fight or flight)

Sometimes an optional sensory component exists.

- A **sensory** component—sights, sounds, et cetera, which intrude and serve to trigger the emotional response

When executives understand emotions and the context in which they are experienced, businesses can plan for and better manage the behavior linked to them.

Emotionality is distinguished from rationality because the latter only involves one of these four components: *thinking*. Unlike an emotion, thinking may, but is less likely to, have a sensory component. That's because we frequently think in "the abstract." In contrast, there are often specific circumstances or events that bring an emotion into being and give it a time-sensitive urgency that thoughts rarely have.

More importantly, a rational thought remains fairly abstract. A thought will be likely to cause a sensory, bodily sensation only if it triggers an emotion. Meanwhile, surely the single most important distinction for business is that thoughts, unlike emotions, aren't action-oriented. They don't necessarily cause anything to happen.

In short, rational thought involves conscious, deliberate, evaluative assessments. A thought is about *arriving* at a judgment. Think of it as a dog riding in a car with its head out the window.

Emotions might be best summed up as a cat-fight: sudden, hairy, intense.

In contrast, it's as if an emotion happens *to* us. They're more like spontaneous events that unfold inside us. So think of emotions as a dog finding itself in a fight with a cat. Everything's relative. Chaos reigns. The dog's just happy to survive.

Now we are halfway through establishing a comparative framework for emotions. On one side of emotions are rational thoughts. What's on the other side of emotions? The answer is moods, which in comparison are far less intense than emotions because they aren't associated with a triggering, sensory stimulus. The strength of emotions is that they help mobilize the body to get through an emergency. As revealed in our faces, emotions have an onset, a peak and typically fade in a matter of seconds. Moods tend to linger for hours or days and again live more in the abstract—like thoughts. Unlike rational thoughts, however, with moods the feeling component is in play along with the thought itself.

Joy	Amazement	Rage	Loathing	Grief	Terrified
HAPPINESS	**SURPRISE**	**ANGER**	**DISGUST**	**SADNESS**	**FEAR**
Satisfaction	Curiosity	Annoyance	Boredom	Pensiveness	Worry

Red = high-intensity / Blue = low-intensity

(Plutchik)

Fig. 3.1 Emotional Intensity Spectrum Once contempt is incorporated into its related emotion, disgust, a set of six basic emotions emerge. Those six can then, in turn, be expanded on by taking into account higher and lower intensity versions of them.

A Wider Range of Emotions
It's possible to expand the set of core emotions to anticipate more situations.

Now that emotions have been defined as highly prone to triggering stimuli that lead to action, we're alert to the need to tread carefully in interactions with others. How consumers and employees get treated on a daily basis *will* have consequences. But before we can factor emotions into strategic and tactical business planning, there is still one step left. We need to have as wide but accurate a range of emotions to talk about as possible. Only then can we address the variety of human behaviors likely to arise in different situations.

Aiming to leverage only the core emotions on Ekman's list could begin to seem limiting. It's a little bit like asking an agency to draft a creative brief on par with da Vinci's *Mona Lisa* but telling them they can use just a pair of colors to do it.

Fortunately, two simple steps help create a wider array of emotions to utilize in planning and analysis. First, realize that the emotions showcased in Chapter 2 exist on a spectrum. While emotions are much more intense than moods, they also vary in regard to their own degrees of intensity, as Figure 3.1 indicates.

Second, think of Ekman's core emotions as the primary colors, which, when mixed in different combinations, create all the other colors. Emotions rarely occur alone; they are usually felt in combination with another emotion. In fact, the number of action units in Ekman's system that reference only one emotion are the exception, not the rule.

By plotting the primary emotions on both a horizontal and diagonal axis, Sensory Logic created a chart, illustrated in Figure 3.2, that shows how secondary emotions are formed. Every secondary emotion is a combination of two primary emotions. (Here, Ekman's core emotion of contempt appears as a combination of disgust and anger.) For example, to understand how *out-*

	Surprise	Anger	Disgust	Sadness	Fear
Happiness	Delight Relief	Pride Vengeance	Morbidity	Nostalgia Yearning	Guilt Hope
	Surprise	Outrage		Embarassment Disappointment	Awe Alarm
		Anger	Contempt Resentment	Sullenness Envy	Jealousy
			Disgust	Regret	Shame Prudishness
				Sadness	Despair Distress

green = positive emotions
red = negative emotions
gray = neutral emotions

Primary Emotions and Secondary Combinations

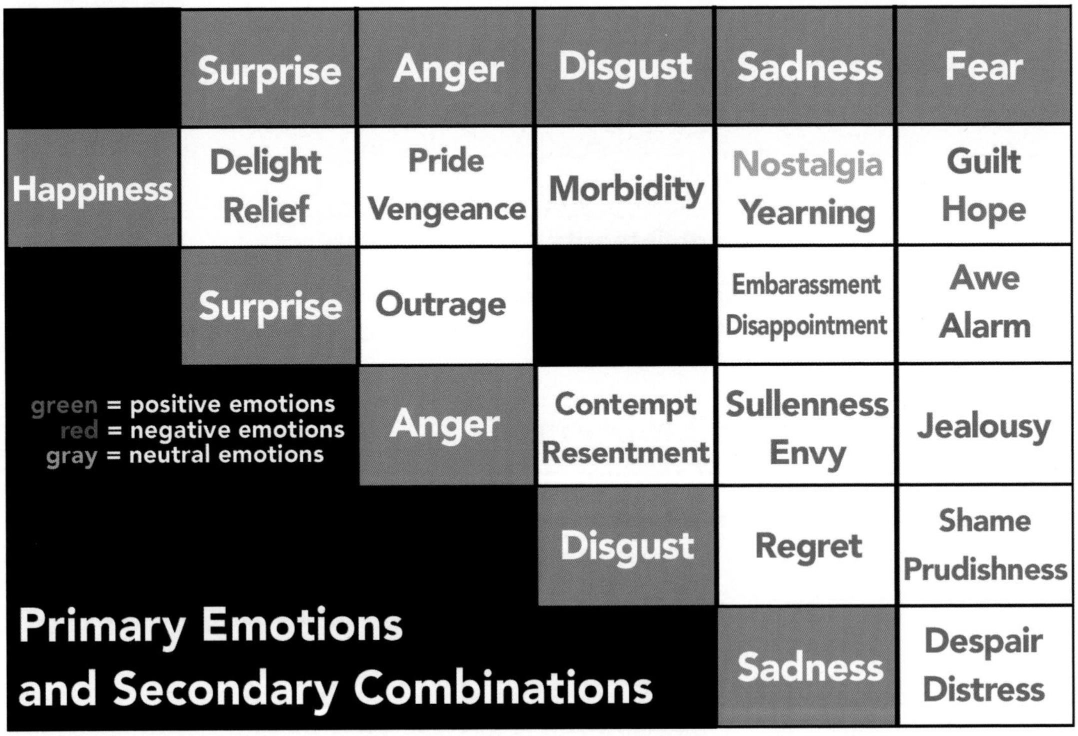

(Zeitlin)

Fig. 3.2 How the Primary Emotions Combine to Create the Secondary Emotions
When the primary emotions combine (as they usually are in real life), a much richer palette of human emotional response emerges. Quite obviously, the bulk of the secondary emotions are negative in orientation, reflecting people's innate desire to survive by choosing either fight or flight.

rage is formed locate outrage in one of the white boxes that denotes the secondary emotions. Next, find the corresponding primary emotion in a blue box above outrage on the horizontal axis, in this case *anger*. After that, locate the other primary emotion directly to the left of outrage, also in a blue box, in this case *surprise*. Now it is easier to understand that outrage is a combination of anger and surprise.

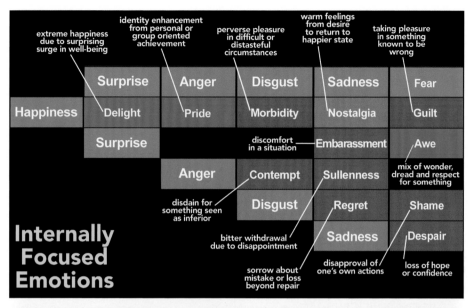

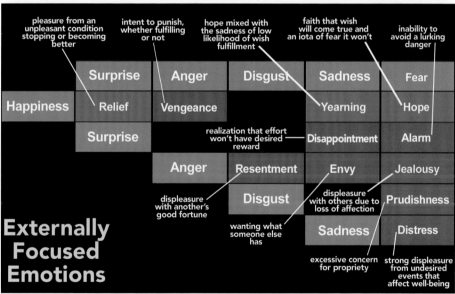

Fig. 3.3 Internally and Externally Focused Secondary Emotions

When we take all combinations into account, the initial list of emotions grows from Ekman's seven to 30. This chart provides a much richer palette of emotions to work with. Whether used as an inspiration for innovative marketing or as a tool for motivating employees, these primary and secondary emotions offer universally measurable benchmarks against which specific goals can be scientifically quantified. They will be referenced in subsequent chapters as we discuss how they may apply to various issues.

While there are only seven core emotions, in interpreting human responses it's possible to blend the core emotions to create a broader array of feelings that provide specific insights.

Of the 30 emotions listed here, notice that even given the most generous of interpretations, only seven of the emotions listed are positive in orientation. Two others—surprise and nostalgia—are neutral. The remainder are negative to some degree, again reflecting the drive to survive that keeps us particularly alert to bad news.

Internally Versus Externally Focused Emotions
Some emotions we effect, while others reflect external forces dominating us.

In Chapter 2 we defined each of Ekman's core emotions, the ones that are labeled here as the primary emotions. Now it's time to briefly define the other, secondary emotions so that they can also serve as a reference point (Fig. 3.3).

With 24 of them to cover, some sort of categorization will no doubt prove helpful. Let's break them into two sets: the 13 internally-focused versus the 11 externally-focused emotions (Roseman; Ortony 1988). By internally-focused, what's meant are emotions that are either caused by the person experiencing them or are inwardly directed. These emotions typically relate either to self-esteem issues or how we internalize our responses to changing conditions based on the expectations we held going into a situation.

An example of an internally focused emotion is pride, which involves how we feel about our own accomplishments. In contrast, vengeance is an externally-focused emotion because the person feeling it wants to harm somebody else.

That leaves the 11 externally-focused emotions. These are the emotions caused by external circumstances or where the emotion's energy or resulting actions get directed at somebody else. Concerns about status and the fortunes of other people—especially when linked to how well our own goals are being realized—tend to cause these emotions.

How Emotions Influence and Reveal Behavior

Specific emotions signal that specific behavioral outcomes are likely.

With a working definition of emotion in place and specific definitions for the primary and secondary emotions established, it's now possible to start modeling how specific emotions lead to specific outcomes. Thanks to facial coding, it's also now possible to know what exactly consumers and employees are feeling. But in order for this amazing new knowledge to make an actionable difference on behalf of business practitioners, it's necessary to close the loop by linking emotions to behavior.

In short, we need to know: What do each of these emotions mean in terms of understanding and influencing people's behavior?

For simplicity's sake, we will focus on five behavioral results. As a reader's guide to Figure 3.4, here's a summary of what the academic research indicates about how emotions influence a handful of key, recurring business-oriented behaviors:

- Related to attention is what kind of outcome orientation people have based on the emotion they're feeling. The choice is basically carrot or the stick, reward or punishment. Here *happiness*, *anger* and *sadness* are related because all three of these emotions involve being

	Primary Emotional States					
Behavioral Result	Happiness	Surprise	Anger	Fear	Sadness	Disgust
Outcome Orientation	High focus on receiving reward	Split focus between reward and punishment	High focus on receiving reward	Split focus between reward and punishment	High focus on receiving reward	High focus on avoiding punishment
Level of Attention	High	High	Medium	Medium	Low	Low
Action Bias	High: strive for results	High: strive for results	High: prompts retaliation	Low: delay/freeze	Low: delay/freeze	High: engage in avoidance
Risk Tolerance	High risk, low reward	NA	High risk, high reward	Low risk, low reward	High risk, high reward	NA
Decision Making	Quick (not concerned)	Cautious (uncertain)	Quick (impulsive)	Cautious (wary of outcome)	Cautious (delay)	Quick (get it over with)

(Roseman; Smith; Frijda; Raghunathan; Loewenstein; Tiedens; Mackie; Bodenhausen)

Fig. 3.4 A Profile of Feeling/Action Interdynamics

strongly focused on getting the reward (*happiness* is the best because the reward we seek is either in sight or already in hand). The polar opposite is *disgust*, where avoiding the punishment of a negative condition is everything.

- In regard to level of attention, advertisers and executives, for instance, are right to emphasize the positive in order to get the audience's attention. Research indicates that only *happiness* or *surprise* ensures a high attention level. Losing hope and interest as reflected by *sadness* or *disgust* brings about the lowest attention level.

- When it comes to getting something done, each emotion also involves a different action bias. Four of the six emotions under study here drive people to action, but the type of action varies. Feeling *happy* or *surprised*? We'll strive for results. *Angry*? We're seeking revenge. *Disgusted*? We can't get away fast enough. *Fear* and *sadness* are, in contrast, the emotions that slow us down.

- For consumers and employees alike, risk tolerance is a major consideration. The mantra "No pain, no gain" only makes sense to an audience that feels like the mantra is right for them. We'll take the risk of trying to secure a gain more often if we're *happy*, *angry* or *sad*. The difference between these three emotions, however, is that when we're happy we tend to take a risk even if the reward is low. With *fear*, the risk is considered low because danger already exists. Finally, with *sadness* we feel like we've got nothing to lose.

- Finally, decision-making styles also vary by emotion. Feelings provide information. They also influence how we process information. If we're feeling *happy*, *angry* or *disgusted*, we go quickly—either because we're not concerned (happy), impatient (angry) or discouraged (disgusted). In contrast, feeling *surprise*, *fear* or *sadness* leaves us more paralyzed.

Overall, these findings indicate why the business world needs to take emotions seriously. They shouldn't be ignored because they influence and at times even dictate outcomes. Moreover, simply describing a person as feeling positive or negative isn't good enough either. As we've seen from these five behavioral results, two negative emotions like anger and sadness, for instance, can lead to very different outcomes.

Simple categorizations like positive or negative simply aren't insightful enough to help strategize. As Figure 3.4 makes evident, the various negative emotions can lead to sharply contrasting behaviors.

Motivations:
what spurs us on

Synopsis: Emotions don't exist in a vacuum. Some sort of stimulus is forever tempting our emotions to turn on, provided it's powerful enough. But while the stimuli will vary, the argument has now been made that the key motivations underlying why and how those stimuli strike us don't vary and haven't varied across the course of human history. The four core motivations that have been identified from research will be emphasized here.

Key take-away:
- Four core motivations cover the reasons why people take the actions they do.

Understanding Needs That Drive Human Behavior
Four core motivations cover the reasons why people take the actions they do.

On learning how the core emotions can influence our behavior, it would also be helpful to know about the core motivations that cause our emotions to turn on. In *Driven: How Human Nature Shapes Our Choices*, Lawrence and Nohria, two Harvard University organizational psychology professors, have analyzed human motivation. While their focus is on the workplace, i.e., company employees, their conclusions apply to consumers as well.

After an extensive review, the authors propose that there are four basic human motivations: to defend, acquire, bond and learn. While these motivations will be explained in greater depth momentarily, in essence they can be defined as follows:

- **Defend**: the oldest, most primitive need is pure instinct: survive.
- **Acquire**: while not a matter of survival, feathering the nest adds to comfort.
- **Bond**: having allies provides both pleasure and security.
- **Learn**: akin to the spiritual/self-growth atop Maslow's hierarchy of needs.

Depicting the order or interrelationship of these four core motivations is open to interpretation. In Figure 3.5 and 3.6, as well as in all of the application chapters to follow, I've decided to diagram the four motivations a little differently than in *Driven*. Lawrence and Nohria depict each core emotion as occupying a corner of a four-sided diamond. This format could suggest that

Much like Ayers Rock in Australia, the core motivations that drive human decisions and emotional responses are speculated to have been around since the beginning of time.

the diametrically opposed motivations of defend/acquire and bond/learn cancel each other out. Yet nothing in their book makes that claim.

In contrast, I've sought to avoid such a misunderstanding by showing the oldest, in effect, most negative motivation—defend—in the center of the diagram. It is obviously protective in nature and likely to be closely related to fear. As a result, placing *defend* in the middle makes sense because nothing is more basic, more central, to humanity than the urge to ensure our survival.

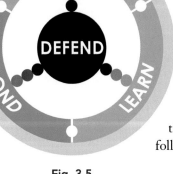

The other three motivations are, as Lawrence and Nohria observe, more proactive in nature. So they've been arrayed around the more constrictive *defend* motivation. Meanwhile, all of the motivations have been linked to make the point that—like the primary or core emotions, and the way they can blend to create secondary emotions—the four core motivations may likewise either interact or work independently of one another and will be depicted accordingly in the examples to follow.

As complex as that may seem, the bottom line, however, is simple. Lawrence and Nohria propose that, taken together, these four core motivations form a complete, universal set. Let's follow their reasoning.

Fig. 3.5
Four Core Motivations

Motivation #1:
Defend

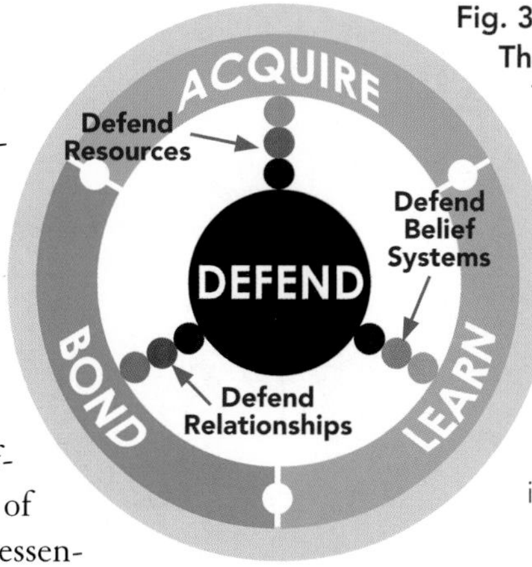

The most fundamental motivation is to ensure our survival. Protecting ourselves from danger and creating security is as basic as it gets. In addition to preventing physical harm, this motivation also encompasses defense against psychological harms like lower self-esteem or stress: a combination of mental and bodily harm. While essentially negative and reactive, the defend motivation can be viewed positively to the extent that it preserves useful achievements and guards against making rash changes.

Fig. 3.6
The Defend Motivation
The single most primal motivation is to defend our existence. Reactive in nature, this motivation can nevertheless interact with the other, more expansive motivations to arrive at goals broader than individual survival.

The reactionary defend motivation can likewise be understood in relation to the other motivations. For example, when attacked we seek to protect: *resources* (belongings that we have acquired), *relationships* (loved ones with whom we have bonded) and the *belief systems* (values we've learned during life). See Figure 3.6 for details.

In the end, however, the defend motivation stands alone in the center of the diagram because it's markedly different from the other three motivations, which are more expansive in nature, inspiring us to extend our horizons. The motivation to defend risks a fight to the death in a classic evolutionary win/loss scenario. In contrast, the other three motivations provide an opportunity for win/win situations in which everyone enriches his or her physical, social and mental well-being.

Here then is what the more evolved motivations are about:

Motivation #2:
Acquire

When not harnessed on behalf of benefiting one's immediate family and other loved ones, acquire becomes the selfish me-myself-and-I motivation. At its most basic level, this motivation ensures our survival by prompting us to gather essentials such as food and shelter. At a more advanced level, however, the goal is to gain control of objects and symbols of power that improve our status relative to others. Often, this motivation also entails accruing money and allies to bolster our identity and make life more secure and pleasant. People seem to have a natural desire to establish dominance within hierarchies, which is why the fear of disgrace is this motivation's dark underbelly.

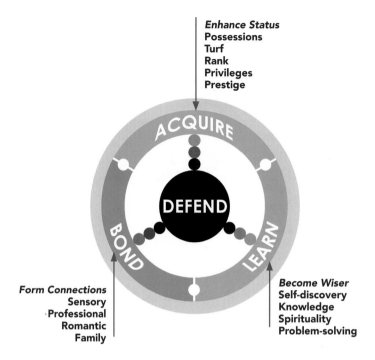

Enhance Status
Possessions
Turf
Rank
Privileges
Prestige

Form Connections
Sensory
Professional
Romantic
Family

Become Wiser
Self-discovery
Knowledge
Spirituality
Problem-solving

Fig. 3.7 The Proactive Motivations. Listed above are special goals or points of focus related to each of the other three, more proactive core motivations.

Motivation #3:
Bond

The collective of me is we. Bonding is based on the reality that a life shared with others can be more fulfilling as well as more comfortable. Moreover, from a more strategic vantage point, opportunities to be part of a community and engage in reciprocity can result in mutually supportive, long-term relationships. Everyone seeks acceptance.

Motivation #4:
Learn

While the motivation to acquire is *materially* expansive and the motivation to bond is *emotionally* expansive, the motivation to learn is *intellectually* and *spiritually* expansive. It's based on our innate curiosity about the world around us. It can be thought of as non-material foraging. At a rational level, learning is about collecting information to plan and predict likely outcomes. But at heart, this motivation explains our quest for spiritual, ideological and aesthetic ways to appreciate and make sense of the world around us.

In summary, those are the four core motivations companies should always bear in mind. Why? Because to create and communicate initiatives that will engender long-term commitment from consumers and employees alike, companies must link their initiatives to motivations that are essential and eternally relevant.

The Emotionomics Matrix:
introducing a strategic model

Synopsis: With both of the human factors of emotions and motivations explained, it's now time to introduce the deliverable referred to at the start of this chapter: the Emotionomics Matrix. In literal terms, it refers to the integration of emotions into economics. But in richer, operational terms, the Emotionomics Matrix is meant to give the business world a way to take into account what motivations cause people to act and how people's feelings will, in turn, further influence their actions. In this section let's first define the Emotionomics Matrix and then show it in practice, using as a case study the marketplace battle involving upscale beer.

> **Key take-aways:**
> - The Matrix reflects the reality that behavior can arise from a mixture of factors.
> - Underlying the growth of upscale beer is a drive for authentic uniqueness.

Defining the Emotionomics Matrix
The Matrix reflects the reality that behavior can arise from a mixture of factors.

The purpose of the Emotionomics Matrix is to use it to strategically frame business issues in a way that gets beyond pure rationality. To achieve that goal, the Matrix must be at once both simple enough to understand and use and flexible enough to reflect the reality that behavior arises from—and is guided by—a mixture of the motivations and emotions already introduced in this book.

In the application chapters to follow, the Matrix will be repeatedly employed to help frame the discussion of the three key business issues each chapter is organized around.

But first let's explain what exactly the Emotionomics Matrix is. While the four core motivations are central to it, the Matrix would be woefully incomplete if it didn't take into account emotions. So Figure 3.8 shows how it might be possible to assign a place within the Matrix for each of Ekman's core emotions based on which motivations are the most likely to invoke them. While these are not rigid assignments, the objective is to give readers some sense of how the core motivations and the core emotions may be related.

In subsequent examples, each business issue will be framed in terms of which motivation or pair of motivations are most relevant. The issue's placement relative to the motivations will then be shown by an arrow labeled with the emotion that is also most relevant to the issue. Most times, the emotion deemed most relevant or revealing of the business issue being discussed will be the one business people should strive to *create* in their targeted audience, whether it be consumers or employees. But at other times, it will be the negative emotion they should seek to *diffuse* so as not to imperil their goals.

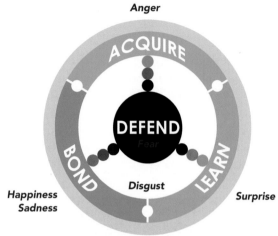

Fig. 3.8 The Emotionomics Matrix
How do emotions and motivations pair up
most naturally?

- Defend and fear form a likely combination, given concerns about survival.
- Acquire and anger fit together because anger often involves seeking control.
- Learn and surprise make sense together because of the discovery process.
- Bond fits together with both happiness and sadness as we either celebrate being with those we care about or are sad about missing them.
- Disgust can involve rejecting an idea (learn), person (bond) or object (acquire).

But we're getting ahead of ourselves. First, let's look at how the Emotionomics Matrix operates by taking it through a practice run.

The Emotionomics of Upscale Beer
*Underlying the growth of upscale beer is a drive
for authentic uniqueness.*

Anheuser-Busch, Miller and Coors were worried. The increased popularity of wine, martinis and micro-brews was cutting into the opportunity for growth. Wine consumption had increased by 63% since 1991. Beer sales were relatively flat and beer's share of the total alcohol market had dropped from 56% in 1999 to around 53% in recent years. Even more worrisome was that in 2005, for example, mass-market beer sales were down .3% overall while the country's craft brewers recorded a 9% increase in sales volume for the year (Daykin; Quaid).

The solution? If you can't beat them, join them.

Mass brewers have done so in numerous ways. They've been buying microbreweries, signing distribution deals for both foreign and craft beers, revamping their own current offers and creating new ones. Their underlying strategy is to have an offer whose status enables it to compete with cosmopolitans and merlots by providing more authenticity and sophistication than mass-market beer.

But knowing *how* best to enter the growing upscale beer market depends on understanding *why* the shift from beer to wine is taking place in terms of the motivations and emotions in play. So let's use the Emotionomics Matrix (Fig. 3.9) to look at three key issues mass-market beer companies are seeking to address.

Fig. 3.9 Emotional Solutions for Craft Style Beers

Acculturated Labeling

Arresting New Bottle Shapes

ACQUIRE

DEFEND

BOND

LEARN

Unique Aromas and Flavors

Opportunity #1: Unique Aromas and Flavors

To offset the lack of enticement some consumers might usually associate with non-craft beer offerings, the big three beer companies have begun to provide new, upscale beers with rich aromas for the nose and more tantalizing flavors for the taste buds. Anheuser-Busch has introduced B-to-the-E and Tilt, which feature sweet flavors, caffeine, ginseng and guarana, a Brazilian stimulant. That edge helps to battle a rival like SAB-Miller's entry, Leinenkugel's Sunset Wheat, which uses coriander to create a unique taste. Another notable contender is Sam Adams' Utopias, described as having a cognac-like aroma and a taste that's slightly fruity with maple syrup "notes." With a current asking price of $100 for a 750mL bottle, Utopias promises the drinker something that can't be found in a bottle of malt liquor.

Emotion and Motivations – From a human factors point of view, let's start with the underlying emotion most relevant here: how the **yearning** for fulfilling sensory sensations can be met. A blend of sadness and happiness, yearning transformed into unalloyed happiness must be the emotional goal of beer companies seeking to overcome a legacy of less than exciting offers. The pertinent motivations are **learn** and **bond**. Why? Because companies seizing the opportunity will, first, get consumers to learn about their enticing aromas and taste bud treats; second, they will then get consumers to form a sensory bond with their offer through experiencing it.

For the past 15 years, major beer
producers were growing nervous
with flat sales, a rise in wine consumption
and a drop in total market share.

Wine, on the other hand, enjoyed a surge in popularity
to the tune of a 63% rise in consumption since 1991.
It was different, classy and aesthetically pleasing.
Vintners toasted each other all the way to the bank.

Opportunity #2: Arresting New Bottle Shapes

The wineries have moved to easy-open screw-tops, cans and party-friendly boxes to remain upscale but soften their image. What can the beer companies do? Well, since we see the beer's packaging before we experience its smell or taste, the shape of the beer bottle is a good means of signaling that a new, non-advertising form of differentiation has arrived. Anheuser-Busch's Celebrate packs a double punch. It appears under its Michelob brand as an oak-aged, dark vanilla beer and its bottle looks more like a bottle of champagne than beer. But for an even more extreme positioning, again look to Sam Adams' Utopias, which come in a bottle styled like a copper decanter and resembling a trophy.

Emotion and Motivations – In this case, the emotional goal is clearly **surprise**. Beer companies want to differentiate their offer by having consumers feel surprise on encountering the new packaging, followed by yearning transformed into happiness upon sampling the beer it holds. The advantage isn't just limited to pleasing consumers. Motivationally, the goal is that they will discuss these new unexpected shapes with fellow beer connoisseurs, also eager to **learn** about and then **acquire** the new "finds" on the market.

Opportunity #3: Acculturated Labeling

One big advantage that wine and martinis enjoy is that they often carry more social cache than beer does. To counteract that perception, the big breweries have learned from the microbreweries and the wineries by adopting more exotic labels and names. Sometimes those names are classy: Coors sells Blue Moon Belgian White Ale. Sometimes they're healthy-sounding, even organic: Anheuser-Busch has Wild Hop Lager. A cool label can help, too. Dogfish Head Brewery has commissioned the award-winning artist Tara McPherson to create labels for its Fort and Chateau Jiahu beers.

Emotion and Motivations – Sometimes the emotional goal isn't about proactively achieving so much as it is about avoiding a negative. This time around the emotion to diffuse is **contempt**. That may not be how beer drinkers feel about themselves, but it could be what they suspect other, more seemingly sophisticated drinkers could be feeling about them as they sit together in public places like bars. Therefore, the motivations involve wanting to **defend** oneself by being able to **acquire** more self-esteem through the "good taste" status other forms of alcohol enjoy.

We've come to the end of Section 1. Now readers should have all the foundational knowledge required for the application chapters to follow. Chapter 1 covered insights from brain science about people's decision-making process. Chapter 2 established facial coding as a tool to measure and, therefore, manage people's emotional responses. Finally, Chapter 3 built the Emotionomics Matrix that will provide a psychological context for the various business issues awaiting discussion. So let's move on, first to the marketplace and then to the workplace, looking at opportunities for emotional buy-in.

Who says drinking beer isn't an art?
Dogfish Head Brewery is a craft brewer that cares about more than the taste of its beers. Dogfish Head adds to the consumer's experience through its labels—some of which (like the two above by Tara McPherson) are created by award-winning artists.

PART TW2

MarketplaceApplications

4 branding

Branding is 200 proof emotionality. And what's better evidence than the sale of vodka—an odorless, colorless, tasteless liquor—where brand equity, aided by a great name, great packaging and great advertising, is essential to creating loyal customers.

OVERVIEW

Branding is primarily emotional in nature and, without the benefit of a tool like facial coding, also almost hopelessly abstract. After all, the essence of brand equity is that a company has managed to create a sense of loyalty among its customers. What is loyalty if not a *feeling*? Devoid a tool like facial coding that measures loyalty in emotional as opposed to rationalized, verbal input survey terms, companies are hard-pressed to know if they really enjoy brand equity or not. To help them achieve true emotional buy-in, this chapter will focus on:

- **Reflected Beliefs**: The first key to building brand equity is for companies to pursue a customer-centric brand strategy that protects the emotional health of their relationship with consumers. To do so requires, in turn, ensuring that consumers see their deeply-held, personal beliefs mirrored in the brands they purchase. As a result, companies should reflect the target market's beliefs, linking their beliefs about themselves to an enduring belief in the brand. The best strategy is always to sell people on themselves. That's because building on what's already been internalized works best.

- **Belonging**: A second brand equity key is to provide status so consumers enhance their self-identities vis-à-vis potential membership in groups to which they aspire. To that end, build a bridge facilitating people's adoption into those very groups. That is, people should feel not only that the brand fits them, but that it fits the social group to which they hope to belong. With both "me" (beliefs) and "us" (belonging) covered, a brand is in a more strongly fortified position to guard against status-induced defections.

- **Telling a Story**: While the first two keys to brand equity are strategic in nature, the third one is tactical. It's about creating a brand story rich enough to engage consumers. To do so, tell a story that builds a brand/customer relationship by offering a vivid personality people can relate to, and by creating hot-button associations. Over time a combination of personality and associations will help intuitively guide consumers to a brand, provided that they don't become concerned that they've invested their time and money on a company whose story lacks enough power.

Now let's look more closely at how to build brand equity, starting with the values to be found lodged in consumers' hearts.

Reflected Beliefs:
keep consumers' values in view

Synopsis: This section is about encouraging companies to make a practice of reflecting beliefs because everything consumers see in the world gets "bent" through the prism of the values they espouse. Companies should figure out what values emotionally matter most to their target markets and then be sure to deliver on them. To bring that point alive, the rest of the section looks first at why customer relationship management (CRM) is a half-hearted approach to knowing consumers and then at beliefs on the global scale as well as closer to home.

Key take-aways:

- A beliefs strategy means consumers no longer think about which brand to buy.
- CRM provides data without any intuitive feeling as to what it all conveys.
- Given the strength of both religious and secular beliefs, never defame them.
- Figure out which values are for real and which are less imperative.

Staying Power
A beliefs strategy means consumers no longer think about which brand to buy.

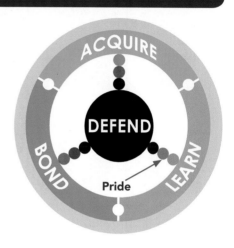

Despite the wave of business books and articles heralding the concept, very few companies are actually customer-centric. All too often, they choose the *what* (their products, services, et cetera) over the *who* (their customers). Too often the goal of getting ahead of rivals ends up having only a tangential relationship with getting closer to customers.

Instead, companies need to focus on the people they serve. That's because those companies that do pursue a genuine customer-centric brand strategy will enjoy a significant advantage as a result of greater emotional equity that will drive sales. Yes, be true to the essence of the brand. But at the same time be forever on the move, proactively understanding and mirroring the target market well enough so that the company can get and remain closer to it.

Emotion and Motivations

Pride is the key emotion here because consumers want brands that reinforce and enhance, not disrespect or ignore, their self-identities. In other words, consumers have belief systems they inevitably want to protect, having invested themselves in making sense of the world. To seize on this opportunity, companies must tap into consumers' motivations to **defend** their worldviews, which of course arose from what they have been able to **learn** from life's circumstances.

Let's explore this *who* versus *what* dichotomy more fully.

Customers are the who of brand strategy. A solid, self-sustaining strategy mirrors customers' preferences. Having such a strategy entails speaking to them on their level: who they are and associate with, what they do and value. An adept "mirror" brand drives an emotional connection so deep that consumers no longer think about what to buy.

They simply buy the brand that makes them feel comfortable, happy, proud and successful.

In contrast, a company with a *what* brand strategy focuses on what kind of functional offers it has to sell. A company blindly driven by a bottom-line focus inevitably regards customer contact as mere transactions. The relationship-building opportunity that could exist is lost, as customers simply become a revenue stream.

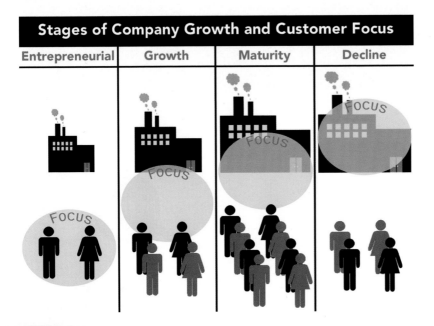

Fig. 4.1 The Center of Focus Shift

As a company grows in scale, it tends to become increasingly distracted by internal dynamics, losing sight of customers in the process (Slywotsky).

Remember *competitive differentiation means nothing to consumers unless it's focused on what's in it for them.*

Done correctly, branding is more than a barrier to competition or a price-booster and profit-generator. Why? It's because brand worth literally becomes internalized and accepted as an extension of the beliefs and values of its loyal, hard-won constituency. Trust and faith add intensity to the quality of branded offers, making them less subject to erosion. Consumers buy brands that provide emotional reinforcement, notably pride, in who they are and the decisions they make.

Thus consumer beliefs and brand equity go hand-in-hand because both are concerned with the long haul. They're about staying power. Core beliefs are built on core emotions, the templates that drive business outcomes. Forget about changing beliefs. A brand makes headway to the extent that it ties into beliefs and avoids what isn't credible or relevant. How can a company know that its approach is on track? By gauging consumers' core emotional responses.

The Company

Comprised of:
Offerings, brand equity and market distribution channels

Brand Strategy:
Where consumers are at, where they're going, and where they want to be.

The Audience

Comprised of:
Loyal consumers, new targets and employees

Audience Make-up:
Core beliefs and emotions

Fig. 4.2 Beliefs and Brand Strategy: How Companies and Target markets Match
The key is realizing that brand strategy should be intimately related to the beliefs of the target market. Unless the company knows where its market wants to go, it has no chance of knowing where to direct its brand strategy.

While truly reaching the target market is vital, consider the difficulty that inward-looking companies have communicating the essences of their brands. Mission statements often prove to be companies talking to themselves, and positioning statements aren't much better. Without the prior legwork done to know customers' beliefs, how can a company make a meaningful, lasting connection with them?

Even if a company is on the right path, how can it know for sure by relying only on rational, verbal input from its target market when branding is primarily emotional in nature?

In the following example, Sensory Logic tested a resort and adventure travel company's vision of *what* it offers by scrolling its mission statement across a computer screen for a group of subjects, one by one. We wanted to learn how the *who*—the target market—would actually respond. In short, we looked for when, how much and what type of emotional response occurred (Fig. 4.3).

Very Positive	Blue
Positive	Green
Neutral	Orange
Negative	Red
No Response	Black

We will guide you through a world of active travel, providing access to places in nature and cultural experiences around the world where extraordinary things happen to individuals from sun-up to sun-down. We are committed to assisting you to realize your dreams for memorable, unique and ultimately body-and-soul satisfying experiences . . . again and again.

Fig. 4.3 Facial Coding Response to Positioning Statement

The text in blue and green are the parts of the positioning statement to which test subjects responded positively. What worked? The company was on-message and on-emotion when it could credibly promise an offer of individualistic adventure that would carry to day's end and please body and soul alike. In other words, the offer appealed to its target market when it reflected that audience's values and affirmed the importance of their being dynamic, independent and rejuvenated.

In contrast, the text in orange and red indicates times the positioning statement left people either feeling ambivalent or that they might be encountering empty rhetoric, thus undermining the company's positioning strategy. Meanwhile, fully half of the statement invoked no response, signaling emotional irrelevance. In short, this draft of the statement was going to need some more work if the company was going to gain real buy-in.

CRM and Its Future
CRM provides data without any intuitive feeling as to what it all conveys.

Because customer relationship management (CRM) emphasizes *what* over *who*, it's too bad that the most common approach to the brand/customer relationship nowadays relies on the various CRM software packages. That's a good first step toward customers. But the current CRM tool kit never makes the whole journey (Rigby). It starts by recording and organizing individual transactions. Then it determines how much the customers spend, how often they buy and where and how they make purchases.

But in the end, CRM really only manages to glean customers' transactional histories. Moreover, this data is helpful only if actually utilized. Depending on consumer participation, yes, CRM can provide a list of demographic attributes that allow for segmentation by age, gender, income, job, education, et cetera.

Customers, however, have much bigger stories to tell. Executives who understand that an emotional connection is central to the creation of a viable relationship will want to get a bigger perspective. Without a way to get a feel for what the data really means, isn't CRM software merely a glass half full? The missing void could be filled with vital emotional insight, which would inform management, designers, marketing staff, sales people and others at a more comprehensive and per-

"To give emotions the scant attention they get in CRM applications is to ignore the most influential force in buying behavior. Change CRM to read CDM—customer data management—and you have a more accurate descriptive name for what CRM is really all about: moving more product less costly. It is less about serving customers than many claim, a lot less!"

—David Wolfe

tinent level. Such insight in tandem with trans-actional history would provide the knowledge required to build a more powerful connection between a company's brand and its customers.

Without a way to understand what CRM data means emotionally, it's a glass half-full solution. It needs to be topped off with an emotional kick.

Beliefs—
Religious and Secular
Given the strength of both religious and secular beliefs, never defame them.

A good way to start determining any target market's beliefs is to examine how different societies mold people's worldview. Companies engaged in global marketing, take note: in *The Clash of Civilizations and the Remaking of the World Order*, Harvard University professor Samuel Huntington argues that since the fall of the Berlin Wall, the world has divided it-self into eight different power blocks. They're organized around language and religious value systems, requiring companies looking to achieve optimal emotional buy-in to customize their approach.

Just how prominent is religion in defin-ing these power blocks? It's extremely perva-sive. Even in the West, where religion is less prominent, 85% of Americans believe God ex-ists. Moreover, the percentage of "born-again" Christians in the U.S. has risen 12% in the past two decades to 45% (Phillips).

Contrary to how it is sometimes depicted, America is not godless. In fact, 85% of Americans believe God exists. The main message here is that religion is a big part of people's beliefs. Brand strategy should take this into account and accordingly avoid offending the sensibilities of any potential customers. This holds true for any belief.

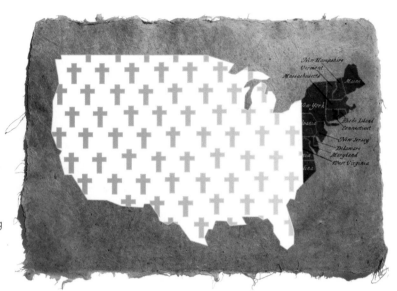

This map represents the degree to which America is a religious nation. Only a fraction of the country isn't spiritually motivated.

Therefore, branding directors and advertising agencies should be deeply attuned to religion's influence and its role in consumers' value systems or they risk giving offense. Pride isn't a trivial emotion. As a mixture of happiness and anger, pride has an edge to it. It contains an element of defiance, a don't-tread-on-me spirit. Given the emotion's quality of certainty and triumph, a brand wants to be a facilitator of this emotion rather than an obstacle. No company wants to be seen as an enemy of its target market's belief system.

In short, reflecting beliefs needs to be a front-and-center strategy. That's true because beliefs result from a lifetime of learning and constitute the essence of selfhood, which a person will adamantly defend—sometimes even to the death.

For his part, Huntington emphasizes three global mega-trends. The first two involve the relative decline of Western countries' economic strength, especially America's, in the face of the rise of Asian countries, China in particular. American and East Asian cultures share few values in common, except hard work, as illustrated by the percentages of the populations endorsing the importance of the eight values in Figure 4.4.

Likely to boast seven of the top ten world economies by 2020, Asian countries are quick to emphasize how the virtues of Confucian culture have bolstered their successes. Their leaders herald order, collectivism and restraint over the self-indulgent individualism they see rampant in Western society.

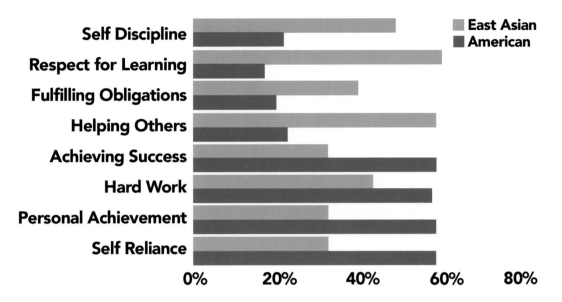

Fig. 4.4 Value Orientation Differences Between the U.S. and East Asia
In regards to the percentage of citizens endorsing these eight values, American and East Asian cultures have little in common except honoring hard work. Brand strategists must therefore be careful to customize their approaches (Hitchcock).

Huntington's third trend? The Muslim share of global population is expected to surge to 30% by 2025, making the differences in values between the predominantly Christian West and the Muslim world even more prominent. To disregard the differences between the two is to disregard a potentially huge market.

Closer to home, let's now look at two examples of how consumers' belief systems affect the outcome of brand marketing efforts. But in doing so, bear in mind that great brands organically evolve and have few, if any, tangible levers companies can pull to effect quick, deep-seated changes. A brand is hard to manipulate because a brand message involves no call to action, no need for audience participation. In practice, branding becomes the accumulation of a series of tactical steps, with emotional testing essential to avert long-term drift brought about by otherwise potentially undetectable short-term missteps.

American Beliefs Involving Cars and Sex
Figure out which values are for real and which are less imperative.

The first case involves a major U.S. auto manufacturer that ran ads with themes emphasizing family safety and environmental awareness. While people claimed that the environmentally conscious ad had greater Impact, emotional data captured through facial coding revealed a large enough drop-off in interest that safety was actually slightly ahead in both Appeal and Impact (Fig. 4.5).

It seems that being "green" sounds good. But when push comes to shove, people want to protect themselves and their families more than the species at large. As a result, the green advertising may be more suitable as a subtle, incremental building block of help to the company long-term.

The second case involves another company in the automotive sector. This company planned on running some "sexy" TV spots, joining a growing trend. But it wanted to be sure it wasn't going to offend women by doing so.

The good news? That would be the company realizing it would be smart to test the spots before launching them in order not to risk alienating a "segment," i.e. women, who represent over half the planet's population and, therefore, aren't exactly a niche market.

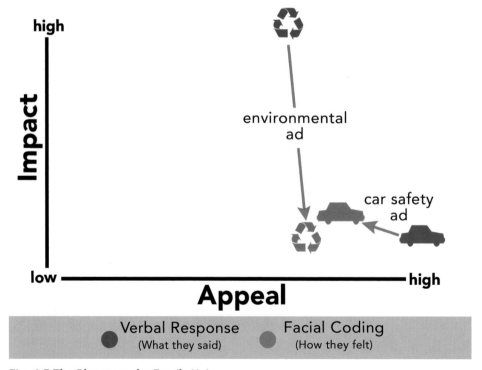

Fig. 4.5 The Planet vs. the Family Unit
Though people claimed to be more affected by the environmentally conscious advertisement, facial coding revealed that the family-oriented ad was stronger in both Appeal and Impact. In other words, they liked it more and responded more intensely to its message.

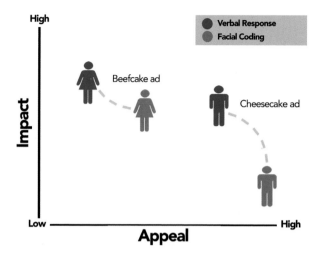

Fig. 4.6 Gender Differences in "Sexy" Spot Response

No surprise: men found the "cheesecake" commercial much more appealing than they were willing to acknowledge. But perhaps given the dulling surplus of titillation on TV, they were actually less impacted by it than they stated. In contrast, the women liked the "sexy" commercial less than men did. But they were also a little more impacted than the men as well as more pleased by the "beefcake" commercial than they admitted.

The bad news? The "cheesecake/beefcake" spots elicited a lower degree of positive response from the study's female subjects. Clearly, women didn't find the content as compatible with their value system as men did.

Why in commercial terms would it be important to know that women were likely to find the commercials distasteful? Consider these statistics (Barletta; Sharpe):

- Women are estimated to be responsible for 83% of all consumer purchases, including: 80% of healthcare decisions, 91% of general household purchases, 94% of furnishing purchases, 92% of vacation expenditures, and 62% of car purchases.

- Today, over 30% of women earn more than their husbands.

- Women also control over 50% of the private wealth in America (a number certain to rise given their longer life expectancy).

In cases like the two examples just discussed, the antidote to common branding errors is to learn where the target market is really coming from. Then a company's brand strategy is less likely to be off-base. Equity grows from staying as close to one's customers as possible, reflecting their beliefs to build a viable, sustainable, emotional connection.

Two decades ago, a study found that only 1% of magazine ads contained implicit sexual activity. A decade later thinly-veiled depictions of intercourse had risen to 17%. Meanwhile, the percentage of sexily dressed women went from 28% to 40%, while men in varying states of nudity rose from 11% to 18%. No known current study has addressed the topic, but surely the trend continues to grow. . . whether in accordance with people's value systems or not (Davenport).

Belonging:
where status and security meet

Synopsis: Because brands are social in nature, we rely on them to reinforce our sense of membership in a tribe. Companies whose brand position is so broad that there's no "us" and no "them" become, in effect, all things for all people, which is impossible and, therefore, meaningless. This section opens by affirming the need for the brand to serve as a bridge to a consumer's desired community. Then it looks at two segmentation factors that companies have a hard time navigating well: age and race.

Key take-aways:
- In branding, the desire to achieve "in-group" status is paramount.
- For seniors, emotions become ever more the currency of persuasion.
- People's subconscious bias is to rely on their own tribe.

Across the Great Divides
In branding, the desire to achieve "in-group" status is paramount.

Meryl Streep reportedly said that she thought life would be like college (full of lively, intellectual discussions), but found it to be more like high school: clique-ish with everybody jostling to fit in. Douglas Atkin nails the importance of creating a "we" in his book, *The Culting of Brands*. He defines a cult brand as "a brand for which a group of customers exhibits a great devotion or dedication. Its ideology is distinctive and it has a well defined and committed community. It enjoys exclusive devotion (that is, not shared with another brand in the same category), and its members often become voluntary advocates."

In other words, great brands leverage our innate impulse to belong to an inner circle that affirms who we want to be, with three factors being especially significant here.

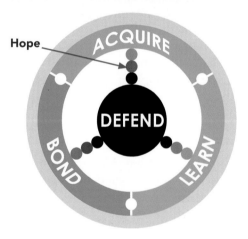

Emotion and Motivations

Hope is the key emotion for those who see a brand as a tribal destination. A brand that nurtures and reinforces our identity by helping us to affiliate with others is invaluable. On the Emotionomics Matrix, this opportunity lies between the motivations of to **acquire** and **defend**. The former is related to status and power and the latter to protecting ourselves against getting hurt because of rejection by a group to which we aspire to belong.

Great brands play to our inner desire to break through barriers and become part of a group that represents who we are as well as who we want to be.

The first factor is that, in response to the evolutionary desire to impress others, great brands make it possible for us to feel unique, special and worthy of affinity in the eyes of whatever our preferred group happens to be. To that end, the key step is to take a position a little bolder than that of rivals. Being average just won't get a brand noticed anymore. If a brand's positioning isn't both readily perceivable and important to people, the brand is at risk.

The second factor is to remember that a brand's edginess and the reflective glory it theoretically casts on loyalists isn't, ultimately, as important as whether the social fit is both right and authentic. After all, our social aspirations have to be plausible for them to be sustainable, rather than mere pipe dreams.

The previous two factors involved groups that we as individuals decide to join. They're distinctions that we pursue on our own. But sometimes the brand community we belong to gets decided for us, at least to some extent. Thus, the third factor involves non-electable signifiers like age and race, which we'll look at next.

Age and Age-ism
For seniors, emotions become ever more the currency of persuasion.

The new consumer majority consists of people beyond the midpoint of life. Brand strategists, take note: the level of spending by those over 45 years of age will soon exceed that of people between the ages of 18 and 39 by one trillion dollars. Meanwhile, those over fifty years of age represent 44% of adults and control 70% of the country's wealth. This is where age-ism becomes evident: despite those statistics, only 10% of all branded advertising expenditures target older consumers (Wolfe).

As we age, the word-oriented left hemisphere of the brain overloads more easily, but the right hemisphere's ability to process visual images holds steady. So companies will find the senior market less attuned to rational, persuasive arguments. What's the better approach? The answer is emotional, visual, subjective appeals that play to older people's rich networks of long-term memories and associations.

Once again, emotional measuring is the key. How much of a difference can one's age make in calculating likely buy-in?

Quite a bit is what Sensory Logic found in a study involving equally wealthy investors segmented by seniority. The underlying brand strategy issue? Would a company's famous name provide enough equity to put people at ease with an online offer requiring them to share financial information?

Though they might still need a little help crossing the street, the elderly no longer need help when it comes to purchasing power. The 50+ segment of America controls over 70% of the nation's wealth and represents 44% of adults.

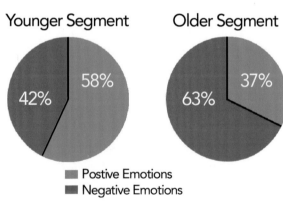

Fig. 4.7 Age Differences in Online Buy-In

When it came to determining true willingness to participate in banking activities online, Sensory Logic found some interesting responses. While both groups professed great willingness to provide the personal, even intimate information required, the emotional response of the younger segment was over 20% ahead of the older segment and neither segment was as comfortable with the concept as they said they were.

For younger people this proposition proved to be less worrisome than it was for older people. The latter group worried far more about matters like ease-of-use, program quality and, especially, online security. In the verbal responses, there was essentially no difference between the younger and older segments in regard to the question, "Are you willing to provide personal information?" But the facial coding revealed that the older group was actually far less willing to do so than they claimed (Fig. 4.7).

Race and Racism
People's subconscious bias is to rely on their own tribe.

Nowhere does the idea of "tribes" surface more strongly than in regard to issues involving race and racism. For instance, an academic study investigating racial stereotypes concluded that people are hardwired to prefer their own race with bias unconsciously permeating people's attitudes (Wartik). Intriguingly enough, however, as we saw in regard to research shared in Chapters 1 and 3, different emotions can lead to different outcomes.

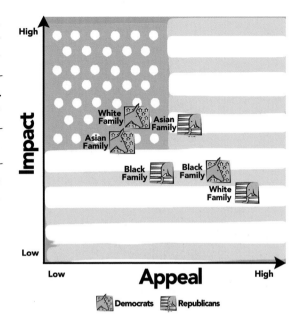

Fig. 4.8 Racial Preference and Party Affiliation

A financial services company had us test three print ads which were textually identical but had families of different races in them. Party affiliation was the key demographic variable. Although more than half of the Democrats analyzed were Caucasian, they were most positive about the African-American family shown to benefit from a financial services offer meant to assist families buying a first home. In contrast, the mostly Caucasian Republicans felt more supportive of their own race.

Specifically, students in this study who were coaxed into *anger*, for instance, were more likely to have negative reactions to members of other racial groups than they were to people of their own racial groups. In contrast, *sadness* actually eased the degree of bias (perhaps because being "down" inspired greater sensitivity). Not surprisingly then, its opposite—*happiness*—proved to be like anger because it increased the students' rapid-response rejections of "outsiders."

At times, clients have directly asked Sensory Logic to check for issues related to racial bias.

In one case (Fig. 4.8), the stakes involved determining how best to appeal to U.S. Congress members and their staffs in order to protect the company's government charter. The specific focus was testing three print ads to see how well they promoted a program to assist first-time home buyers. In another case (Fig. 4.9), the company feared it might offend Asian-American sensibilities. Why? The risk was that a TV spot showing a disheveled, Caucasian executive meeting his Japanese counterparts might signal disrespect.

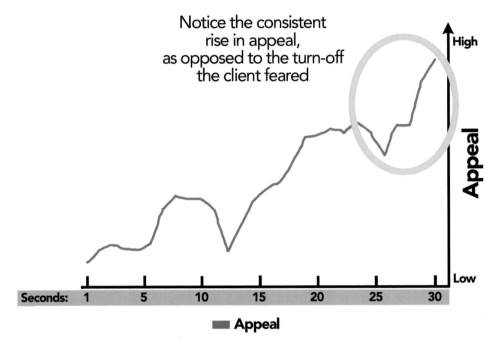

Fig. 4.9 Asian Persuasion

A TV spot in which an American is revealed to have food in his teeth didn't offend Caucasian Americans. Nor, according to the sizeable Asian-American segment included in the study, did it seem like a blow against the dignity of the Japanese delegation with whom he was meeting. Instead, both groups contributed to a consistent rise in Appeal as opposed to the turn-off the company wanted to guard against.

What's the overall verdict based on these two cases alone? The first case would definitely suggest that people's instincts are to pull back to their own racially defined comfort zones. The second case, however, would offer some hope that people aren't so thin-skinned as to make dialogue impossible.

As for the implications in terms of creating a sense of belonging, it would appear that brands trying to signal in-group status across great divides like age and race must be realistic enough to tread carefully. In a contest between the hopeful motivation of acquiring status and power and the protective motivation of defending oneself against getting hurt, it's hard to imagine that the more primitive, *fear*-oriented part of the brain doesn't hold sway.

Telling a Story:
selling familiarity and comfort

Synopsis: Stories engage us, so companies should tell stories lively enough to build an extra, protective layer of value around their offerings. Here, we'll go through the steps required to build a robust story. After establishing the importance of storytelling, this section will examine its key story components: personality and associations. Finally, three quick case studies will make the point that associations and beliefs collude in ensuring that brand equity works.

Key take-aways:
- To avoid being a blank slate, a brand must exude a personality.
- Since a warm, attractive personality is vital, gauging awareness isn't enough.
- Brand equity resides in neural networks forged through associations.
- Confronted with new, disruptive information, we favor the familiar.
- Pride gets in the way of accepting apologies or reexamining our beliefs.

The Brand as Storyteller
To avoid being a blank slate, a brand must exude a personality.

A great brand is a myth perched atop functional attributes that deliver on the brand's promise and make the story feel like reality. In other words, if a brand delivers emotionally, its myth is transformed into reality for its tribe. So an offer must comply with the brand's promise, or both risk being destroyed. Like a myth, a brand is hard to start, hard to establish and difficult to dislodge.

Emotion and Motivations

The inverse of pride is shame. A brand story is always vulnerable to a scandal. But shame is often too strong an emotion to describe the reaction of previously loyal customers who end up feeling like a brand story they adopted as their own has failed them. More accurate is an emotion like **disappointment**. It is felt when consumers conclude that a brand story they listened to and accepted in their hearts isn't worthy of support. In terms of the Emotionomics Matrix, companies can guard against that outcome by crafting a story that enables consumers to **defend** their self-esteem while retaining the desire to **bond** with the brand.

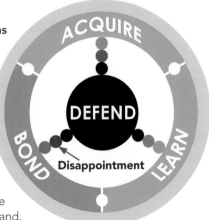

Fig. 4.10 Brand Story Elements
In order to successfully tell its brand's story, a company must make sure that all elements of the tale relate to the target market and appeal to their desires. The above example is a common ploy used to incite foreign travel. The goal is to show a scene that intended customers can not only project themselves into but also desire to take part in.

If consumers' faith in the brand's story gets broken, they'll see the brand's message as an epic lie. Then the fall from success will be horrendously fast. To avoid taking this plunge, a company must ensure that there's substance behind their brand's promise.

That being said, brands—especially great brands—are ultimately more about their implied, emotionally-oriented promises. The functionally based benefits that initially created a need for a company will fade over time. This progression happens for two reasons.

The first is that whatever technical or operational innovations originally provided the company with an advantage will eventually suffer from competitors adopting a "me too" stance.

The second and far more positive reason is that over time robust brands move from framing their offer's appeal in terms of facts to framing the appeal in terms of fiction, which doesn't mean telling lies. Instead, what's meant by fiction is that over time the branded story supersedes the literal offer and becomes the value proposition. A brand is no longer a platform for the rationally oriented offer. Instead, the brand has acquired emotional power that doesn't reside in facts; it resides in faith, enjoyment and ease of connection.

As a result of this shift from nonfiction to fiction, brand equity accrues to the extent that a company's brand story provides the two main components of a successful story: an attractive personality and positive signature associations by which the company becomes familiar and comfortable to members of its target market.

Failure to provide these elements makes the company a blank slate, depriving it of the potential for a stronger consumer connection that exudes warmth. Into that space can step competitors better able to establish themselves as something other than another "faceless" giant, an oversized company nobody wants to hug. To avoid that fate, a company benefits from a brand story that can grow stronger in the hearts and minds of consumers.

Leaving aside associations until a little later, let's concentrate for now on what it means for a company to develop a distinct brand personality for the products and services it offers.

First up, remember the formula: recurring emotions form the basis for traits, which in turn create personality. So in addition to belief systems and seeking to belong to a tribe, another primary reason why branding is deeply emotional is that it involves developing a distinct brand personality. The ability to make that happen helps a company because:

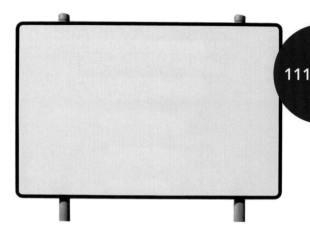

Failure to provide consumers with a compelling brand story leaves a company at risk of being a blank slate.

- It enables consumers to symbolically express themselves, their ideal selves or selective dimensions of themselves in relation to the brand.

- It ensures a relatively stable and distinct context for a company's offers, strongly differentiating them from those of other companies and cementing consumer preferences and usage.

- It provides a common denominator to aid in marketing a brand globally, across cultures.

Given these crucial benefits, companies should—but often don't—seize on the opportunity to develop robust personalities. Instead, they only go half-way toward that goal. In *Emotional Branding*, Marc Gobé characterizes how branding falls by the wayside in perfect terms by observing that, "American Airlines has a strong identity but Virgin Airlines has personality."

Recognition and awareness are enough to have an identity. But to project an engaging, attractive brand personality, a company must not only become a familiar face, but the face of a friend. Only then can a brand be on its way to creating an emotional shortcut in the brain. Trust enables consumers to relax and more intuitively select an offer. With more goods and branded advertisements to look at than time in the day, this subconscious, emotionally-based differentiation is a gold mine in persuading the consumers of today's global economy.

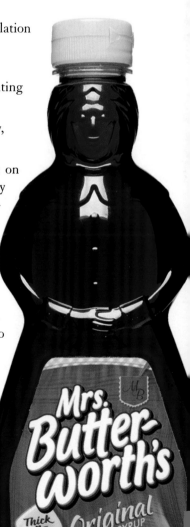

Talk about personality in action. What's more comforting than Mrs. Butterworth? Undoubtedly, the mental image of the kind, grandmother figure makes the syrup taste that much sweeter.
(picture from Pinnacle Foods)

In short: if a business' goal is to gain customers, why have a generic identity? As Gobé says, "A brand is brought to life for consumers first and foremost by the personality of the company behind it."

Personality in Action

Since a warm, attractive personality is vital, gauging awareness isn't enough.

Branding isn't a feature or even a benefit. It's a relationship based on an emotional connection. Therefore, pure economic models miss the mark. So do brand descriptions, which attempt to quantify brand value based on formulas involving awareness, saliency and so forth. Why are they inadequate? The reason is that they don't—and can't—quantify in emotional terms how it feels to be in that brand relationship from the consumer's perspective.

Depending on whether there's a good personality match, we do or don't fall in love. To prove this point, Sensory Logic decided to look at brand effectiveness using facial coding to quantify personal chemistry. In other words, we wanted to see how much of a spark there is between a company's projected personality and consumers.

So we recently tested *Advertising Age's* Top Ten Icons of the 20th Century to learn which ones retain emotional brand equity among consumers of the 21st century. Do these famous American brand icons still provide the comfort and reassurance people desire? And since we're talking about relationships, are there gender differences in how men and women relate to these icons?

Here's a summary (Figs. 4.11 and 4.12) of what Sensory Logic found. It addresses both the Emotional Response Rate (how *interested* people are in the icons either positively or negatively) and how much Appeal the icons have (amount of *preference* or likeability):

Overall Emotional Response Rate

Brand	%
Marlboro Man	82%
Elsie the Cow	80%
Betty Crocker	73%
Aunt Jemima	73%
McDonald	73%
Doughboy	66%
Energizer Bunny	66%
Michelin Man	61%
Green Giant	55%
Tony the Tiger	54%

Gender Differences (% Response)

Brand	%
Marlboro Man	37%
Green Giant	33%
McDonald	33%
Betty Crocker	31%
Aunt Jemima	31%
Michelin Man	21%
Doughboy	18%
Energizer Bunny	18%
Elsie the Cow	17%
Tony the Tiger	7%

Fig. 4.11 Brand Icon Emotional Response Rates Overall and by Gender

These charts show the response rates that each brand icon created overall and by gender. The gender differences reflect which gender had more of a response, and to what degree.

Blue = male

Pink = female

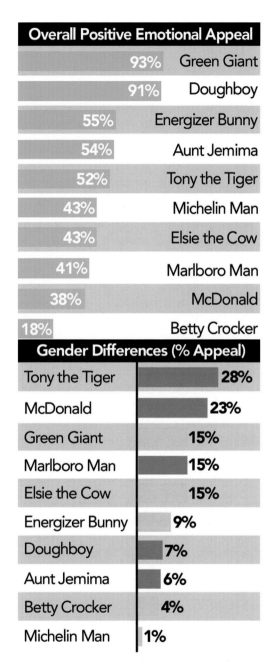

Overall Positive Emotional Appeal	
93%	Green Giant
91%	Doughboy
55%	Energizer Bunny
54%	Aunt Jemima
52%	Tony the Tiger
43%	Michelin Man
43%	Elsie the Cow
41%	Marlboro Man
38%	McDonald
18%	Betty Crocker

Gender Differences (% Appeal)	
Tony the Tiger	28%
McDonald	23%
Green Giant	15%
Marlboro Man	15%
Elsie the Cow	15%
Energizer Bunny	9%
Doughboy	7%
Aunt Jemima	6%
Betty Crocker	4%
Michelin Man	1%

Fig. 4.12 Brand Icon Preference Overall and by Gender

These charts show the level of preference (positive emotional response) that each icon created overall and by gender. The gender differences reflect which gender had more of a positive response and to what degree.

Response Rate: Overall

- Even after being pulled from the national spotlight, the Marlboro Man is still the most emotionally captivating— thanks to 100% male response. Every man tested felt some reaction to the Man as a symbol of what it means to be a man.

- Otherwise, however, the masculine icons fared badly. The female icons did no worse than tie for third, while Tony the Tiger, for instance, had a response rate almost 30% lower than Marlboro's cowboy.

Response Rate: by Gender

- The Marlboro Man, Green Giant and Michelin Man are manly men, with more stopping power for guys. In contrast, Ronald McDonald and the Pillsbury Doughboy generated cross-over interest by getting more of a rise from women than men. Not surprisingly, both Betty Crocker and Aunt Jemima did likewise among women.

Preference: Overall

- Best liked was the Jolly Green Giant, followed by the Pillsbury Doughboy. No other icon came close. Way at the bottom was Betty Crocker, thereby validating General Mills' decision to change its packaging by replacing the rather grim-looking Betty with a spoon!

Preference: by Gender

- Emotional Response Rates split by gender: men had more of a reaction to male brand icons and women to female brand icons. But no such split occurred in regard to preference. Best at creating equal degrees of Appeal from men and women alike was the Michelin Man.

Why Associations Matter

*Brand equity resides in neural networks forged
through associations.*

A recognizable personality gets the brand story rolling. But ultimately the story unfolds based on the clues we consciously or unconsciously pick up when interacting with a brand. As for where the brand story unfolds, well, it's mostly hidden. Ultimately, as Al and Laura Reis note in *The Origin of Brands*, "Branding occurs only in the mind and has no physical reality."

This fact makes branding hard to manage because branding effectiveness is primarily subconscious, emotional and dependent (at least in part) on neurology.

As noted in Chapter 1, neurons that fire together wire together. In practical terms, this scientific insight means that experiences rewire the brain by fusing neural networks. As a result, what we've *seen* predisposes us to what we *can and likely will see* next time around. Memory builds around hot-button connections that grow more dense and weighty if repeatedly forged and reinforced (Fig. 4.13).

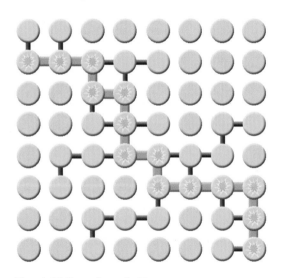

Fig. 4.13 Branding via Neurons
Constantly used neural pathways create stronger, quicker connections (Banich).

So in addition to featuring strong, impression-generating personalities, companies should also strive to reinforce their brand stories by creating mental landscapes rich in associations. A case in point is McDonald's. Despite some problems in recent years, founder Ray Kroc built it to last by drawing on what he learned about storytelling from fellow World War I Red Cross member, Walt Disney.

Is it pure luck that McDonald's is the place children want to go? Hardly. Carefully crafted associations have been skillfully embedded in the minds of America's youths for decades (Fig. 4.14). What Disney and Kroc knew is something that every brand director needs to know: brands are for tribes, but they must nevertheless be executed at the individual level because that's how strong, internalized emotional responses get born.

Once upon a time in business, grand, large-scale strokes like national TV commercials worked just fine. But now they aren't enough unless reinforced by paying attention to how all the little details of a consumer's real-time, less scripted, interactive perceptions of the brand unfold across multiple touch points and on multiple occasions.

How Associations Work
Confronted with new, disruptive information, we favor the familiar.

In practice, branding becomes a matter of trying to leverage the power of a psychological phenomenon known as top-down vs. bottom-up processing (Schermerhorn; Compton).

In essence, the top-down wins most often because the power of emotions means that existing beliefs influence, shape and even dominate how we react to any new sensory input such as advertising for example.

Why does that happen? The explanation is that fired and wired neurons don't just build a network—they build the entire context in which we mentally see our lives. As a result,

Inexpensive French Fries
Value Meal
Fast Quality Yellow

Golden Arches

McDonald's

Fun Ronald
Happy Meal **Kids**
Toys Charity Work

Fig. 4.14 McDonald's Associations
McDonald's has worked hard over the years to make sure their brand name is associated with certain elements. That we think of these same words when we think of McDonald's is no accident.

we're mentally and emotionally invested in what has come before (Fig. 4.15). Our brains favor suppressing any new sensory input—or bottom-up content—that conflicts with what we have already accepted and internalized. Who has perhaps most memorably noted this tendency? One candidate would have to be the famous author and social critic Upton Sinclair, who remarked: "It's hard for a man to understand something when his salary depends on his not understanding it."

Everybody has biases and vested interests that limit our perceptual powers. Therefore, unless a new perception is really disruptive, top-down contextual processing dominates bottom-up content processing. That happens because the top-down version quickly, subconsciously and emotionally frames a stimulus in three ways:

- First, it emphasizes what has been important in the past.
- Second, it often downplays what doesn't fit with established values in order to avoid cognitive dissonance.
- Third, the emotions and motivations invoked help define the meaning found in new perceptions.

Associative, Top-Down Processing in Action
Pride gets in the way of accepting apologies or reexamining our beliefs.

To show how all this mental modeling really works, let's look at three examples where the *context* of brand equity stands in conflict with sensory *content,* causing emotions to be the decisive factor in how a company fares.

Fig. 4.15 Top-Down Processing Typically Wins
Readers, remember the games you played as a child? How about the one with the little wooden shapes you had to fit through a corresponding hole? The first few times you had to try out different holes to see which one fit the shape. But soon you knew which block went with which opening. That's the difference between bottom-up and top-down processing. In bottom-up, the brain is learning and forming associations with stimuli. In top-down, the associations built previously are instantly accessed, then used as filters and to guide subsequent action.

Case #1: Wal-Mart

The first example concerns Wal-Mart, which has used the power of positive, associative, top-down processing to its advantage. For starters, Wal-Mart is famous, of course, for its omnipresent slogan: "Always low prices. Always." The choice of that slogan is already in itself a triumph of top-down processing. It affirms the widespread and widely accepted notion that low prices is a valid—if not the single most important—criterion in choosing where to shop and what to buy. In other words, the slogan affirms the context, framing the way in which we look at and evaluate our shopping options.

With the primacy of price belief reinforced through the slogan, the context has been established. Wal-Mart is then ready to move on to step two of its top-down positioning strategy. Now it's time for sensory input—new, experiential perceptions—to reinforce the implicit mental equation that reads: "Low prices are important, and I find them at Wal-Mart."

Truth be told, however, Wal-Mart doesn't always have the lowest prices. Yes, the slogan doesn't promise that the store does. But with the context of low prices being important as its overt

Wal-Mart's strategy is all about top-down processing. By highlighting the low prices of gotta-have products like flat-screen TVs, the company links Wal-Mart and low prices. Consequently, everything else in the store falls under the halo of lowest prices always. That's how you become the biggest retailer in the world.

strategy, the slogan invites the mind to equate Wal-Mart not just with low prices, but with the lowest prices as a means of essentially telling people: "You will be smart to shop here. You will get low prices, even the lowest prices. And you can do so without having to take the time and make the effort to shop elsewhere. Here you can not only practice price comparisons, but also secure the lowest actual prices for your purchases."

As a result, not having the lowest prices could threaten Wal-Mart's brand equity and its bottom-line profitability. Moreover, that threat is real because, as a study has documented, Wal-Mart doesn't always have the lowest prices (Wellman). Instead of offering the lowest price generally, the company relies on top-down processing and, on a daily basis, selectively undercuts some big brand items (by 15% to 25%) when the items have high household penetration and high purchase frequency.

Those items are known as *signpost items,* and they are a decisive factor in how Wal-Mart plays the pricing game. Signpost items matter because consumers often really don't know whether a price is a low price for an item. So they tend to rely on the retailer's reputation and on prominent and popular items to form an overall impression of a store's prices, thereby preempting bottom-up processing.

As a result, Wal-Mart can get away with content—not always having lowest prices—that stands in conflict with the assumption that Wal-Mart is the place for lowest prices. Why does the strategy work? The answer is, in effect, brand equity. The contextual equation that Wal-Mart is the place for lowest prices overrules content, aided by two factors:

- The first is that signpost items reassure shoppers that the store is, indeed, the one and only place they need to go to in order to get items at the low prices their top-down processing has come to accept as the key criterion. Signpost items help suppress the chance that shoppers will begin to notice a disconnect between the promise of low prices and the reality, thereby switching to bottom-up processing instead.

- The second is that shoppers are eager to accept the signpost evidence in support of an equation they've already bought into. That's because acceptance saves them time and energy (versus shopping many stores) and because emotional equity gets tied to brand equity. In other words, by now Wal-Mart is so well established that countless shoppers have come to accept the idea that Wal-Mart is the place for lowest prices. Over the years they've spent their money at Wal-Mart in the belief that Wal-Mart has the lowest prices, and now they are emotionally loathe to disrupt that belief because it would mean they've been wrong and people hate to admit mistakes. Consumers have in that sense become partners to the strategy and are complicit in its success.

Or another way to say all this is that while rivals' prices are actually competitive on most items, Wal-Mart emphasizes certain items and then makes sure they are steadily advertised, on display and in-stock. This strategy ensures that signpost item *content* supports brand equity, top-down processing *context*: customers equate Wal-Mart with bargains and shopping there with getting the best price in town. Customers feel sure of themselves as they make purchases. Their neural networks are telling them they are smart shoppers and, therefore, smart in general.

Case #2: Automotive Sector

In this defensively-oriented case, a U.S. automotive manufacturer came to Sensory Logic after paying for an extensive national print ad campaign that included an apology for previous lapses in quality. We tested the reception of this particular ad by three segments: recent purchasers (Owners), people who were indifferent to the brand (Apathetics), and those who would not consider it (Rejectors).

How was the apology received? Badly. The average percentage of positive emotional response was a measly 22%. Even worse, the Owners' collective facial coding results were barely ahead of the other two segments despite the fact that fully one third of them considered the company the leading quality provider in the category. What went wrong? Let's look at the strategy and

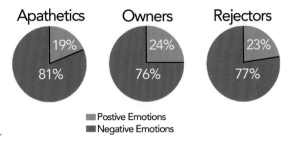

Fig. 4.16 The Wrong Road

Always know what one's apologizing for. This example shows the emotional responses of three segments to an ad by an automaker. The ad was an apology for the sub-par quality of its previous vehicles. That's great. . . UNLESS YOU ALREADY OWN ONE OF THOSE CARS! Then, not only does it feel like you were lied to when you bought the car, you were an ignorant sucker as well. Furthermore, those who weren't owners simply had their initial belief that the car was inferior reinforced. All around, it was an advertising failure.

outcome in contrast to Wal-Mart. Both the retailer and the auto company start with a contextual belief that consumers buy into: in Wal-Mart's case, *primacy of price*; for the automaker, *primacy of quality* as consumers' key criterion in making such a major purchase (Fig. 4.16).

Then Wal-Mart makes its customers feel like winners by giving them enough signpost item content to support their belief that they've made the right choice to shop at Wal-Mart. In contrast, by making the overt apology the automaker was providing content evidence that the primacy of quality belief wasn't being honored. Therefore, the loyalists who had bought in the past were, in effect, being told that they were losers for having made the wrong choice by deciding to buy the company's cars.

Market Segment	Occasional Users	Supporters	Wavering Supporters
Upbeat TV Spot	52% (80%)	69% (83%)	44% (60%)
Defensive TV Spot	47% (75%)	31% (77%)	42% (65%)

Fig. 4.17 Pharmaceutical Product Scandal Results

Green numbers indicate the percentage of positive facial coding response. **Black** numbers reference positive verbal response. Based on our study, the defensive commercial—had it actually been aired— would have decimated the ranks of supporters without bolstering the ranks of the other two segments. Interestingly enough, verbal input alone barely hinted at the shame and embarrassment supporters would have felt because of using and trusting in a product that was shown to be subpar. Their level of affirmation—31%—was less than half what it was for the upbeat TV spot.

Case #3: Healthcare Sector

The third example had a more positive outcome. In this case, the company came to Sensory Logic after a wave of publicity cast doubts on a pharmaceutical offer's safety. The company and its ad agency were considering two versions of a TV spot—one more defensive than the other. The percentage of positive self-report rating results hardly varied across segments. But the facial coding results were clear: the company should not run the defensive spot. On our advice, the company wisely shelved it.

Given the data from facial coding, we determined that this spot would decimate support from its key audience and not gain ground with the other segments. Ironically, this defensive measure was intended to be so widely disseminated that the likelihood of this new sensory stimulus being hard to ignore was high. The net result would likely have been to disrupt the advantageous, top-down processing associations that had previously brought the company success with its supporters. In this case the context was the *primacy of safety*. The risk was that the company would be providing content evidence strong enough to potentially disrupt the implicit equation by which the company's offer was viewed as safe.

The bottom line, emotionally speaking? As these three examples show in regard to telling a brand story, people want tales in which they get to be a hero rather than a fool. Wal-Mart aside, the other two cases highlight the danger of causing disappointment in consumers who had purchased and believed in the brand. When that happens, the loyalists' relationship with the company gets put into jeopardy, threatening a hasty, nasty unraveling of the hope and pride so fundamental to success.

"It's more intuitive than analytical. We have gone from something easily measurable—how many people are aware of your brand to something far more difficult to measure—how do people really feel about your brand."

—Scott Bedbury

Conclusion

Nothing in business is less tangible, and therefore more purely emotional, than branding. All the levers for changing brand equity exist. But where? While the literal answer points to consumers' minds, the underlying answer is in their hearts. To be effective, a strong brand strategy must accomplish the following:

- Reward customers for their loyalty by mirroring the beliefs that frame their top-down processing. Figure out what values emotionally matter most to the target market and make sure your brand can truly deliver and represent them.

- Remember that a brand is social in nature because we rely on it to reinforce our status as members of the tribe with which we identify. The community we join serves as a bridge to adoption by giving us the extra confidence to declare the brand our choice. In contrast, amorphous brands lacking symbolic power don't help consumers impress other people or help orient them to the group that feels right.

- Tell a story that involves a vibrant brand personality whose enduring traits resonate in harmony with the key associations by which consumers know and accept the brand with enthusiasm. A company whose name doesn't invoke mental imagery is in trouble.

An Action Plan

To make sure that the company's brand is emotionally healthy, here are some important points to remember when assessing effectiveness:

- ☐ Create a story so that customers and employees want to say "we" or "us" when talking about the brand. Strive for a sense of membership.

- ☐ Brands should project a destination that is greater than reality. At the same time, don't forget that a brand should over-deliver emotionally not over-promise rationally. If a company has excelled at accomplishing this goal, rivals will use its brand as a benchmark.

- ☐ The brand/customer relationship should feel like a friendship. A great brand creates a group of friends who share an emotional bond.

- ☐ Use research to determine whether the company's brand delivers a strong story so that consumers intuitively respond: this is where I want to be. Given the mind's preference for images, find key visuals that work effectively on an emotional basis. Provide an intellectual alibi to support the emotional brand story.

5

offer design, packaging and usability

Ooh! Ahh!
The exclamations heard when people
see fireworks are what a company wants
consumers to experience emotionally
when they encounter or use its products.

OVERVIEW

As Tom Peters writes, "Design is about emotion." That's because well-designed offers work if they hook people emotionally with an enticing promise that proves to be rewarding in the end. How to accomplish that feat? Vividly establish the offer's superiority by pleasing the senses and creating a compelling emotional benefit. The original, intuitive connection must be so strong that it motivates consumers to try something new and is remembered fondly enough to induce repeat purchase decisions. To help companies accomplish those goals, this chapter will focus on:

- **Winning Superiority**: At the concept stage, the goal should be to make consumers feel like they've won when they purchase something. To truly be considered by consumers, an offer must ignite fantasy as they envision an emotionally enriching outcome. There's too much abundance and lack of true differentiation in the marketplace to approach design any other way. Therefore, the key is to protect the offer's conceptual "wow" element from compromises that would rob it of the ability to awaken a latent desire or create a new one.

- **Sensory Payoff**: At the sensory stage, the goal should be to get consumers to investigate a new offer through perceptions that trigger subconscious emotional responses. More specifically, utilize the sensory bandwidth of sight, hearing, touch, taste and smell as an opportunity to ignite interest. The packaging must accomplish this first because it is the final touch point before purchase. Then it's up to the offer itself to seduce the buyer by continuing the sensory excitement begun at the store. In a crowded marketplace, an offer's failure to be stimulating in sensory terms will also make it emotionally invisible.

- **Functional Fulfillment**: At the usability stage, the goal should be to ensure that consumers don't experience design flaws that test their patience and prevent or limit repeat sales or usage. If rationally-oriented, utilitarian ease of use is neglected, an emotional backlash is inevitable. Usability properly anticipated reduces frustration with trying to use the offer. That step also enables the offer's use to be emotionally gratifying based on easy, enjoyable functionality that doesn't reduce the offer's uniqueness.

Now let's look more closely at how to design an offer with an interruptive call to action that actually gets acted on, starting with the concept stage.

Winning Superiority:
nurturing a "wow"

Synopsis: Conceptually, consumers will be more readily enticed if the offer isn't merely utilitarian but, rather, strikingly unique: the result of inspiration instead of the dutiful necessity of getting the job done and the deal made. As this section will discuss, what often gets in the way are compromises that take precedence over creating true excitement. In contrast, success stories will likewise be shared that range from designing a specific product to an entire hours-long experience of an offer.

Key take-aways:
- Too often, let's-make-a-deal compromises obstruct bold, enriching designs.
- The basis of great design is to be both awe-inspiring and emotionally relevant.
- The highest level of offer design is to create a story-like experience.

Is this guy cheesy? You bet. But he perfectly represents the feeling of awe that should be a company's goal when designing offers.

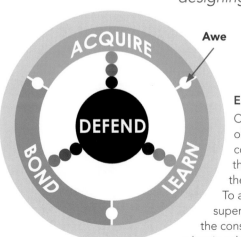

Awe

Emotion and Motivations

Creating **awe** is the emotional objective. The substantial lift consumers gain by acquiring an offer that inspires awe is a huge payoff that they will seek time and time again. To achieve the wow that comes with superiority, great designers will tap into the consumer's motivation to **learn** while also whetting the urge to **acquire**. What consumers find out about the offer must motivate them to want to own it and enjoy its power.

Overcoming Design Obstacles
Too often, let's-make-a-deal compromises obstruct bold, enriching designs.

More than any other facet of a company's operations or output, the design of a product, service or experience possesses the potential for delight. Why is that the case? First, direct, intimately personal exposure gives companies the opportunity to invoke any or all of our five senses in order to cause consumers to notice, comprehend and ideally enjoy the offer. In other words, unlike advertising, where only sight and possibly sound can be leveraged, an offer that uses the entire sensory bandwidth allows for greater exposure. Second, actually laying our hands on a new offer makes tangible the hope that comes with anticipating new experiences. Third, many offers and especially the successful ones will be repeatedly encountered, thereby expanding their influence on our lives.

As a result, offer design has the ability to touch a consumer's inner self to a greater degree than any other part of the company/consumer relationship, save customer service.

Creating an emotionally engaging offer should be a high priority for every company. Maybe it is for many, but the statistics seem to suggest otherwise (Berkowitz; Cooper; Kotler 1994) :

- Over 30% of a typical company's profits are projected to come from new offer launches.

- New offers fail 90% of the time.

- Moreover, in trying to improve the odds of success, companies often rely on extensions or other forms of knockoffs that make only 10% of their "new" offers actually new.

In other words, these dismal figures mean consumers aren't biting—despite companies playing it safe with knockoffs instead of introducing truly new offers. No doubt a large part of the problem is today's highly saturated marketplace. But isn't it possible that there are other reasons, too?

Specifically, there are five likely mistakes responsible for design failing to live up to its emotional potential. Constant among them is that designs may fail to create an emotional high for consumers, who too often are forgotten, lost or simply ignored in the equation. Here are the five reasons why designs fail and, more importantly, how that can be prevented from happening.

In order to be truly effective, design must first face up to and overcome a few hurdles.

1. Feature-itis
(too many features)

A consumer's mind prefers to take short cuts. It does so by quickly categorizing stimuli based on pattern matching aided by repetition. As a result, the high percentage of offer extensions and other forms of knock-offs are somewhat justified from not only a financial (cost savings) point of view but also from a psychological perspective. After all, something entirely new or overly complex creates extra mental work. And guess what: consumers rarely reward a company that makes them work harder.

At the same time, however, most extensions and knock-offs aren't succeeding. Clearly a fresh approach is required. Therefore, for new or even slightly new offers, companies need to track the Emotional Response Rate and the degree of Appeal to ensure that people won't emotionally jump ship. Why might that happen? Either because the work of assimilating them is too taxing or because the offers simply aren't of much interest (which serves as the underlying basis for the other four reasons why designs fail).

Let's concentrate here on the first problem: hard to assimilate. What's the likely culprit behind this problem? It's *feature-itis*: a company's tendency to over-think and over-execute the design of a product, service or experience—thus fatally weakening the opportunity for consumers to respond with happiness or joy.

Music. Games. PDA. Computer. Espresso maker? Pocket knife? (Just kidding.) Talk about feature-itis! Does anyone remember when cell phones were used TO MAKE CALLS?

Because ignoring consumers' emotions is never a wise business move, the solution is to radically simplify the design. Don't get caught up in explaining the offer's rational benefits. Instead, lavish most of the design energy on targeting the sweet spot that will provide the single most attractive benefit. Do so by understanding problems faced by consumers. These are problems consumers want offers to solve. Then think of scenarios in which the company can provide solutions to those problems. The scenarios should involve actions that elicit positive emotions (such as awe or hope) or promise to meet emotional needs. Use these emotional access points as the basis for inventing the advantage the company's offer can best deliver.

2. Cost-Cutting
(too few features)

While every company considers design, it's usually cost-cutting analytics that dictate final production. But no matter what offer a consumer considers, that offer will be incomplete unless it implicitly addresses the business version of Sigmund Freud's pleasure principle. In other words, there has to be a pleasing emotional payoff: a What's-in-It-for-Me (WIIFM). Otherwise, consumers won't buy.

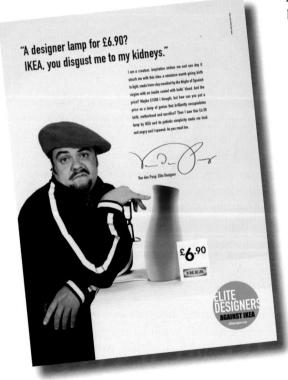

Why a paper bag? Because it's a great example of what can happen if all the features are taken out of a design. . . in this case a fancy woman's purse. In losing the fine-grain, pebbled Italian leather, 18-karat gold accented hardware, myriad internal pockets and matching clutch just to keep costs down, a company ends up with nothing more than a paper bag. And when's the last time consumers got excited about one of those?

"A designer lamp for £6.90? IKEA, you disgust me to my kidneys."

£6.90

IKEA

ELITE DESIGNERS AGAINST IKEA

Ikea's Spoof on Hoity-toity Designers

The solution that gets consumers attracted, buying and satisfied echoes the point made in regard to feature-itis: provide a solution to a problem or shortcoming. The additional point to be made here, however, is that companies should also figure out the rational benefit—the intellectual alibi—that best provides justification for purchasing the offer. But in doing so, they should remember that people feel before they think. As a result, the key emotional benefit should come first in developing the design. It may be that what consumers desire most in emotional terms is just what rationally-oriented or cost-cutting analytics recommend a company skimps on. Given competing agendas, the smart choice that will ultimately drive sales is the one that's emotionally based.

3. Myopia
(selfish features)

A designer's quest for artistic glory may be the reason why the end-user's emotional needs are being ignored. An ingenuous design consumers can't readily comprehend will rob it of emotional punch; just as a joke isn't nearly as funny if it has to be explained. If an engineer is the culprit, a desire for functional superiority may mean the onset of feature-itis. In these and other ways, a company's natural bias for starting from its own inwardly-oriented and potentially myopic perspective can keep consumers from getting the features they want and the emotional connection they desire.

What's required for love of an offer to flourish? The answer is reciprocity and an emotional hook. While the engineer is the "Can it be done?" person and the marketer is the "Will it be done?" person, the designer should ideally be the "Should it be done?" person who looks out for the end-user by knowing which concessions don't matter and which will kill the design.

Determining and eliciting consumer emotion is key. So skip focus groups whose members can only tell the company where they're at, not where they're going. Aim at knowing how potential buyers feel in order to determine what they will do. In conducting research, try to find the early adopters whose emotional model matches that of the company's largest target market. A strong, non-verbal emotional connection with consumers will indicate that the company is fulfilling their unexpressed preferences in a way that will make them willing to consider purchasing the offer.

4. Tunnel Vision
(irrelevant features)

Many offers fail because they were designed in response to a competing offer, to utilize factory capacity or to reposition existing offers. In short, the design is driven by the economic criteria of the business instead of the goal of fulfilling the consumers' emotional preferences. For example, while health-care providers tend to emphasize technology and medicines, patients are concerned with service and information.

Talk about an irrelevant feature. Though this packaging example is slightly over-the-top, features that have nothing to do (or no direct connection) to the offer are simply clutter to the consumer. And what's hard to understand doesn't get purchased.

The solution is to stake claim to imaginative power. If there's no magic to be had, the consumer won't buy. When it comes to offer design, delivering on core competencies isn't nearly as important as ensuring relevance. A company's best bet is to exaggerate the emotional benefit for the target market. Make sure the offer connects with people by determining the one thing the target market remembers two weeks after exposure to the offer. Then adjust the design to eliminate irrelevant features in order to sharpen focus on this crucial feature.

5. No Vision
(only safe, rationally driven features)

A great design, we love. A bad design, we hate. And a safe design, we don't even see. Sadly, it's easy to hate something and way too easy to build something invisible. Often a company will put effort into developing an offer that ends up being invisible because a focus group has said, "Well, I would consider that." Consumers fall back on giving utilitarian-oriented descriptions of what they would buy. However, most communication isn't verbal and great design isn't rational. A prospect's report that something is "acceptable" isn't acceptable. The effort a company puts into developing an offer that's been verbally identified as "acceptable" will produce apple sauce instead of apple pie.

> *"In a world of largely saturated markets and many alternatives, astonishing the customer (through superior design) is the path to exceptional growth and profits."*
>
> —Robert Heller

On the other hand, a company is headed toward a solution when, consciously or not, consumers see the offer as projecting a personality to which they have a positive emotional response. Aim for a personable design, while making sure that the offer's personality aligns with the end-user's preferred self-image.

Proven Winners: Concepts That Work
The basis of great design is to be both awe-inspiring and emotionally relevant.

Given all the competition, form-follows-function is no longer an adequate mantra for gaining market share. Great design needs to go deeper than rationalization. Over time, it has to please our senses and win us over emotionally. But first it has to capture the imagination. What are the essential ingredients to success at the offer's concept stage? Two independent studies provide us with answers.

The first (Cooper) found that the number one success factor is having a unique, superior offer. Offering greatness results in a 90% success rate. Is there a caveat? Yes, the superiority must involve something consumers care about. What's the additional proof? A second study (Madique) showed that success is also based on as deep and rich an understanding of consumer needs as can be ascertained.

Let's look at three successes as well as at one partial success.

Success #1:
The New Love Bug

One example of imaginative power is the Mini Cooper. Like any really great offer, it captures the imagination by establishing a fantastical sense of superiority. No, that doesn't mean to suggest the offer is false or doesn't work. Rather, the offer inspires awe by daring to provide a plausible promise that doesn't just endorse the status quo.

After all, it is a ridiculously small car—which makes its wide-eyed, pronounced headlights all the more noticeable.

Fig. 5.1 The Ridiculously Small Mini
Sometimes the small dog wins the fight. The Mini Cooper has managed to sell 40,000 units a year because people simply love the charm of it.

And speaking of exuding a sense of differentiated superiority. . . how was it launched? By being mounted atop SUVs and driven around 21 cities with signs on top that read: "The SUV backlash officially starts now." Now *that's* an offer certain to annoy some people, but enthrall others. The approach says, in effect: express your uniqueness and values by buying this car. You could be here, too—above the hum-drum SUV fray, living a superior life of fun and fantasy.

Success #2:
Babes in Toyland

A second example of imaginative power in action is from the $20 billion toy industry. The sector has always leveraged the way children focus on the faces of others—something they do from the moment of birth. Nothing illustrates the emotional way kids relate to toys better than a girl's connection with her dolls. And for years no doll was more loved than Barbie.

Then in 2001, MGA Entertainment introduced its Bratz line of dolls as a hip alternative to Mattel's offer. Barbie smiles. The Bratz pout. The differences, especially the Bratz' air of superiority, go on from there. In short, the Bratz capitalized on the emotional needs of young girls in search of fun and attitude better than Barbie did, and financial rewards followed from taking a slightly more extreme position.

Fig. 5.2 Barbie is literally under attack from the Bratz gang.

Its parent company reported sales of over $2 billion in 2005. It's estimated that Bratz now has over 30% market share.

Success #3:
The $2,000 Washing Machine

Premium goods have surpassed $400 billion in annual domestic sales with expected growth of about 15% a year (Silverstein). The explanation for the rise has to be emotions, at least in part. Clearly, paying lots of money for an offer isn't "rational." Driven by consumers' willingness to pay more for goods in the categories that are most emotionally meaningful to them, new luxury goods have upended the traditional price/volume demand curve.

A case in point is Whirlpool's upscale Duet product line. The line retails for three times the average washer/dryer set. Surely nobody wants to pay $2,000 for a washing machine. Talk about a purchase that's purely functional and not emotional, right? But in actuality Whirlpool's innovative, European-style machines have sold very well to enthusiastic owners and the premium washing machine category has grown by 9% (Silverstein).

In testing that Sensory Logic did on the Duet line, we found that despite some verbal expressions of doubt, the emotional responses of subjects were strong and positive with high Emotional

Incorporating sleeker designs and more aesthetically pleasing materials, Whirlpool's Duet® retails for three times the average washer/dryer combo. The premium washing machine category has grown by 9% overall.
(picture courtesy of Whirlpool)

Response Rates. Consumers were extremely interested in learning about additional innovations and the wider array of color options being considered.

Charles Jones, Whirlpool's V.P. of Global Consumer Design, was quoted about our research in *The Wall Street Journal* (Zaslow). About consumers he observed, "They'd say, 'I don't know if I'm comfortable with this,' but their facial expressions were saying, 'This is pretty cool!' It saved us from going down a number of blind alleys." This focus on design has helped Whirlpool's stock price rise 31% since introducing the new upscale Duet washer and dryer set in 1999.

Partial Success:
Ergonomic Handles

Finally, here's an example of an offer design that can work well—depending on which target market is being addressed. In another study involving the household, Sensory Logic moved from the laundry room to the kitchen and pitted an ergonomic, upscale OXO Good Grips® spatula against a basic, utilitarian "Fred Flintstone" model (Fig. 5.3). Unlike the Whirlpool study, which involved only women, in this case the sample was split between men and women—as were the results.

Verbally, women didn't indicate a preference either way. Indeed, their strong "wow" preference for the softer and more flexible OXO spatula only became clear after analyzing the emotionally-based facial coding data. Interestingly, men somewhat similarly to women, were verbally unenthusiastic about the crude model. But unlike the women's results, the men's facial coding data showed a win for the no-frills flipper over what they apparently took to be the frou-frou OXO Good Grips® model.

In other words, the outcome would suggest that men enjoy feeling manly. In this case, it's likely that psychographic segmentation is everything. Those men who are comfortable with their soft side and fit the so-called "metrosexual" profile may be exactly the right target here.

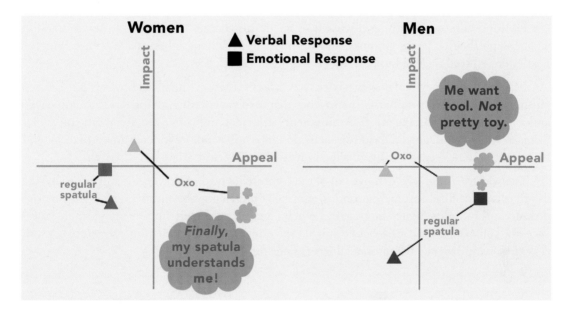

Fig. 5.3 Getting a Handle on Gender
OXO's Good Grips® are great. They're ergonomic, stylish and comfortable. But that doesn't mean they are for everyone. Testing we did on the product showed that, emotionally, men actually preferred a regular old steel spatula to the fancier (and more feminine) Good Grips® model.

*"It is only shallow people
who do not judge the world by appearances."*
—Oscar Wilde

Designing the Experience
The highest level of offer design is to create a story-like experience.

The previous examples were about products, but when addressing imaginative power in action we need to acknowledge the design of services and experiences as well. After all, America has moved far away from being the producer of things: only 12% of our economy is manufacturing-based anymore. About 80% of both the country's economy and its workforce belong to the services realm (Pine 2004). Therefore, the topic of service deserves a more in-depth discussion, which comes in Chapter 8.

However, almost everything discussed so far in this chapter also applies to services and to what Joseph Pine II, James Gilmore, and Bernd Schmitt, among others, have been calling the next, more evolved stage of business: the providing of experiences.

As first Walt Disney, and now Starbucks have shown, there are financial rewards in creating a sensory and emotionally immersive experience that involves a setting, characters (the employees) and a plot (experiencing the offer). Amusement park rides and coffee are merely the offer platforms to which these companies add specially designed opportunities for consumers to feel—and, in essence, become—emotionally satisfied in ways that they can't attain anywhere else.

The way for a company to move out of the commodity trap—which is to say, beyond having its offers regarded by consumers as undistinguished, interchangeable entities, vulnerable to price pressure—is to differentiate emotionally. When engaged customers find meaning in an experience, the collaborative outcome between what the offer *presents* and what it *represents* to consumers emotionally provides the ultimate degree of customization.

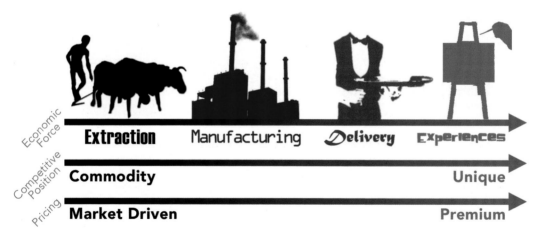

Fig. 5.4 The Progression of Economic Value
Pine and Gilmore see four stages of growth: the agrarian extraction of natural resources, the industrial manufacturing of standardized goods, the service and delivery of customized care, and now akin to Disney, the staging of memorable, personal experiences that are creatively designed to provide more emotional payoff.

In short, while service is a transaction, an experience should be more encompassing.

Consider American Girl Place. We could label its two locales, Chicago and New York City, "stores." But while consumers can buy the popular dolls, books, furniture, and clothing on-site, there's also a doll-hospital admissions center, a hair salon, a restaurant and places set aside for souvenir photo shoots of *American Girl Magazine*. The "store" even contains a 150-seat theater, which helps explain why the average customer spends two and a half hours in the building. To call it integrated marketing is only half-correct. It is really more like integrated offer design.

The intent is to make the enrichment of the customer's life the end "product." At American Girl Place, there are many features but no likelihood of feature-itis because the optional activities are clear and emotionally relevant.

A coffee shop. So what. There's plenty of those.

Except this isn't just a coffee shop. It's an ING DIRECT Café. Though it does serve java, ING has created major oases in the middle of cities and staffed them with certified financial planners. The goal is to provide customers with a peaceful environment where they can check their stocks, get financial advice and enjoy a nice cup-of-Joe.

Sensory Payoff:
the way to the heart

136

Synopsis: The key here is to create enough sensory excitement that consumers get emotionally intrigued and can overcome any previous disappointments in the category. As reflected in the content of this section, sensory engagement typically starts with the packaging as experienced in-store but then moves on to the offer itself, which is usually experienced at home.

Key take-aways:

- Great packaging is about eyeballs and fingertips, leveraging sight and touch.
- A great offer design has a payoff for each part of our three-part brain.

Wrappers That Work: Enticing Packaging
Great packaging is about eyeballs and fingertips,
leveraging sight and touch.

The goal of establishing an offer's superiority is conceptual in nature and happens consciously in consumers' *minds*, inspiring fantasies about how the offer will be emotionally satisfying. But the next opportunity, overcoming marketplace invisibility through sensory sensations, happens more subconsciously. It is an unfolding in consumers' *bodies*. After all, the whole proposition of getting consumers to discover and investigate a new offer starts with engaging them. We're talking eyeballs and fingertips—the basics. The sensory bandwidth must be leveraged to ignite and sustain emotional interest in the target market.

This sensory intrigue must occur twice: once through packaging and again in actual usage. Let's concentrate on packaging for now.

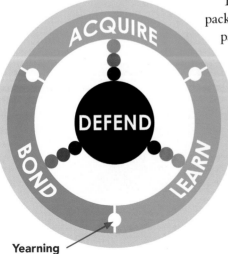

Yearning

Emotion and Motivations

Yearning is the relevant emotion here, as consumers, burned by disappointments, dare to hope again. This rekindled desire is less about trying to **bond** in the social sense than it is about a me/new toy relationship. The other motivation is to **learn**, as consumers gain a better experiential understanding of the offer.

"With its thousands of images and messages, the supermarket is as visually dense,
if not as beautiful, as a Gothic cathedral. It is as complex and as predatory as a tropical rain forest."
—Thomas Hine

While ultimately functional, product packaging must be as full of sensory enticement as possible to induce sales opportunities. Packaging's dual personality—emotionally stimulating in store, rationally satisfactory after purchase—is necessitated by the difficulty of grabbing people's attention. In any retail setting, shoppers are now bombarded by so much sensory input that their minds immediately and subconsciously filter out what's not important to them.

Just like our ancestors on the ancient savannah, shoppers must be able to answer essential questions: where will sustenance come from, and what is better to avoid? Moreover, they must be able to do so quickly and automatically.

That brings us to our next issue: just how small the window of opportunity really is. It is estimated that designers have .06 seconds, on average, to make an impression on a shopper in the grocery aisle (Hine). Nor are volume, competition and limited time the only hurdles. For packaging to function effectively in such a short amount of time, it must do so while typically appealing to only two of the senses: sight and touch.

For inspiration, consider Red Bull.
Not only did Red Bull create the energy drink category, it owns it with worldwide sales of $1.5 billion annually (Reis). What makes Red Bull so effective? Let's start with the offer: it's not just a drink but a highly relevant way to improve performance during times of stress. Positioning? Red Bull says it all connotatively by packaging in smaller, 8.3 ounce cans that suggest potency and fit nicely in consumers' hands.

It's believed that 70% of what we look at in stores is packaging (Nelson). But what exactly are we looking at? At Procter and Gamble they call it the "first moment of truth." Soon, an offer is either in someone's hand or passed over. This figure visually summarizes eye tracking data we captured from subjects looking at a store's toothpaste shelf. Areas shown in red had the most attention.

In other words, packaging needs to catch the eye and welcome the hand. At the sensory level, an offer's visual obscurity is the kiss of death. As people are primarily visual beings, we look at things to establish most of our impressions. So if a packaged offer doesn't visually engage consumers at first glance, it's either too complicated or has settled for look-alike invisibility. In creating an effective package design, quick comprehensibility and a firework-like pop are everything.

Then after pleasing the eye, it's time to invite touch. Make the offer tangible in such a way as to invite consumers to hold it in their hands. But remember that once a package is held, people's emotional brains—the second part of the brain in evolutionary terms—will assign value. So be

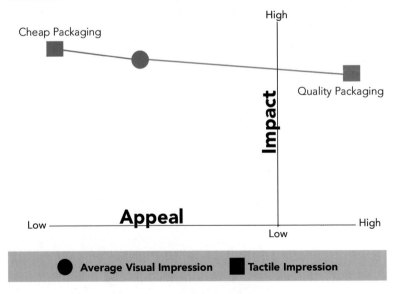

Fig. 5.5 The Effect of Package Quality on Emotional Response
The difference between great and cheap packaging? A sale. As seen in this study on healthcare product packaging, there is a distinct difference in perception. The cheap packaging says, "You don't think my health is important." The heavier, more substantial packaging says, "You're concerned about quality and will look out for me." The bottom line is that flimsy packaging may save money on the factory floor but will definitely cost money on the sales floor.

sure to make the perceived value an emotionally positive one.

Packaging must build trust and reassurance both visually and physically because even though consumers might not be able to directly see the packaged offer prior to purchase, they must nevertheless understand or feel the offer is worthwhile to buy. Successful packaging can fulfill this last requirement in multiple ways. Packages can influence through the use of clever color schemes, size, material quality, unique shapes or weight.

A Pleasing Offer Experience

A great offer design has a payoff for each part of our three-part brain.

When it comes to getting the offer home from the store, out of its packaging and to actual usage, all previous sensory experiences are mute. Enticing quick-moving shoppers to stop and, within just a few nanoseconds, "consider" the purchase is over. The goal now becomes deepening and enriching the sensory-emotional experience. To learn how to do so, let's return to our model of the three-part brain and its implications for offer design.

How does the target market respond emotionally to the shapes, proportions and spatial relationships in the company's offer?

More universal; greater sensory bandwidth	*all senses*	hard/soft strong/weak new/old simple/complex
Visual & Other Sense Perceptions	*sight/ sound/ touch*	tight/loose chaotic/orderly
	sight/ sound	high/low fast/slow full/open
	sight/ touch	big/small tall/short heavy/light wide/narrow thick/thin in/out rough/smooth damp/dry relaxed/tense angular/curved straight/jagged vertical/horizontal
Entirely Visual		light/dark
	sound	loud/quiet
Non-visual Sense Perceptions	*smell*	fresh/stale
	taste	spicy/mild
More limited; less sensory bandwidth	*smell/ taste*	sweet/sour
	touch/ taste	warm/cold

Fig. 5.6 Sensory Archetypes

The chart shows dichotomous pairs of sensory attributes and where they fall in terms of engaging all or some of the sensory bandwidth. At the top are pairs that engage our sight and other senses. At the bottom are non-visual pairs that engage less of the sensory bandwidth and are thus less likely to be effective in a shopping environment (Lakoff).

Learning the 27 universal and hardwired sensory archetypes in Figure 5.6 will help a company design offers more effectively by enabling it to invoke the patterns people already intuitively know and can relate to readily.

At the sensory level, appearances matter. But the key here isn't just aesthetics in a pure visual sense; it's essence and satisfaction. Strategic advantage doesn't lie in the form-follows-function mode, but rather in *form-follows-soul*. In other words, without ignoring functional utility, decide on what the offer is really about in terms of its key emotional benefit and then choose which of the sensory archetypes can best help deliver on that benefit.

In general, at the emotional level strive for attachment. The secret of lasting love and enduring relationships is pleasure. Without it, no sparks will fly. And without sparks, nothing will endure over time.

Finally, at the rational level ask oneself: are the functional qualities substantially addressed? Are consumers able to justify the purchase to themselves and others, using an intellectual alibi? Does the offer as designed readily provide such an alibi?

For a real life example of just how much in conflict the sensory, emotional and rational levels can be, let's look at a study Sensory Logic did comparing two car interiors: one of an upscale American car and one of an upscale German car. As these results show, subconscious, sensory-emotional responses can be at odds with consciously stated preferences (Fig. 5.7). In this case, the people we tested in Detroit probably knew on a rational, reflective level that American pride and jobs could be at stake in their expressing preferences for a foreign-made car.

So they rationally sought to ally themselves with the American car. Thus, they consistently rated its design attributes as better, even though their own emotional responses indicated that, new car smells aside, they liked the German car more.

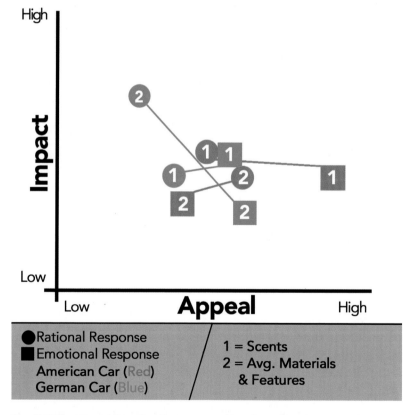

Fig. 5.7 Emotional Results: German vs. American Car
Scent of a woman? Try scent of a car. On an olfactory level, the American car won easily. But when the eye and hand were involved in evaluation, experience belied adverse verbal responses toward the German car and revealed high Appeal in favor of it. On average across a half dozen categories involving materials and features, the German car was consistently felt to be better—despite comments and ratings indicating the opposite.

Functional Fulfillment:
joy, not frustration

Synopsis: A well-designed offer takes into account not only the sensory and emotional levels, but also the utilitarian needs that occupy the rational level. Otherwise, the potential for emotional enjoyment will get sabotaged by rationally-oriented frustration related to inadequate functionality. Protection against that fate lies in usability testing, but especially testing that gauges efficiency and accuracy alongside the emotional aspects of the usage experience.

Key take-aways:

- An offer that taxes our emotional resources isn't going to be viable for long.
- True customer satisfaction is sensory-emotive and must be tested accordingly.

Emotion and Motivations

An offer that makes consumers feel less capable creates displeasure in general and **anger** in particular as they lose a sense of being in control. This emotional outcome is the exact opposite of what they want. An offer consumers sought to **acquire** because it would enhance their power, status or capability now, instead, becomes something they must **defend** themselves against.

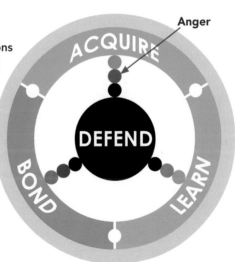

The reaction on this face is one any company wants to avoid. Confusion leading to disgust for the offer is the quickest way to help competitors achieve that bottom line boost they've been striving for. After all, why buy what can't be understood?

Effectiveness of Use
An offer that taxes our emotional resources isn't going to be viable for long.

At a very rational level, consumers want the offers they purchase to work easily, correctly and with as little effort as possible. For example, who isn't happier knowing that Microsoft Office now requires only four clicks to insert a text box, whereas the 2003 edition required 26 clicks?

Sounds like companies just need to address fairly utilitarian and traditionally logical issues, right? Let's not fool ourselves. Emotions are at play here—front and center. The moment we're confused. . . poof! In a cluttered world, nothing spells an offer's doom more quickly than its being hard to assimilate. Every offer needs to sell itself without the aid of complicated, detailed advertising and instructions for use. In development, consider this question: can a person encountering this offer without previous knowledge figure it out and be captivated by the outcome?

Designing for maximum ease and pleasure of use requires minimizing and defusing the potential for anger that could arise if usability proves to be a hassle and, therefore, robs consumers of a sense of self-control during the usage experience.

It's essential that consumers grasp how an offer works quickly and intuitively. Non-visual instructions won't be of much help, especially when written by a non-native speaker who lacks grammatical fluency. Even when instructions are well-written, the truth is that words alone often aren't enough to avoid an emotional disconnect should the going get tough. The key to success is ensuring that consumers are able to form their own mental image of how the offer works.

In the end, the real reason why the intuitive sensory approach to functionality is so vital is emotional in nature. That's because, first, frustration floods people and causes them to short-circuit and shut-down when they feel unable to comprehend something new. Second, emotions control our muscles, hence our behavior, robbing us of adeptness when rage takes over.

Imaginative power. Superiority. The symbolic role of the offer in people's lives. None of those qualities will be sustainable or matter if a consumer is frustrated with the offer and comes away feeling as if the original, conceptual promise wasn't fulfilled.

> *"In the 1980's, in writing* The Design of Everyday Things, *I didn't take emotions into account. I addressed utility and usability, function and form, all in a logical, dispassionate way—even though I am infuriated by poorly designed objects. But now I've changed. Why? In part because of new scientific advances in our understanding of the brain and how emotion and cognition are thoroughly intertwined. We scientists now understand how important emotion is to everyday life, how valuable."*
>
> —Donald Norman

After all, if an offer looks great, feels great, and performs terribly, then a company's marketing and branding dollars have been wasted and amount to nothing more than a very expensive opportunity to frustrate the customer. Making sure the offer lives up to expectation, both in terms of design and post-purchase usage, is the best way to ensure customer loyalty.

Usability Testing to the Rescue
True customer satisfaction is sensory-emotive and must be tested accordingly.

Fortunately, in recent years the usability movement has become stronger as companies realize that part of championing design is making sure the outcomes please consumers. November 3, 2005 was the first World Usability Day, with 35 countries participating in the Usability Professionals Association's inaugural event meant to promote user-friendly design.

It couldn't have come a moment too soon.

Over the last 40 years the average American has grown in size so much that the trend has implications for all sorts of offers, not the least of which are new motor vehicles. As *Chicago Tribune* columnist Jim Mateja notes, "Hard to believe, but the last time attention was paid to how the size of people affects the size of the passenger cabin was when John, Paul, Ringo and George were an opening act in the '60s." Mateja was writing about how Ford is updating its models using mannequins to help designers account for the increased size of the average buyer.

What explains the new commercial focus on user-friendly design? According to Randolph Bias, author of *Cost-Justifying Usability*, the return on investment for companies who do so is estimated at 100-to-1 (Baig). In other words, ease of use is good both for consumers and for the company's bottom line.

As the Apple iPod's clean, easy-to-use design proves through market domination, intuitive and easy-to-use offers simply sell better. Ikea is another example of simplicity in action. The instructions that accompany its assemble-yourself offers don't even bother with words. Instead, they rely on pictures and the fact that the designs are well thought out and easy to assemble.

Ensuring that consumers don't suffer sensory confusion leading to an emotional disconnect should be obvious. Perhaps companies will take this information one step further and realize that design discussions involving designers, engineers and marketers are incomplete unless they include those who will service the

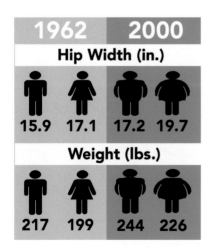

1962		2000	
Hip Width (in.)			
15.9	17.1	17.2	19.7
Weight (lbs.)			
217	199	244	226

Fig. 5.8 Americans Are Getting Bigger
The sizes stated here account for the upper limits of all but the largest of us. Companies that create consumer comfort by acknowledging expanding waistlines set themselves up for bulging bank accounts (Mateja).

offers. That's because an offer that can't be feasibly supported at the customer service stage *post*-launch needs to be reevaluated *pre*-launch.

The good news is that usability testing is being increasingly performed, and for good reason: the quality of offers impacts the quality of consumers' lives.

But now for the bad news: the challenge facing standard usability testing is that best practices means moving beyond evaluating only a consumer's rational responses. After all, at the point that really counts—the experience of the offer—satisfaction lives in the sensory impressions and the customer's heart, i.e., his or her intuitive, emotional response to that experience.

On its own, consciously constructed, verbal input can't help you assess the quality of your offer or how easily and enjoyably consumers use it. Donald Norman is on track in *Emotional Design* when he notes that questionnaires are "poor tools for learning about behavior" because "most behavior is subconscious and what people actually do can be quite different from what they think they do."

Actions do speak louder than words

This cliché phrase is why observations, especially those done utilizing facial coding, can be of decisive help. Gauging *emotional buy-in* in this way and then using verbal input to identify the *intellectual alibi* can serve as an effective one-two combination. Then designs and revisions can be undertaken by drawing on a more complete picture of the situation.

Otherwise, usability testing too often gets reduced to capturing just speed and accuracy, proxies for gauging efficiency. The problem is that neither variable tells how consumers have internalized the usage experience, nor how they truly feel about the offer.

To fully grasp the implications of this frequent shortcoming, consider a pair of examples. The first one involves testing Sensory Logic performed at the conceptual level for a new feature that could seriously impact the machine's usability. The innovation seemed good, rationally speak-

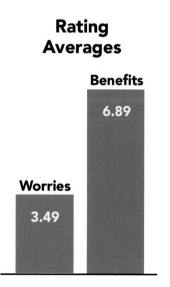

Rating Averages

Benefits
6.89

Worries
3.49

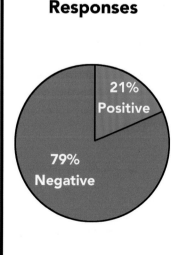

Emotional Responses

21% Positive

79% Negative

Fig. 5.9 Offer Attribute Response
Asked to evaluate a potential feature on a major home appliance, respondents provided verbal responses that saw the feature as a benefit by a ratio of two-to-one. But emotionally, that same feature was greeted by an almost 80% negative emotional response.

ing. Asked to rate potential advantages versus drawbacks, subjects saw more of an upside than a downside by nearly a two-to-one ratio. Furthermore, only 5% of the subjects voiced concerns that the additional feature might be "just another thing to go wrong" (Fig. 5.9). Emotionally, however, the subjects responded with lots of doubt and no strong positives.

The second study was conducted in Japan for a healthcare offer. In this case, Sensory Logic videotaped subjects interacting with the offer. Their facially coded expressions were caught on video and the visible reactions were segmented into five stages: 1) viewing the packaging; 2) reading the instructions; 3) opening the package; 4) applying the offer; and 5) smelling the offer's fragrance.

Figure 5.10 shows the breakdown of emotional responses for all subjects Sensory Logic tested as well as a screen shot of a participant at every step of the process.

The results show that the best received steps of the offer/use cycle were the initial contact (89% positive) and smelling the offer (72% positive). As one might expect, reading the instructions didn't prove enjoyable (93% negative). But our biggest concern was that opening the packaging proved to be a *100% negative experience* for subjects, the possibility of joyful anticipation having been overtaken by responses mostly driven by frustration and dislike. Moreover, this strongly negative reaction threatened to create adverse momentum heading into steps four and five.

Fortunately, the results revealed both current strengths and the largest opportunities for improvement. Armed with those insights, the company was then in a position to take the steps it deemed necessary to generate the best possible emotional buy-in to their offer.

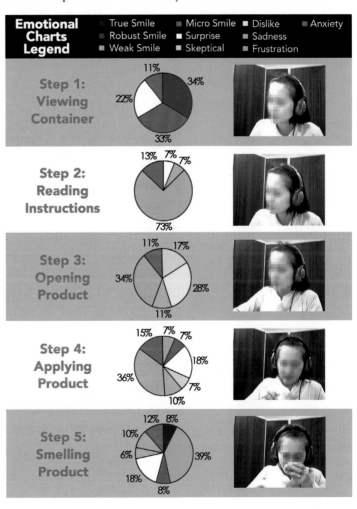

Fig. 5.10

Step-by-Step Emotional Responses to Product Testing

Conclusion

We've all experienced both the highs and lows of offer design, packaging and usability. The ideal is for companies to create offers that intuitively grab and please us and that we can readily understand. Unfortunately, all too often consumers experience the opposite and fear disappointment again. To be effective in the design phase, the following must be accomplished:

- At the concept stage, aim to create awe. This mixture of fear, curiosity and most of all delighted respect for what the offer can do is vital. Without an emotional breakthrough there's no staying power or connection—only another "deal."

- At the sensory, encounter stage, make hope spring eternal. Do so by engaging the senses, sparking a belief first in the packaging and then the offer in order to bypass the intellect and induce engagement. By inviting intimacy, commitment will follow.

- At the usability stage, protect consumers' fragile faith in the offer. This can be done by knowing that we love an offer only if it loves us in return. Bad design violates the love pact by creating a sense of betrayal when the offer doesn't fulfill its promise.

Sensory Facts % of Daily Needs**	
Sight	70%
Sound	10%
Smell	27%
Touch	19%
Taste	31%

**How well does the offer fulfill customer expectations and needs?

An Action Plan

To make sure that the company's offer design, packaging and usability efforts are emotionally healthy, here are a few check-ups to do when assessing effectiveness:

- ☐ Convene consumers to talk about the company's products, services and designed experiences. By listening carefully or, better yet, by quantifying the emotions underlying their words through facial coding, the company can learn valuable information about both its offers and those of its competitors. Then look for differences that reveal opportunities for differentiation.

- ☐ Discern the emotional needs of the company's largest buyer segment, and then discern whether those needs are being met. In essence, learn consumers' values, aesthetic sense and the nature of their relationships to the company. Specifically, learn how they respond emotionally to shapes, proportions and spatial relationships. Learning those patterns will help the company design more adroitly.

- ☐ A company's offer is emotionally healthy if its life cycle is different from the offers of the rest of the industry. To maintain an edge, identify consumers who didn't repurchase to learn why they didn't feel rewarded.

- ☐ With regard to packaging, let the emotional connection and positive sensory experiences continue to guide changes that might be necessary to fit a distribution system or other company-centric utilitarian requirement. Stay loyal to pleasing the external consumer audience—the one that pays the bills (their feelings should never be ignored).

- ☐ With regard to usability, resolve any problems that reduce the emotional connection consumers make with the offer. Utilitarian usage issues are a hurdle to be overcome, but never at the expense of ignoring the potential for originality or at the cost of undermining consumers' allegiance to the offer.

6 advertising

Advertising's goal is to shed a brilliant spotlight onto a previously unseen or ignored offer. The mantra is for consumers to see it, want it, need it.

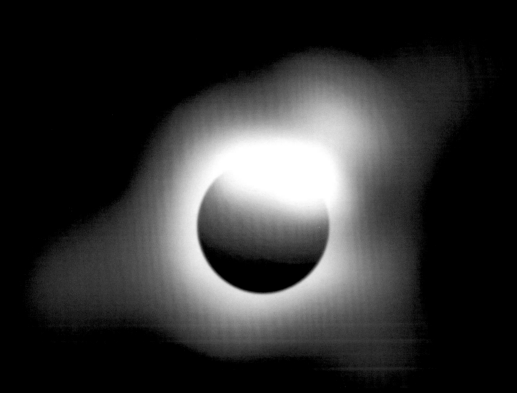

OVERVIEW

The best advertising addresses the enduring human desire for something big, new and positive. Plain and simple, advertising relies on enduring consumer hope. Fail to deliver on the promise of new, enhanced possibilities and the heart can't fight through the skepticism the mind will have about getting pitched to, yet again, in an advertising-soaked world. Done right, however, advertising generates images that consumers deeply feel, as well as see, helping to tilt the choice in a company's favor the next time they're shopping for what it sells. To help companies present emotionally resonant advertising, this chapter will focus on:

The best advertising addresses our eternal search to find something:

Big.
New.
Positive.

- **Being Absorbing**: In traditional terms, the first step to success is to generate awareness. But awareness by itself isn't enough because recognition isn't of economic value. So agencies are right in pushing the envelope in order to create stopping power on the way to securing Emotional Potency. The bottom line is that awareness doesn't indicate the potential—and necessity—for emotional buy-in, which starts with the ability to slip past people's emotional filters by eliciting a strong emotional response.

- **The Invisible Line**: The second step, consideration, also needs to be recast. What's the underlying issue? Keeping the creative output on the right side of an invisible line so that the offer's Appeal doesn't suffer emotional damage and limit consideration. In other words, to support economic gain creativity needs to be defined as the creation of emotions in consumers that promote consideration rather than rejection of the advertised offer. That positive outcome can only happen if the agency has a grasp of where the invisible line is between pressing "hot buttons" effectively enough to be engaging but not pressing them so hard that the target market ends up being offended instead.

- **Reassurance**: The third step, persuasion, is of all the traditional terms the one most fraught with baggage. Too often, it really serves as a code word for guaranteeing sales, which, in reality, is asking too much of advertising. Providing reassurance is a more credible and achievable goal. Removing barriers to acceptance is vital. The key is gaining and keeping the target market's faith in advertising through images and concepts linked to those it already emotionally endorses.

Now let's look more closely at how to creating advertising that breaks through the clutter and makes a connection, starting with the link between securing attention and generating emotional involvement.

Being Absorbing:
what stopping power entails

Synopsis: Advertising needs to be emotionally absorbing. Otherwise, it's irrelevant and stale. In this section, we'll look at how big the challenge to connecting with consumers has become, and review the five decision-making stages advertising must impact to be effective. But only the first two stages will be emphasized for now, as the discussion moves on to contrasting rationally-oriented awareness with emotionally-oriented stopping power as the first step to success.

> **Key take-aways:**
> - The mind is geared to filter out stimuli, requiring emotion to break through.
> - Current methods for gauging awareness really only capture recognition level.
> - The goal of measuring stopping power leads inevitably to Emotional Potency.

Emotion and Motivations

Awe is the key emotion as advertising must be absorbing enough to interrupt and interest consumers as well as be able to enter their long-term memories. A lesser emotional response may not be substantial enough for the days, weeks or even months until the purchase decision is at hand. The dominant motivation is consumers' desire to **learn**. Even at this initial step, the drive to **acquire** the advertised offer is also an emerging factor.

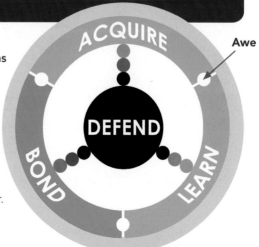

Overcoming Indifference
The mind is geared to filter out stimuli,
requiring emotion to break through.

How big is the challenge of trying to secure the awareness—let alone the enduring emotional engagement—of consumers? Huge, of course. People are awash in information and only too glad to tune out what they don't need, which is why it is increasingly difficult to create a successful ad.

Over a five-year period during the late 1980s, for instance, separate market research firms tracked the percentage of U.S. and West German viewers who remembered the last commercial they had seen on television. The decline was over 40% in America and nearly 20% among the Germans. More recently, a third research firm found that in cluttered markets like the U. S. and Japan, TV commercials are only half as capable of increasing awareness as they are in countries with far fewer commercials being aired per week (du Plessis). And that's just looking at the marketplace.

How about the mind? In that case, even under the best circumstances establishing awareness is difficult. As discussed in Chapter 1, the human brain takes in 400 billion bytes of information per second through our senses but only consciously processes 2,000 bytes. That dramatic ratio should make it evident that when it comes to awareness, keeping the door shut—not open—is far and away our basic impulse. In other words, filtering or screening out takes precedence over input.

As 400 billion bytes makes clear, the mind has remarkable elasticity when it comes to absorbing data. The problem lies in processing it all. Perhaps the authors of *The Attention Economy* put it best when they described sensory input as being processed in a large funnel (Davenport), the narrow spout of which is what behavior actually results from the influence of so much input (Fig. 6.1). Let's add a little more detail to the five key stages of their metaphorical funnel to get a grasp on how emotions and advertising interact.

People today are drowning in information and only too glad to tune out what isn't relevant or entertaining.

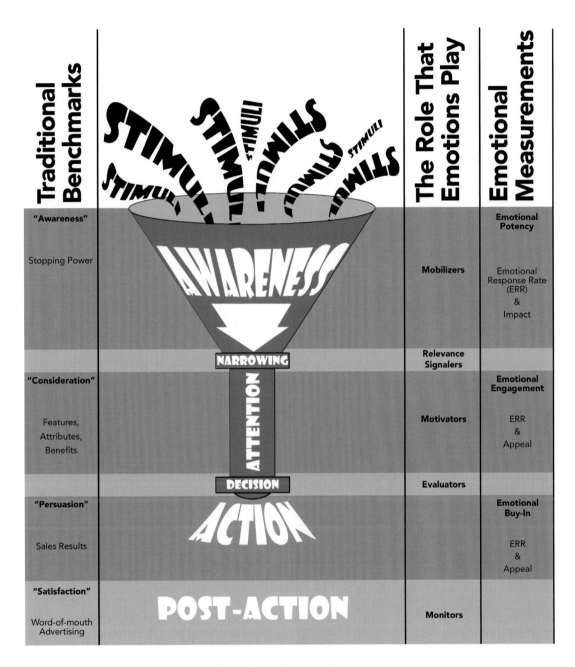

Fig. 6.1 How Attention Works: Traditionally and Motivationally

This chart diagrams how stimuli are funneled through the attention process. On the left side are the traditional ways to think about the process. On the right is listed first the role that emotions play in each step, and second how Sensory Logic measures the emotional significance of each step in the attention process.

Stage 1: Awareness –This stage is about noticing something, becoming aware of it. Advertising proliferates in hopes that consumers will recall some of it. If properly diagnosed, recall is the first place in the funnel where emotion matters. That's because we remember something for only one of two reasons: it either sparks an emotional response or easily corresponds to something we've already retained. At this earliest stage, *emotions serve as mobilizers*. They're like an early-warning system, alerting us as to whether we might want to approach or avoid the advertising in question for innate, subconscious reasons we might not be able to articulate.

Stage 2: Narrowing –Survival instincts help explain the next, slightly narrower part of the funnel. To function most effectively and ward off threats, people have to focus first and foremost on what they feel will matter most. Thus at this stage, *emotions serve as relevance signalers*. They turn on—and stay on—when a goal is at stake. To be viable, which means to avoid being winnowed out at this stage, advertising must enhance or protect our lives.

Stage 3: Attention –This is the consideration stage. Here *emotions serve as motivators*, fueling our response as we contemplate the advertising. As will be discussed in the middle part of the chapter, this is where creating sustainable interest is vital. Advertising that isn't ultimately very likeable or appealing will drop from consideration. That's typically for reasons related to the execution: either the effort required to comprehend the advertising is too taxing or else, more strategically, the advertising fails to square with people's emotionally-based belief systems.

Some of the best "advertising" in the world is conducted through street signs. They consistently create awareness, elicit relevant memories and responses and help us make instantaneous decisions that are acted on.

Stage 4: Decision –This is as far as research can go in validating, prior to launch, whether advertising is likely to drive marketplace response. As will be discussed in the last part of the chapter, companies are looking for purchase intent or other forms of persuasion. In emotional terms, what they want to know, based on *emotions serving as evaluators*, is what's the gain versus harm equation? Emotions are judges of value. In judging the advertising, consumers are also judging whether the branded offer is worth pursuing.

Stage 5: Action –Only the post-launch tracking of sales results is truly relevant here. By this point, *emotions have reached the critical point of serving as enactors*. We take action either to change or regain the status quo. As a means to an end, the advertising will have caused people to resolve, evade or mitigate a situation that the advertising promised the offer could help us handle. Remember from Chapter 1 that only the sensory and emotional parts of the brain attach to muscle activity. The rational brain serves as a lobbyist, which is why functional benefits don't matter much unless they acquire emotional significance (often thanks to the advertising).

Finally, after all is said and done and the consumers' monies are spent, emotions and advertising have one final rendezvous. That happens because *emotions also serve as monitors*. As part of being evaluators, they monitor the degree or quality of the progress we've made as a result of the action we took. Here informal word-of-mouth advertising becomes an important alternative source of information because, as noted by many business people, there's nothing worse than great advertising on behalf of a terrible offer. Spurred to buy only to be disappointed, we then emotionally and financially withdraw—in favor of investing our time and money elsewhere.

Gauging Awareness through Rational Means
Current methods for gauging awareness really only capture recognition level.

Now that we have a sense of how—driven by emotion—people notice, focus and expend their mental energy and money in response to the presence of advertising, let's move on. Next up for review are the practices most commonly used to gauge advertising's effectiveness during the awareness stage. Inevitably, the advertising agency's client fears that all its costs for creative development and media placement will accrue without a discernable rise in sales. To address the very real and valid concern that advertising seemingly evaporates into thin air, agency planners and traditional researchers have arrived at three primary methods to assess awareness:

As part of being evaluators, emotions monitor the degree or quality of the progress we've made as a result of the action we took.

In other words, emotions provide our gut-level responses to decisions we've made and allow us to keep an eye out for offers that don't live up to their promises.

That way, we won't be duped again.

- **Assessing Exposure** —One method of forecasting awareness penetration is for agency planners to proactively gauge the likely exposure level. By trying to choose the right media outlets and time slots as well as the optimal frequency of exposure, they seek to gain the most awareness for the least amount of money. What are the problems here? First, there's the fact that buying placement doesn't guarantee exposure. Next, no one can agree on what number of potential exposures best facilitates breaking through the clutter. Moreover, there are also disputes over what rate of exposure will best slow down the rate at which people may forget the advertising they've seen.

- **Assessing Viewership** —A.C. Nielsen monitors the raw number of people taking in a particular TV program and, advertisers hope, also the program's advertising spots. But future challenges to tracking viewership will be to ascertain exposure to the new, less easily tracked media that is filling today's stimuli funnel. There's also the unresolved issue of whether a TV set on in the house guarantees actual viewership, especially in an age of zipping and zapping, let alone TiVo and the mute button.

- **Assessing Recall** —The goal here is to answer the question: "Does anyone remember your advertisement?" It's an attempt to learn whether consumers noticed and remembered a company's advertising. In practice, the question is typically handled one of two ways. The first is by describing an ad to a group of people to see if they can confirm their awareness or knowledge of the ad (aided recall). The second is by mentioning the brand and asking people to provide any recent examples of advertising for it (spontaneous recall). The possible limitations here consist of: a) the interviewed subject's ability to describe the advertisement, b) the interviewer's judgment that the subject's description is a satisfactory fit, and c) the fact that the subjects' descriptions reflect only limited, conscious, rationalized feedback unrelated to a real-time response.

In short, these three methods may provide adequate means of gauging stage one awareness as they are suitable for quantifying recognition. They give a company some idea of whether its advertising will be or has been noticed. But these more rationally-oriented measures aren't in sync with what breakthroughs brain science have taught us about the importance of emotion in driving response. In addition, they are inadequate for stage two narrowing because they don't get at what feels most important or most relevant to consumers among all the advertising they experience. To address that need, the terms and tools involved in the debate over awareness must shift in ways we're ready to discuss next.

> *It's better to be looked over than overlooked.*
>
> *—Mae West*

From Recognition to Emotional Potency
The goal of measuring stopping power leads inevitably to Emotional Potency.

In acknowledging how the awareness-to-action funnel actually works, companies can't afford to settle for merely generating recognition. And here's why. What is recognition? It's awareness. It's merely having noticed the advertisement. Now, emotions may be turned on enough at this first stage so that they're mobilizers, prompting people to at least recognize and retain the advertising to some degree. But achieving measurable recognition won't prepare a company's advertising to survive the next stage on the way to being truly effective: being emotionally absorbing because it's meaningful.

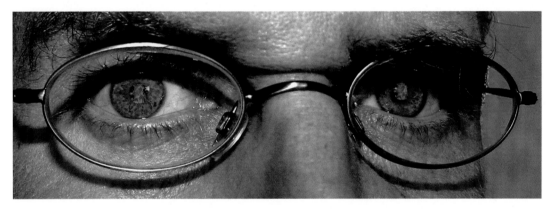

Without intense emotional interest, awareness is simply looking.

That stage is where the funnel starts narrowing and where emotions serve as relevance signalers. As a result, more than awareness must be gauged because, importance is signaled by the depth or extent to which consumers' emotions get invoked.

Therefore, more reflective of what is happening in stage two narrowing—with its requirement to be emotionally absorbing—is terminology that goes beyond the meaning of recognition, recall, et cetera. The term the advertising agencies have always (rightly) favored is an ad's "stopping power," which is a term to describe whether or not an advertisement grabs people's attention by stopping them in their tracks. Stopping power beats surface-level awareness in value because it speaks to changing behavior.

Stopping power beats awareness in value because it speaks to changing behavior.

How to know that the company's advertising has that potential, however, requires a new tool like facial coding, geared as it is to tracking behavioral response (as shown on a person's face). More specifically, given what we discussed in Chapter 2, Sensory Logic proposes that deeper-level awareness (narrowing) can be determined, in large part, by quantifying the extent of an ad's Emotional Potency.

There are two different measures that help to do so:

Emotional Response Rate —As previously stated, this is the percentage of the subjects that responds emotionally to the advertisement. In other words, it's a matter of learning *how many* people get absorbed or caught up by the stimulus to which they've been exposed.

Impact —This measure reflects the strength of the emotional response felt by the subjects who had a response. It's a matter of learning *how intensely* people are affected by the stimulus to which they've been exposed.

Let's illustrate the difference, first in theory and then in practice. Imagine that 40% of the sample population in a given study reveals at least one emotional expression on their faces while watching a 30-second video clip shown on the company's website. That percentage is the Emotional Response Rate: the percentage of subjects whose emotions have been brought into play. Equally important, however, is knowing the strength of the emotional response in that 40% share of the subjects. Lots of true smiles, lots of delight, will result in an Impact score higher than if those smiles are wan, micro-smiles.

That's in theory. Now it's time for a real-world example, but with the real company names changed.

Outdoor advertising is the perfect example of where Emotional Response Rate and Impact matter. Unlike its cousin the print ad, people probably experience a billboard at 70 mph in a car, with the radio on and without a chance to linger. The results shown in Figure 6.2 are for an actual award-winning "Zen Cola" billboard that shows a rival, "Other Cola" delivery man eating lunch in a diner, pouring a Zen Cola into the can of Other Cola that he knows he should be drinking.

The eye tracking results are pretty provocative in their own right. They show people's eyes concentrating first on the action—the two cans and soft drink being poured—then on the Other Cola logo on the delivery man's uniform, then to the Zen Cola logo in the lower right corner, then back to the two cans and the offer again.

In short, the gaze of consumers is going where Zen Cola would want it to go, and perhaps even in the ideal sequence. Alone that knowledge is more a matter of awareness than of emotional potency. In this respect, the outcome is even better. Over two-thirds of the subjects we sampled had an emotional response to the billboard, and among those people the smiling, happy reaction was robust enough to secure a high Impact score. In other words, the execution tested as being highly likely to break through to consumers emotionally so as to set up nicely the next proposition: driving consideration.

Fig. 6.2 A Great Gaze Fixation Pattern and On-Target Emotional Response

Hearken back to our discussion of eye-tracking hot spots in Chapter 2. The above illustration is a depiction of a real billboard Sensory Logic tested. The order in which test subjects viewed the visual elements (represented by the red arrows starting at the face), contributes to the Impact of the ad and creates great branding. Subjects saw the man, the cola switch, and realized—via the logo on his shirt— that he is an employee from the "Other Cola" company who would rather drink "Zen." Then they fixated on the "Zen" brand logo at bottom right before going back to the humorous cola switch, which brought a smile to their faces as a compliment to the surprise they felt on first noticing the logo on the disloyal delivery man's uniform.

The Invisible Line:
why knowing the target market matters

Synopsis: The basis for choosing an advertising agency should be that it helps the client by knowing the target market best. More specifically, its creativity should help bridge the gap between company and audience. When is an execution interruptive or merely offensive? Where should the line be drawn? This section looks at the balancing act between the agency's innate desire for interruptive edginess and the client's need within that edginess for the offer to be liked. The interplay between the measures of Impact and Appeal will be examined, including how belief systems and likeability influence consideration.

Key take-aways:

- Creating a relationship with the target market requires a mix of Impact and Appeal.
- The key to success is to stay focused on the target market and its belief systems.
- Consideration always trumps stopping power in deciding where to draw the line.
- With messaging, believability not comprehension drives consideration.

Balancing Act
Creating a relationship with the target market requires a mix of Impact and Appeal.

To reiterate: traditional means of assessing target market awareness of advertising doesn't tell a company if that audience has experienced any real, in-depth emotional response to it. Moreover, awareness alone certainly doesn't explain *how* it's been received. As such, a company can't bank on awareness. For instance, it's hard to ignore Carrot Top's flaming red hair in a telephone commercial. But taking note of his presence is hardly the same as responding positively to an ad that uses him as a spokesperson.

Therefore, determining how to break through is crucial. The ideal approach will both break through and captivate—in order to facilitate consideration. That's important because in the move from stages one and two to stage three, attention, the focus is now on sustaining consumer interest by establishing a relationship with target market members so that the advertised brand offer eventually gets on their shopping lists. As a result, Appeal, the ability to create liking and preference, ultimately becomes more important to success than generating Impact alone.

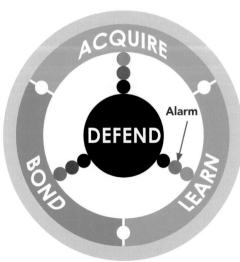

Emotion and Motivations

Alarm is the key emotion, which must be avoided here. Why? Because a target market tensing with worry in response to the approach used in the ad won't be inclined to internalize its content. Since consumers' belief systems are in play here, the challenge of being edgy but not too edgy falls between **learn** and **defend**. Seeking to protect their worldview, consumers will be open to new stimulation only if it doesn't endanger what they've come to accept over time.

In short, advertising involves a careful balancing act. Just as too little Impact means it won't be interruptive enough to attract interest, too little Appeal means it won't be able to sustain that interest.

Someone who profoundly understood the dynamics between Impact and Appeal was Sigmund Freud's fellow psychology pioneer, William Wundt. His research led him to conclude that, when aiming to connect with people, one needs to target a sweet spot that is either the right degree of complexity *or* novelty, but not a combination of both. The reason is clear-cut: people won't look favorably upon a company for making them work too hard to follow along. Instead, they'll just give up. The equivalent of arsenic in the marketplace is advertising that involves a *high* degree of *both* complexity and novelty, leading to lots of impact but also to Appeal that runs into negative territory.

Meanwhile, the other part of achieving maximum Appeal is either to pair simplicity with novelty or to pair complexity with familiarity so people can be enticed but not overwhelmed. Once again, the underlying reason should be clear-cut: simplicity makes something new easier to digest, just as familiarity gives people a handle on a more complex approach. So include either simplicity *or* familiarity, but not both at once because the dull result will be a low level of Impact.

But that's in theory. In practice, getting the balance right is admittedly more difficult—for reasons we'll explore next.

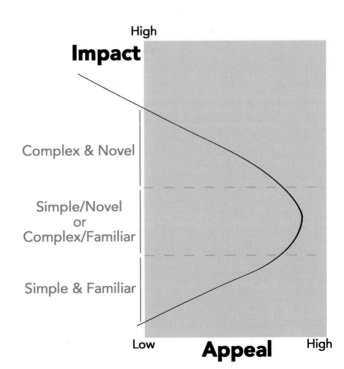

Fig. 6.3 Wundt's Curve: the Sweet Spot

Psychologist William Wundt's research led him to discover that people respond differently to certain combinations of information. Achieving maximum Appeal happens when a simple idea is presented using a novel approach or a complex idea is introduced in a familiar manner.

Belief Systems at Stake
The key to success is to stay focused on the target market and its belief systems.

The business reality of advertising is always inherently messy, with egos, budgets and turf battles all pieces of the puzzle. But the point here is to emphasize balancing Impact and Appeal to induce the optimal level of stage three attention. And that goal leads us to three different, often competing belief systems. Of the trio, only one, the target market's, should really matter in the end. But first, let's look at the other two players in the drama because they typically weigh in long before consumer preferences become a real factor in the outcome.

Who are those two players? The agency and the client, of course, with the former as creative instigator and the latter as paymaster and thus the final judge of what consumers will witness. It's an inevitably uneven relationship, about which Luke Sullivan, a long-time copywriter at Fallon Worldwide, wistfully jokes: "About 20% of your time in the advertising business will be spent thinking up ads; 80% will be spent protecting them; and 30% doing them over. The elevator cables in your client's building will fairly groan hauling up all the people intent on killing your best stuff."

To illustrate how frayed and counterproductive the client/agency relationship can become, consider some recent results from an annual survey that studies the situation. As Figure 6.4 shows, perceptions of teamwork are skewered, with clients seeing it as improving far more than agencies do. Hassles and tension are seemingly forever increasing. Meanwhile, neither side believes that the best possible work is emerging from the process.

The underlying problem is that the two parties come from very different perspectives, complete with different belief systems. As Figure 6.5 seeks to explain with intentional exaggeration, advertising agency personnel and their clients are typically locked in an art versus commerce clash.

What's the solution? It's remarkably simple: focus on the target market's belief system and the emotions related to that belief system. Good orientation requires being on-emotion for the audience in question. Fortunately, the measuring of emotions through facial coding helps facilitate this goal.

How is the business world doing in regard to understanding and reflecting consumers' belief systems? The answer is not very well. Consider these statistics:

☹ 91% of women believe that advertisers don't understand them and 58% are seriously annoyed by portrayals of their gender (Barletta).

☹ 79% of men are alienated, barely able to recognize themselves in the advertisements portraying their gender ("Secrets").

For *Advertising Age* critic Bob Garfield, responsibility for this predicament lies squarely with advertising agencies. He sees creatives as all too often primarily interested in proving their "pointless originality" by winning awards and becoming mini-movie directors. Given this focus, they fail to make emotional connections with target markets and waste clients' money.

66%	Increased Teamwork	30%
20%	More Hassles	22%
17%	More Tension	NA

7.3 average client rating of work from 1-10

24.7% projected increase in sales if agency allowed to do best work

53.9% clients that get the best work

Clients

Agencies

Fig. 6.4 Differences in Client and Agency Perspectives
These are the recent results from the Salz Survey of Advertiser-Agency Relations. The situation is improving compared to a few years ago, but clients and creatives are still out of sync (Elliott).

Agency   vs.   Client

Our mantra is, "Break-through creative drives success in the marketplace." Our fear is that creativity is in the eye of the beholder – and despite our talent, we know that the ultimate arbitrator is whoever signs the check. What we want is a free hand. What we dread and get hurt by is heavy-handed interference in what you pay us to be experts at creating. In the worst case scenarios, the clients are unimaginative and clinically unable to express what they're looking for and don't remember what they said in the last meeting.

Our challenge inside headquarters is to validate that what's being created is money well spent. Our fear is that the agency takes a direction contrary to the CEO's vision. In meetings with the agency, we feel like the suits half understand our dilemma, but creatives can't be bothered. What we want is no mistakes. We get axed for signing off on disasters. In worst case scenarios, the agency seems to be full of undisciplined, unfocused romantics who rarely deliver on what we told them was necessary.

Fig. 6.5 The View from Across the Conference Table—These are the stereotypical perspectives that agencies and their clients can too easily fall back into amid the stress of dealing with each other.

Now, maybe Garfield's satirical portrait of creative directors is on target (though maybe it isn't). No matter what, it's hard to put all the blame on one party when *somebody* at the client's company signed off on the concepts.

Here's a case in point. The following graph (Fig. 6.6) shows responses to a potential TV spot for a company whose offer supports the consumer electronics sector. The storyboard in question involved a jogger using the company's offer when she was suddenly mugged. Apparently, the idea behind the spot was to emphasize the offer's desirability by implying that it was so desirable that a man would resort to mugging a woman who had it in order to obtain it himself. Amazingly enough, test subjects said they liked the storyboard fairly well. So this spot remained in the mix of those being considered. Based on positive verbal responses, it even seemed that producing and running the spot could lead to success.

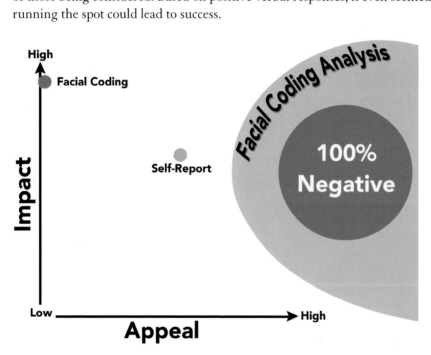

Fig. 6.6 Breaking Through. . . But Broken
These results demonstrate the importance of being on-emotion. Even though the TV spot received favorable verbal feedback, the facial coding showed a whopping 0% positive response. It turns out that although subjects rationally accepted the concept of a woman being mugged to obtain a desirable offer, in their hearts they were strongly against seeing that kind of execution.

The facial coding results, however, told a very different story. For only the third time in Sensory Logic's decade of research, a stimulus recorded *no* positive facial expressions. None. Zero. Zip. Even though the storyboard rated high in Impact, it was strongly negative. Translation: underneath all their rational filtering, the subjects really hated the concept of a woman being mugged.

Wisely, the company didn't take it to full production. But imagine if the company had made its decision based only on verbal, self-reported input. In this case, facial coding was essential. It

> "David Ogilvy is famous for observing, 'The consumer isn't a moron. She is your wife.' Well, David, God rest your soul, that's just not so. The consumer—the average consumer—isn't some ad guy's wife."
>
> —Bob Garfield

provided an objective, scientific tool able to unite the agency and client's mutual interest of staying focused on ensuring emotional compatibility between the company's advertising and the target market's values.

The Way Forward
Consideration always trumps stopping power in deciding where to draw the line.

Despite Garfield's jabs, the reality is that agencies and companies both share the credit and the blame for outcomes that either emotionally connect with consumers or else offend them. Indeed, in many ways the balancing act between Impact and Appeal runs parallel to a careful balancing act between the two parties' respective strengths so that neither creativity nor nurturing the company/customer relationship gets unduly sacrificed. On one hand, the need for stopping power justifies giving the agency's creative artistry something of a free rein. On the other hand, that strength must be balanced against the company's inevitably greater sensitivity to the buying public that enables it to stay in business.

Here then are a few guidelines and related observations to make this emotionally-based balancing act easier to manage.

The first is that in any potential conflict between stage one awareness and stage three attention, opt for the latter. Yes, the stopping power that leads to Emotional Potency is important. A consumer's perspective is always defined by the qualification: "If I don't see it, I sure can't like it." But a company should never sacrifice the long-term value of getting consumers to affiliate with the offer—that is, a chance for sales—in exchange for the short-term gain of generating the kind of stopping power that enshrines the advertising. In other words, the creative shouldn't take precedence over keeping the target market emotionally on-board enough to spur consideration.

Second, establish an "us" versus "them" dichotomy because, otherwise, there's no reason to belong and no membership status with which to entice consumers. A company will often be tempted to cast the net so benignly wide that no one could be offended and imagine *not* being part of the target market. The product manager figures everyone's a potential sale. But don't give in to that thinking because creativity will suffer for it.

Third, for its part the agency will often be tempted to give into gimmicks. But speaking directly to the essence of how the offer emotionally benefits consumers will not only be more appropriate but also more effective.

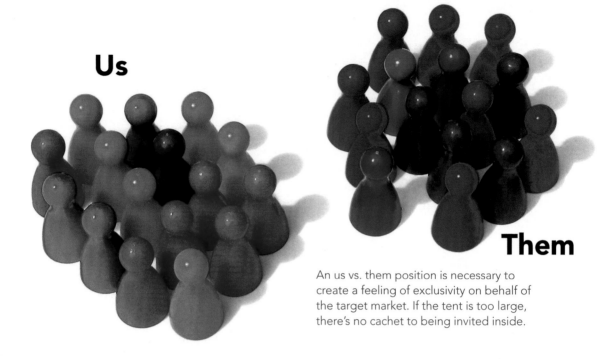

Us

Them

An us vs. them position is necessary to create a feeling of exclusivity on behalf of the target market. If the tent is too large, there's no cachet to being invited inside.

Fourth, in pursuit of stopping power, agencies often commit the stylistic vice of going for too much too quickly. Steve Jobs' motto is that elegant simplicity works. What Warren Beatty said about words, "Take any script and cut it in half," can be applied to advertising imagery and special effects, too. Remember the example of Wundt's Curve, where the combination of complexity and novelty blunts Appeal.

Fifth, as about to be explored in greater depth, negative emotions can be invoked to generate stage one awareness and survive stage two narrowing. But over time, the emotional net outcome must be positive to avoid generating the kind of alarm that will scuttle consideration.

Why Being Heard But Not Felt Isn't Enough
With messaging, believability not comprehension drives consideration.

At the time that this book is being completed, a coalition of the Advertising Research Federation (ARF), The American Association of Advertising Agencies (AAAA) and the Association of National Advertisers (ANA) are involved in an unprecedented collaboration to define and decide how to measure "engagement."

Why has engagement suddenly become the hot new term (Spillman; Manning; Howard 2006)? The business reason starts with the inherent limitations of assessing awareness, as discussed earlier. But it also involves the pressure of how to gauge exposure, response and thus the overall effectiveness of any and all advertising platforms, including new emerging forms and the Internet. Meanwhile, psychologically speaking an ad's ability to engage consumers indicates, in turn, its ability to sustain their interest to such an extent that the awareness-to-action funnel doesn't close.

To that end, a measure is needed that encompasses the traditional benchmarks such as message comprehension, believability and the likeability or acceptance of feature, attribute or benefit claims. As practiced by Sensory Logic, that measure could be Emotional Engagement as a means of gauging effectiveness at the attention stage.

Let's examine why. The coalition's current working definition of engagement is "turning on a prospect to a brand idea enhanced by surrounding context." But as of now, there is no emerging consensus about *how* to measure engagement. To do it properly will require directly addressing the role of emotions in advertising. After all, turning people on to a brand idea is more than just making sure they turn on their TV set. Awareness isn't the key here, because turning them on means that emotions have been turned on.

Generating momentum in favor of a brand idea means that feelings of acceptance become central to the engagement proposition. Conscious, cognitive, verbalized input can only tell if consumers find that brand idea plausible from an intellectual alibi perspective. A tool like facial coding is required to learn whether or not that brand idea will be embraced by consumers, thereby setting up the opportunity for persuasion.

The reality is that whether consumers heard and understood a brand idea isn't nearly as important as whether they find it both believable and likeable, in their hearts. So a second facial coding metric is required. Just as measuring Emotional Potency, based on Emotional Response Rate and Impact, helps to establish the degree to which an ad has stopping power, likewise measuring Emotional Engagement, based on Emotional Response Rate and Appeal, helps to establish the degree to which a branded offer, as advertised, is engaging and a solution worth considering.

For example, consider a test Sensory Logic conducted in which there were four main messages the company hoped to convey through a series of three different print ads. The format or style of the ads was largely identical. Each showcased a person offering a testimonial about a benefit being provided. But as Figure 6.7 shows, the Emotional Engagement results couldn't have been more varied for the trustworthy message considered central to the campaign.

The bottom line? Without faith in the offer, which is an emotional barometer, the persuasion goal about to be addressed loses its viability.

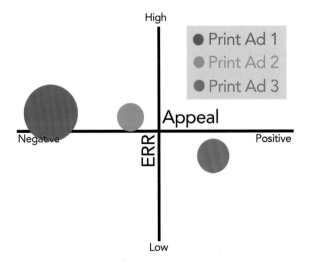

Fig. 6.7 Results for Conveying Trustworthiness

Here we have the Emotional Engagement results for three print ads in a campaign. Given very similar layouts and content, it was the spokespeople who primarily caused the responses to vary. Emotional Engagement is the product of Emotional Response Rate (ERR) and Appeal. The larger the bubble, the more salient the Emotional Engagement—whether positive or negative.

Reassurance:
defusing skepticism

Synopsis: Given the doubt and disinterest sown by today's advertising saturation, defusing skepticism becomes the key to achieving persuasiveness. As this section will explore, Appeal is again crucial. Only with an ad that emotionally nets out with a positive result can progress really be made. That's because the heart must be won over by an ad before time runs out and the rational mind begins to write it off as just another attempt to sell. Finally, this section also looks at two other qualities a persuasive ad exhibits: enough emotional "white space" for the offer's value to register and a corresponding opportunity for the offer to be branded clearly.

> **Key take-aways:**
> - As to emotional net outcome, likeability and persuasion go hand in hand.
> - An over-reliance on rational messaging won't achieve persuasion.
> - Introducing the branded offer should create a positive emotional response.

Plausible Preference
As to emotional net outcome, likeability and persuasion go hand in hand.

It's now time to talk about the third and final goal of advertising: spurring a favorable verdict at stage four decision. As with Emotional Engagement, again the appropriate facial coding metric involves the Emotional Response Rate and Appeal. But this time the metric is Emotional Buy-In because stage four is where persuasion and the goal of achieving a sales lift become the focus.

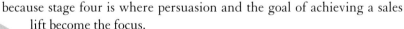

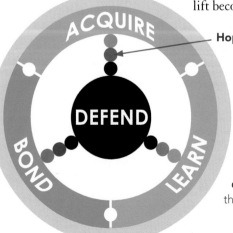

Hope

Emotion and Motivations

Hope is the perfect emotional end-state for advertising to create as consumers contemplate the happiness an offer will bring. The goal is to build positive momentum in the face of doubts that may linger. Two motivations that pull in opposite directions are operating here: an instinct to **defend** or hold onto one's money versus the urge to **acquire** the advertised offer.

> *"Advertising that creates a positive emotional response performs better than that which does not—a fact repeatedly borne out by tracking studies the world over."*
>
> —Nigel Harris, Millward Brown

Since consideration and persuasion are a function of Appeal, it follows that positive appeal (or likeability) is serious business that can ultimately drive sales. Marketers ignore this relationship at their own peril.

Indeed, no less a source than market research giant Millward Brown now believes that likeability is decisive. In *The Advertised Mind,* Erik du Plessis of Millward Brown's South African operations, has pulled together a history of studies validating the argument that "Advertisements that work are advertisements that are liked." The evidence is based on researchers having correlated thousands of interview results with sales data after working in conjunction with the Leo Burnett agency, the Ogilvy Center for Research and Development, and the Advertising Research Federation (ARF), among other sources.

Du Plessis's extensive study of likeability has led him to refine a model that suggests the types of advertising that generally work or don't work, even if the model doesn't involve a tool to access the emotions fueling consumers' responses. Figure 6.8 shows an adapted depiction of this likeability model—including the facially coded emotions appropriate to each of the seven types du Plessis cites.

Fig. 6.8 Adapted Depiction of du Plessis's Model with Emotional Responses

The location of each type of advertising style can be explained as follows:

Positive: 1) Relevant News: delivering new ideas or opportunities is more important than pure information, which quickly grows stale. 2) Empathy: advertising that depicts a lifestyle or dramatization can pull us in. 3) Entertainment: since humor is so culturally dependent, entertainment may be liked without being effective.

Negative: 1) Alienation: opposite of empathy, a depiction that fails to involve us. 2) Confusion: this type of advertising doesn't work because nobody likes to feel stupid while struggling to "get it."

Neutral: 1) Familiarity: works best if there's a little bit of novelty. 2) Brand Reinforcement: placement on chart not shown because it depends on what type of brand equity is being reinforced (positive or negative).

The point of sharing this likeability model isn't to suggest that these seven different types of advertising will work exactly the same way, every time, as depicted here. There will always be exceptions. Nevertheless, by seeing types, emotions and sales effectiveness together, one can get at least a general answer to questions often raised, like: "Which emotions are best to create in your audience?" and "What kinds of ads tend to work best?" Yes, few people set out to create a confusing or alienating ad. But to discover whether a company's ad is truly entertaining or off-putting is why gauging emotional response is important.

Ultimately, however, the goal of advertising is to spur people to action by answering the target market's basic question: "How will my life be better if I purchase this offer?" To do that, advertising can't merely avoid giving offense and hang back, guarding against lack of Appeal. It must also provide reassurance to ward off concerns about credibility.

Every button an ad attempts to push is designed to interrupt a potential customer's day-to-day routine and attract attention. But advertisers should seek to interrupt the imagery already implanted in the target market's collective imagination *judiciously*. Few people enjoy the effort of changing their minds. Dislodging what's already there is inefficient, and often threatens the happiness that hope builds toward. It's not by chance that familiarity is more toward the effectiveness end of the spectrum in the likeability model.

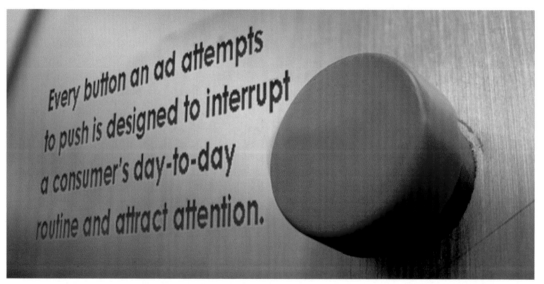

In short, advertising's goal should be to bring the promise of something new—but not *too* new—to the target market's mental doorstep. After all, advertising must work to reinforce, not demolish, its market's comfort zone.

That goal is more easily stated than accomplished, however, because even getting a chance to win somebody over has become a challenge. As Fallon copywriter Luke Sullivan notes, "There is a high wall around every customer. And every day another brick is added." Instead of welcoming advertising or even accepting it, consumers now experience growing intolerance in response to clutter and endless spin, as the statistics in Figure 6.9 make evident.

Therefore, we now see the rise of alternative media and advertising phenomena like Marathon Ventures and BzzAgent. The former puts companies on TV by means of virtual product placements. The latter capitalizes on the fact that family members and friends rate highest as reliable recommenders. As a result, BzzAgent maintains a national network of "volunteers" who create a buzz on behalf of offers they believe in, without a script, in exchange for rewards that include a sample of the offer.

The wicked irony is that, in this very tough climate, companies still need to understand if consumers find their ads persuasive. The ability to attain that goal or an analogous aim like greater purchase intent as a result of exposure to advertising is, however, often difficult to discern. So it's no wonder that an agency and its client may clash regarding the validity and reliability of research measures.

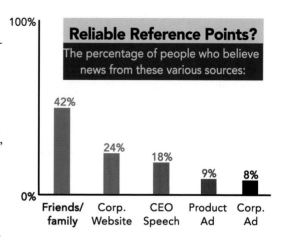

Reliable Reference Points?
The percentage of people who believe news from these various sources:

Fig. 6.9 Growing Intolerance of Spin

As is evident from the statistics, companies like BzzAgent are on the right track when it comes to spreading the word. The conventional wisdom that word of mouth advertising is the most successful has merit. Lowest on the totem pole? Ads put out by corporations themselves—proof that reassurance matters (O'Brien).

Sensory Logic knows this contested territory only too well. Again and again, we've seen highly positive verbal response scores when a question about purchase intent or persuasion is asked. People at Proctor and Gamble have told us that they've even mapped it as an artifact based on how close to the equator the sample country is, with certain places like Morocco, for example, consistently providing scores that prove to be vastly inflated compared to actual marketplace penetration once the offer gets introduced.

Sensory Logic hasn't tested in every corner of the globe yet, but a case that readily comes to mind is a test in which we asked subjects whether, after seeing a particular print ad campaign, they were now more inclined to consider the offer than they had been before seeing the ads. The result was an astounding 98% "yes," which if valid would have made it the greatest campaign in the history of advertising.

Clearly, companies should be cautious here. Asking people who are being paid to participate in a study if an ad enhances their purchase intent—and trusting what they say—is just begging them to embellish reality. It's akin to one's best friend asking, "Isn't my new haircut great?" or a neighbor declaring, "Isn't my baby adorable!"

We've found that the normative average for positive verbal responses regarding persuasion-type questions hovers around 65% depending on the project. The rigorous method of facial coding puts that same number 10% to 30% lower. No wonder Jon Steel, formerly of Goodby, Silverstein and Partners, has written, "If my life depended on picking which is more likely to be true, 1) what people say with their eyes, posture and attention, or 2) what they say with their words, I would choose one every time."

"Magic" Versus the Risk of Message-itis
An over-reliance on rational messaging won't achieve persuasion.

The stage four decision phase is the launching stage to action. That is to say, it's the point in the awareness-to-action funnel where emotions serve as evaluators and consumers use their gut-level instincts in making their purchase decisions. The bottom line here is profoundly emotional in nature: does the advertised offer's value equation feel right to them?

In other words, this is as far as advertising can go in terms of making the sale possible. From here on out, it's a matter of the media buy, the company's brand equity, the offer, its pricing, its distribution channel and, of course, larger marketplace factors like rival offers and how the economy is faring. Short of tracking sales vis-à-vis the timing of an ad campaign launch, it's also as far as market research can go in gauging effectiveness.

But given the pressure for advertising to boost sales, it's incumbent on agencies and their clients not to become so concerned about stage five action that in the process they undermine what the previous stage is really about. In short, they need to leave enough breathing room within the advertising execution for subconscious, sensory-oriented processing to work its magic—joining imagery together—while allowing emotions to play their role as evaluators.

What's the opposite of creating space for emotional "magic" to happen? Encumbering ads with rational messages in an attempt to close the sale. To persuade consumers, companies often load up their advertising with extra messages. But that's a rational approach to what should be an emotional call-to-action. To include this reason and that one, this feature, attribute, benefit, et cetera, and then some more, is asking consumers to work really hard—which is counterproductive to engaging their hearts.

So fast, cheetahs look like meercats!!!

SMALLER THAN AN AMOEBA, MORE POWERFUL THAN A SUPERNOVA!!!

German chocolate never tasted so Dutch!!!

The hottest thing since sliced bread!!!

Instant guacamole!!!

Makes butter look like margarine!!!

Weighs less than an anorexic dragonfly!!!

MESSAGING GONE WILD

In the attempt to drive sales, companies plug myriad features to persuade buyers.

But that's a rational solution to an emotional problem.

If none of the features engages the heart, the only thing consumers get is a headache.

It's difficult to set up more than one or two emotionally-oriented value propositions in the short space of an advertisement. Instead, giving consumers a single, striking reason to care will prove far more decisive than a wave of reasons people will be left struggling to comprehend.

In effect, the problem of *message-itis* is akin to the feature-itis discussed in Chapter 5. Both offer design and advertising can become so complicated that nobody wins: neither the company, the agency, the designer, the engineer, the marketer—nor the consumer.

Over-doing the execution robs an advertisement of the opportunity to make a strong, clean emotional connection with the target market. And yet this error happens all the time because companies are too self-focused. To understand more clearly why the error occurs and then what companies can do to guard against it, let's examine three specific reasons why companies have a message-itis tendency:

- **The Offer's Origins** —The ability to compete for earnings surely originated in bringing to market an offer, probably a product, that was functionally unique and superior.

- **The Company's Goals** —Faith that the offer will sell itself, on its own rational terms, is a factory-driven perspective that follows easily and naturally from a corresponding faith at the company headquarters that the offer is truly differentiated and relevant.

- **A Numbers Mindset** —A message bias is likely to be aided by a company mindset that focuses on production quotas and downplays or even disregards the emotional angle.

Two steps can be taken to help protect companies against message-itis, which is really nothing less than an undue focus on what is being said about the offer. The first is that, fortunately, the compensating strength of advertising agencies consists of *how* something is said. Part of their task is to remind the client that adding a consumer-focused element gives the offer an extra, emotional dimension that can truly lift sales. Given financial pressures, however, most companies are still likely to insist on trying to translate the agency's creative "magic" into numbers of some sort, which is where the second step comes in.

Rationally-oriented, verbal research invites subjects to, in effect, echo the messages in the ad copy. But what a company should really want to know is if any of those messages break through, matter to consumers and lead to acceptance. Therefore, the second step should involve gauging the degree of Emotional Buy-in. For companies interested in purchase intent, while also bearing in mind that actions really do speak louder than words, facial coding provides an alternative set of metrics based on the persuasiveness response evident on people's faces.

In a test Sensory Logic did for a financial services company, subjects viewed an ad, absorbed its official message, then gave the ad in question a healthy verbal response echo of almost 80% positive. But they also took in an unofficial message—a feeling of being manipulated because a child actor was being used to sell a very adult offer. The facial coding outcome was a much weaker positive percentage, with emotional buy-in only half as robust as verbal approval (Fig. 6.10).

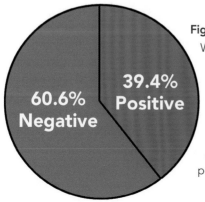

Fig. 6.10 Facial Coding Results for Home Mortgage Spot
Would anybody take advice from a horse on how to drive a car? Of course not. As it turned out in a test we did, people didn't really feel comfortable taking advice on home mortgages from a young child. Though their verbal responses were 80% positive (after all, who can say cruel things about a cute little girl), they felt differently. Their negative emotional response of almost 61% informed us that while the spot was on-message, the use of the little girl was off-emotion because people felt manipulated and therefore lost trust.

Brand Linkage Matters
*Introducing the branded offer should create
a positive emotional response.*

Finally, to discuss persuasion fully requires taking into account the element of timing. The difference between feature-itis and message-itis is that with the latter the key isn't the offer but, rather, the *inherent* offer, namely what the offer will do for the consumers who buy. As a result, there's a future focus to advertising that puts extra pressure on it. Direct TV aside, most advertising is meant to spur purchases that might be days, even weeks away. Therefore, it's necessary for an ad to be easy to remember until the moment when the pertinent purchase decision eventually arrives.

Two factors are important here:

- First, the goal of being memorable is emotional in nature because our memory device, the hippocampus, resides in the emotional part of the brain. Only an ad whose content sparks a memory through an emotional hot-button connection or associatively relates to a memory already embedded in our brain will be retained.

- Second, an ad should aim not only to evoke an emotional response but also help consumers link the offer to the sponsor. For that to happen, at least some portion of the emotional response should happen in proximity to when the branded offer comes into view, especially in the case of TV commercials that take time to unfold.

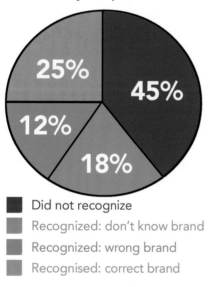

Did not recognize

Recognized: don't know brand

Recognized: wrong brand

Recognised: correct brand

Fig. 6.11 Brand Linkage Testing Results
When 200 viewers were asked if they had seen a commercial, they gave answers that could be grouped in four categories. It turns out that brand recall only happened 25% of the time (du Plessis).

After all, achieving engagement and likeability won't matter much unless consumers know whose advertisement they've found emotionally noteworthy.

Even research conducted using traditional means highlights the importance of creating brand linkage in order to enhance the odds of sales effectiveness. An independent research study involved 200 subjects seeing, among them, a sample of 800 commercials. Afterwards, the subjects were read descriptions of various ads one at a time and asked if they had seen each ad. If they stated that they had seen it, the subjects were then asked to name the brand. Here's what this study found: only one fourth of the commercials benefited from a commercial/brand connection that could help to drive sales (Fig. 6.11).

In other words, the old saying—"Half my advertising dollar is wasted, but I don't know which half"—runs the risk of being twice as optimistic as it should be.

What's the solution to avoiding the misuse of advertising dollars? It's to look at when and where in an ad consumers get emotionally involved. Then achieve brand linkage by getting the branded offer adjacent to some of those moments and execution elements. Sensory Logic calls such instances pivot points. They're the places where there is either the greatest concentration of gaze activity (according to the eye-tracking results), an unusually large volume of emotional responses, or a sharp and often prolonged shift in the Impact and/or Appeal score. There could even be all three results at once.

When those kinds of reactions happen in close proximity to when the branded offer appears, the potential sales outcome is golden. All that's needed now is for the final, net emotional response to be positive thanks to the offer's solution being a credible promise. If so, then the potential buyer has turned on, tuned in and been won over—with the offer and sponsor closely enough linked in memory for the purchase decision to be more likely triggered in the company's favor the next time it comes around.

To that end, consider the second-by-second emotional results of some Australian TV commercials (Fig. 6.12). They provide a revealing look at good versus worrisome results, relevant to the volume of emotional response. Specifically, what should be focused on are the final seconds of

Based on the low brand linkage scores that independent research has seen, the old saying, "Half my advertising dollar is wasted, but I don't know which half," runs the risk of being twice as optimistic as it should be.

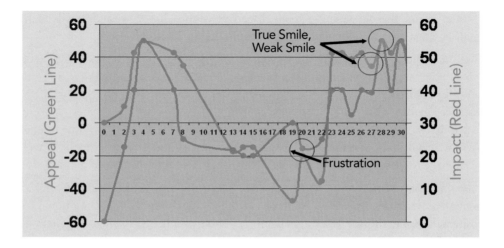

Fig. 6.12 Emotions and Brand Linkage in Contrasting Spots

The top chart shows how being on-emotion and having brand proximity to emotionally engaging pivot points correlate to positive associations for the branded offer. Meanwhile, the bottom chart shows how an off-emotion TV commercial fails to do this. In a study Sensory Logic performed for some Australian spots, we found vast differences in the emotional effectiveness of the placement of the branded message. In the chart above notice how positive pivot points present an optimal placement opportunity for a brand tagline to appear in the final seconds of the spot. True and Weak Smiles abound and provide a positive context for the branding. Conversely, the chart below has an abundance of negative pivot points, and, while the spot ends with some Weak Smiles, the Impact they provide is not enough to overcome the negativity and Anxiety felt throughout the spot.

To achieve positive branding associations, the ideal approach is to correlate the branded offer, logo and tagline with emotionally positive pivot points.

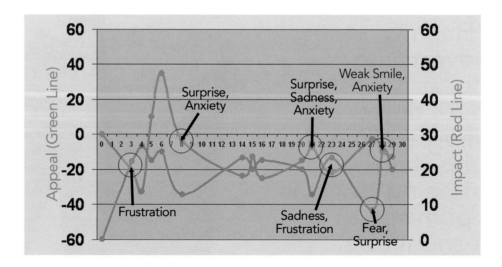

each graph, which detail the Impact, Appeal and emotions present during the appearance of the brand and brand tagline in the commercials.

The top chart shows the results from an emotionally on-message commercial that managed to pull at the heart-strings of subjects. As you can clearly see, the final seconds show an explosion of both Appeal and Impact and the emotions present at the pivot points that were revealed are comprised of True Smiles and Weak Smiles. All in all, as the branding message was delivered, emotions ran high and happy—a perfect combination for brand success.

Conversely, the bottom chart shows the results of a TV spot from the same campaign which, while emotionally stimulating, just didn't have the positive oomph needed to create positive brand associations. Of the six pivot points that occurred, only one has a positive emotional response. And while it occurred during the final seconds of the commercial and, therefore, in synch with the tagline, the Weak Smiles that were elicited were not enough to create positive Appeal.

In order to achieve positive branding associations, correlate the offer or tagline with positive pivot points and end with positive emotions.

Finally, in regard to the shift in Impact and/or Appeal score rule, consider the best brand linkage Sensory Logic has ever seen. We tested TV commercials for a major U.S. automobile insurance provider. One of the spots featured a comical situation in which a husband and wife crash into each other's cars in their home driveway, are mistreated by their current insurance provider, then turn to the advertised company for a better deal and better service.

The whole spot performed very well, with Appeal appropriately dipping during the introduction of the problem and rising during the solution phase. The spot was on-emotion. But what stood out as a major pivot point was the ending. There, likeability skyrocketed just as the branded solution came onto the screen. Now that's a good sign that this brand will be remembered well and fondly enough to drive sales results.

Conclusion

When everything is said and done, what does "persuasion" mean? As science has shown us, it's really about what resonates emotionally and can motivate behavior. To bypass the emotional dimension is to accept the rationally-defensible, good reason as gospel. The informed approach is to remember that priority will be given to ads that feel like they deserve our attention, acceptance and dollars. Consumers will want the rationally-oriented intellectual alibi, but only as a means of justifying what they've already accepted emotionally.

Everybody is interested in the "how-can-my-life-be-better?" story. Rekindling hope is what advertising is really about. To be effective, advertising must:

- Take the biological instead of the logical route. Be memorable by hitting an emotional "hot button" in order to make a connection that reverberates. We remember what we internalize, and what we internalize is part of us—and what is part of us is an opportunity a company can sell us on again and again. Companies that are on-emotion don't need to buy as many repetitive placements to gain the audience's attention, thus saving money.

- Move past a statistical, demographic profile of the target market in order to gauge the audience's emotional profile. Then a company will know where to draw the necessary line between stopping power and offense, effective creativity and risky business. When using humor or sex, for example, be wary that the target market may become distracted or offended by the device meant to ensure stopping power. After all, in business, what's better than a joke? A sale.

- Answer the question, "How can we make our offer—and its story—as emotionally large and pertinent as possible in order to reach the widest target market in today's niche-markets?" The message-itis of rational benefits disengages consumers emotionally and exacerbates the problem of stretching both the creative and media dollars across many rationally-derived segments.

An Action Plan

To make sure that the company's advertising is emotionally healthy, here are a few points to check when assessing effectiveness:

- ☐ Interest is emotional in nature, so play the emotion card to invite consumers in. To learn if the company is in the game, discover whether consumers look forward to as well as internalize its advertising. Because the essence of great advertising is that it disarms the intellect and goes straight to the heart, quantify the advertising's Emotional Response Rate while also verifying whether it is evoking the desired emotions.

- ☐ Learn if the company's advertising survives the key emotional filters—originality, relevancy, likeability and credibility—and has engaged the motivations that drive its target market's emotions.

- ☐ Sample current customers to see if an advertisement for an offer they've already purchased reinforces its value and provides reassurance, thus reducing the risk of buyer's regret (sadness).

- ☐ Bear in mind Maslow's hierarchy of needs and examine, honestly, just how well the company's advertising addresses basic needs first, and then the progressively more complex emotional needs. We all pay attention to what is most necessary, then useful and only then nice to have.

- ☐ Gauge the emotional response to the key visual images in the company's ads. Since most consumers don't want to be sold to, and advertising is selling, the visual is the crucial element in getting past consumers' emotional filters and drawing them in. Secure proof that the visuals evoke the desired emotions, and then the company is at least half way home to a successful campaign.

- ☐ Reconsider how the company uses focus groups. Question the goal of understanding what consumers think. Very few really great creative advertisements will survive a focus-group study intact if the approach is, "Look at this and tell me what you think." The company has just asked the subjects to be rational. So they will try to "look smart" or "be safe" and the company will miss the emotional aspect entirely. Instead, make the goal to understand how subjects will feel.

7 sales

How do prospects feel about being approached? This sign about sums it up. Nobody likes to feel vulnerable.

An emotionally savvy sales partner will make them feel like they're making a safe, beneficial choice instead.

OVERVIEW

Nothing in business relies more on face time and emotions than sales. Promoting likeability and trust is everything. How could it be otherwise when the selling process is really a *buying* process, thus placing a premium on establishing an emotional connection with a potential customer. To help salespeople do a better job creating the kind of rapport that will lead to greater success with prospects, this chapter will focus on:

- **Commitment:** Like people, companies give as well as give off information about themselves. From the job interview through the introductory orientation and training, companies sometimes explicitly—but always implicitly—let their sales force know how they expect prospects to be treated. By adopting relationship commitment as a model, companies can ensure that their salespeople will ultimately be more effective. It is a relationship, after all. The average first sale takes seven calls to close, with 80% of purchases coming after the fifth call (Davis; Coe). So let the sales force know how to treat prospects sensitively and build trust, which is emotional in nature.

- **Unity:** Prospects are on the lookout for signs alerting them to the fact that the salesperson can't be trusted. Every other factor will pale in comparison to this gut-level judgment, which is primarily made on a non-rational basis. The salesperson's conduct must, therefore, involve no miscues. Everything should be consistent from start to finish during the process, with the seller's image and conduct aligning with the branded offer so that the whole package exudes steadfast integrity.

- **Interwoven Rewards:** When sales directors take into account the need for after-sale customer support and healthy sales force team dynamics in their coaching and compensation methods, the opportunity for repeat sales is enhanced as the team will feel like they're in it together and will thus aid the cause. To that end, it's essential that salespeople be incentivized on a broader basis, beyond sales volume alone, including factors like the satisfaction they create among customers and colleagues.

Now let's look more closely at how to honor the buying process, starting with how companies can develop sales forces with the right emotional aptitude.

Commitment:
adopting a relationship model

Synopsis: Enacting a buyer/seller relationship model starts with hiring and cultivating a sales force with the emotional aptitude to build customer relationships rather than "strip mine" for sales. To help accomplish that goal, this section first discusses the opportunity inherent in building a sales force adept at relating to prospects emotionally. Then it highlights the three qualities found in superior salespeople so companies can reduce the costs, financial and otherwise, of salespeople who don't have what it takes to succeed.

Key take-aways:
- Loyalty is based on attending to the emotional aspects of the relationship.
- Great salespeople are characteristically upbeat, resilient and caring.

Why a Relationship Approach Is Superior
Loyalty is based on attending to the emotional aspects of the relationship.

The idea that salespeople should re-orient their thinking and approach prospects using a relationship-based model isn't new. There's been talk about the problems of using a rational, functionally-oriented, features-attributes-and-benefits sales approach for some time now. But the extent to which an emotionally informed, relationship approach to sales has been adopted remains an open question. Without a more comprehensive understanding of why to change and how to proceed, companies will be tempted to stay with what they know, regardless of the disadvantages involved.

Emotion and Motivations

Sales people will be quietly consumed by **guilt** if they know the company's unofficial policy in treating prospects is exploitative in nature. Meanwhile, in motivational terms, they will find themselves pushed toward **acquire** by the company's goal of short-sighted and short-term sales profits, while left to **learn** on their own about possible conflicts between their beliefs and the company's.

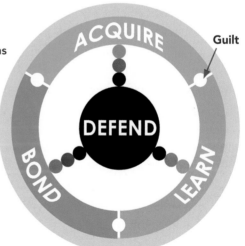

Thus the goal of this chapter is to give directors, managers and their salespeople the perspective and tools that will enable them to implement a true relationship approach.

For that to happen, companies must change how they build their sales forces. What does this change look like? It involves procuring and further developing salespeople who are emotionally savvy. To move beyond a transactional approach, salespeople must understand the emotions relevant to buying.

Commitment.

A beneficial sales relationship is based on it.

Think SAFETY!

For prospects, the sales process centers on one thing: SAFETY. The safety of resources well spent. The safety of affirmation. The safety that they won't be taken advantage of. It is therefore the emotionally savvy salesperson's job to make sure that this overarching need is addressed.

In short, they must be alert to how sensory cues, emotions, motivations, and rationalized intellectual alibis all fit together for the buyer. Moreover, emotionally savvy salespeople are able to align themselves more fully with their prospects due to understanding both verbal and intuitive, non-verbal communication.

Why is that dual understanding so crucial? To answer that question fully, consider the essence of the buying process. From the prospect's point of view, the buying process begins and ends with a feeling that is pure gut reaction: *safety*. Everybody wants to feel secure, especially when being sold to by a relative stranger. We deal with people we like and we like to be in comfortable situations. So more often than not, prospects instinctively pigeonhole a salesperson as either ally or predator and here's why. What's the psychological legacy of having ancestors who spent thousands of years on the savannah trying to avoid an early demise? Prospects sense that if the salesperson is a predator, intent on winning, they must be the prey about to lose.

As a result, the reality of sales is that every prospect is afraid of being ripped off and every salesperson is afraid the prospect won't commit. Developing a reciprocal, non-exploitative relationship will help put to rest prospect fears that inhibit good communication and commitment.

Real change based on better emotional skills can bring success. A recent article in *Bank Investment Consultant* profiles an innovative firm specializing in emotional training for financial sector salespeople. The multi-week program devotes the first 40% of its time to teaching participants how to utilize emotional intelligence (Stock). The pay off? Numbers like these:

- In just two years, a bank's sales force enjoyed a rise in commissions from $16 million to $98 million, with only a relatively small increase in personnel (100 to 125 people) over that same time period.

- At another bank, the emotional intelligence training of new hires alone was enough to boost sales to a figure six times the original forecast—and did so within a single year.

These outcomes reflect the fundamental opportunity available to companies that broaden their sales emphasis from a purely rational or logistical approach to one that will also reflect the impact of emotions. That's because, in essence, there are two flawed assumptions that companies often otherwise make regarding sales that harm their potential for growth.

The first is an assumption that buyers respond calmly and logically when asked to part with their money in exchange for what the sales force is selling. A traditional, functional approach assumes that good techniques during a sales presentation will close the deal or that the disclosure and manipulation of facts will bring success.

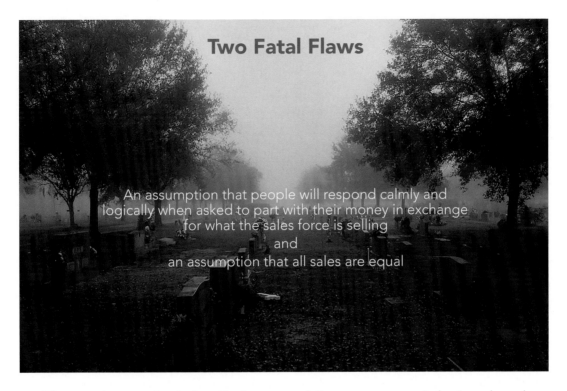

Two Fatal Flaws

An assumption that people will respond calmly and logically when asked to part with their money in exchange for what the sales force is selling

and

an assumption that all sales are equal

The second assumption is that all sales are equal. Long-term success in business depends on long-term sales. In other words, repeat sales hinge on fostering a sense of loyalty and partnership. In contrast, sales that are created by tactics such as pressure are short term in nature and destroy the business relationship model that underlies long-term success.

Moreover, a short-term approach doesn't just hurt a company's relationship with prospects. It also hurts the morale of the sales force. Salespeople who know that it isn't their true goal to look out for prospects' best interests will be susceptible to guilt—thereby undermining their ability to stay emotionally sensitive in their jobs long term.

The solution is to establish a sales strategy based on the twin pillars of identifying and understanding the prospect's emotions as a means of building relationships. Why is the relationship model superior? The answer is that it gives prospects what they want, which is security and comfort. The best feeling for a buyer to have after a purchase is being at ease, without doubt or fear or anger. A truly successful sale results in the buyer being ready and eager to accept whatever change the opportunity provides. There's no sense of failure. Nobody got sold anything. Instead, buyers feel good about themselves and the offer. Why? Because they feel good about *who* they bought from.

Unfortunately, most companies approach the sales process from a seller's perspective. The solution is focusing on the buying process, not the selling process. To understand selling from a buyer's perspective, it is important to understand what the prospect's criteria are and the specific emotions involved as the process unfolds. Yes, every situation will vary to some extent. But in general, there are five steps in the process (Chitwood) as outlined in Figure 7.1.

Step	Buyer Decision Factors	Emotional Goal
Approach	Salesperson (company-offer-price-timing)	Comfort
Dialogue	Salesperson/Company (offer)	Respect
Presentation	Salesperson/Offer (company)	Assurance
Negotiation	Salesperson/Price/Timing (company-offer)	Fairness
Follow-up	Salesperson (company-offer-timing)	Security

Fig. 7.1 The Steps and Emotional Goals Key to the Buying Process
The typical buying process has five steps and also five factors that are not equal in importance. (Secondary factors, per step, are listed in paretheses.) What predominates? The salesperson whose personality and ability to create an emotional connection with the prospect shapes the opportunity for success. All of the other factors get viewed by prospects through the lens of their gut-level impression of the salesperson.

What's noteworthy here? First, in stark contrast to a rationally-oriented seller's approach, which emphasizes the offer, an emotionally-oriented buying approach recognizes the prospect's emotions as central to the process. It's the emotional strength of the relationship between the salesperson and prospect that drives sales. Indeed, the offer doesn't even become a prominent factor until midway through the buying process. Second, it's important to note that the emotional goals cited in Figure 7.1 are all intended to alleviate fear. Prospects want the seller to provide not only the offer but, even more so, assurance that protects and nurtures their self-esteem.

Now that we have the buying process model in place, it's time to discuss what it takes to build an emotionally savvy sales force capable of honoring that model. Let's move on to the topic of hiring right.

Building a Good Team
Great salespeople are characteristically upbeat, resilient and caring.

Adopting a relationship model based on the buying process requires focusing squarely on the prospect and the prospect's emotions. Not everyone can do that well. After all, turning the prospect's fear of vulnerability into relief isn't an easy task. Granted, a company may in theory decide to fulfill the model. But the more important question is whether the personnel hired to implement that model are up to the task.

In *Your Marketing Sucks*, Mark Stevens asserts that 95% of salespeople don't really have what it takes to be a salesperson. In fact, several national tests have shown that 50% of salespeople failed

To create a great sales team, a company has to pick the best apples in the bushel. Making sure that the people who get hired are emotionally savvy is crucial. Facial coding can help ensure that a company doesn't pick a bad apple, thereby limiting its future profitablilty.

simply because they didn't have the right attitude (Gitomer 2003; Anderson). With annual turn-over rate in some sales forces approaching 70% and the average turn-over rate estimated at 18% (Heide), it's hard to disagree: something is, indeed, wrong.

Part of the solution is to hire sales-people who are better at emotions, and for three reasons:

- The first is that hiring emotionally savvy salespeople makes sense because they will experience more success, stay longer, and therefore, reduce the churn that damages the company/customer relationship. Not only do familiarity and rapport help short term; in the long term, continuity makes the opportunity for sales more attractive as the salespeople become increasingly credible as the brand's ambassadors.

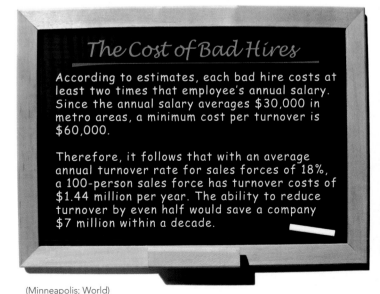

The Cost of Bad Hires

According to estimates, each bad hire costs at least two times that employee's annual salary. Since the annual salary averages $30,000 in metro areas, a minimum cost per turnover is $60,000.

Therefore, it follows that with an average annual turnover rate for sales forces of 18%, a 100-person sales force has turnover costs of $1.44 million per year. The ability to reduce turnover by even half would save a company $7 million within a decade.

(Minneapolis; World)

- Second, high turn-over rates have an emotional cost even on the better salespeople who remain. That's because lots of churn damages morale and internal cohesion.

- Third, high turn-over rates have a financial cost. Companies must invest time hiring and training new salespeople, depleting existing personnel resources to do so. (See "The Cost of Bad Hires" for details.)

Now that we know the stakes, the question becomes: how can everyone do better? In other words, how can companies build a sales force that is emotional savvy?

The first step is to acknowledge that emotions matter. Tom Reilly is on target in *Value Added Selling* when he notes that "Selling is an emotional profession—and emotions play a major role in how salespeople do their jobs." Relevant emotions for salespeople include *pride* in their company and what they sell, *fear* of cold-calling and rejection, and *disappointment* or *joy*, depending on how their sales opportunities turn out.

> "Should one tell you that a mountain has changed its place, you are at liberty to doubt it; but if anyone tells you that a man has changed his character, do not believe it."
>
> —Muhammad

While the first step is a matter of perspective, the key second step is acting on the awareness that emotions matter. Deciphering how well sales force job candidates manage their own emotions and how they will understand those of their prospects helps a lot in predicting the likelihood of their success.

Implementation rests on knowing that selling is largely about character and interpersonal skills—factors ruled by emotion. As a result, companies need to incorporate emotion more into their sales force hiring decisions. Let's look at three emotionally-based qualities that will have a huge impact on whether a salesperson has what it takes to succeed:

- **Upbeat:** A good salesperson is always "up," because someone who exudes the right kind of confidence and success is likely to make a prospect feel "up," too. Enthusiastic salespeople embody hope, which is contagious and will help prospects intuitively relax because a hard-sell approach is less likely to come from a person exhibiting buoyancy.

- **Resilient:** Being in sales and handling rejection go hand in hand. Anybody who can't be persistent and resilient when it comes to coping with adversity won't last long.

- **Caring:** Here the key is having the kind of empathy that builds rapport. Adroit salespeople make prospects feel as though they have an ally. There's no substitute for being likeable, caring and trustworthy.

Find people with those three qualities, and the odds of success significantly improve. In support of that claim, look at the results in Figure 7.2. It shows the differences Sensory Logic found in facial response during salesperson interviews for a staffing company. The company's management told us, after our work was done, whether each salesperson we facially coded was either an average or above-average performer. The goal of the study? To verify that our formula of looking

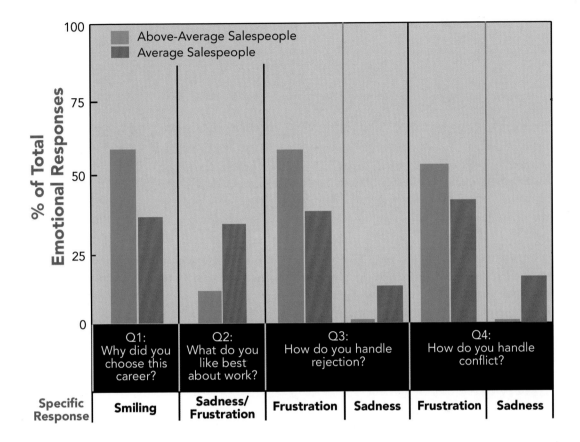

Fig. 7.2 Upbeat, Resilient and Caring: the Three Qualities of a Great Salesperson

This chart shows the results of facial coding salespeople for a staffing company. So what do the specific emotional responses tell us?

- **Upbeat** - Questions 1 and 2 capture optimism in opposite ways. For Question 1, a high level of smiling is present in the above-average performers. For Question 2, these two negative emotions are more than twice as high for the average salespeople, demonstrating their ambivalence toward the job.

- **Resilient** - Question 3 results reveal that above-average salespeople desire progress (hence high frustration) and aren't despairing (low sadness) because rejection doesn't faze them.

- **Caring** - Question 4 results map out similarly to Question 3 because above-average salespeople work through conflict (slightly higher frustration) rather than letting it get them down (low sadness). Here, understanding that disagreement shouldn't lead to a feeling of hopelessness is the key.

190

for certain emotions in response to hiring questions was valid and could be used as a template in evaluating future job candidates.

The verdict:
facial coding does spot winners.

Even without the advantage of facial coding, it's beneficial to account for emotional temperament in hiring. The U.S. Air Force had been dismissing 25% of its recruiters every year because of their failure to meet enlistee quotas (Schwartz). Then the Air Force added a hiring test that screens for five emotionally-related factors: assertiveness, empathy, happiness, self-awareness and problem-solving. Within a year the failure rate for not hiring right had dropped to 2%, saving the Air Force over $2 million in training costs annually while also enabling it to more effectively meet recruitment goals.

Ultimately, making the right hire and encouraging emotionally-sensitive salespeople to use their emotional intelligence with prospects will ensure that a company's sales force is comprised of capable people who enjoy what they do. That path will result in two significant outcomes: 1) feelings of pride in salespeople, and 2) feelings of confidence, comfort and reassurance in those who buy what the salespeople are offering.

Unity:
staying in step with the prospect

Synopsis: Salespeople should always interact with prospects in a manner that builds equity. Then if concerns arise, there's enough trust and rapport to keep the buyer/seller relationship viable, even in difficult cases. This section looks at how to handle that relationship well, from the approach through the negotiation step in the buying process. Highlights along the way include the Great Chain of Buying (how to gauge the prospect's interest) and the Bridge of Consideration (the factors that enable persuasion).

> ### Key take-aways:
> - Ability and willingness to pay are, most often, emotionally based.
> - The key to a successful presentation isn't the offer; it's the relationship building that's involved.
> - The deep-seated explanations for prospect resistance are always emotional in nature.

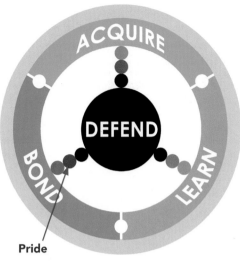

Emotion and Motivations

Pride is only possible when prospects don't feel like they were "sold" or pushed against their will into a purchase that is unsatisfactory. The fear of being pressured causes prospects to put up protective barriers, which explains why **defend** is the key motivation here. At the same time, however, prospects also seek to **bond** with salespeople they hope are on their side.

Approach and Dialogue in the Buying Process
Ability and willingness to pay are, most often, emotionally based.

Because the salesperson is the prospect's focal point during all five steps of the buying process, hiring and training someone capable of honoring the relationship model is vital. But now it's time to discuss enacting that model. Of course securing sales is still far from a certainty. After all, what's new is scary. Change is scary. Prospects ask themselves: "Why should I change? Why should I meet with somebody new like you, the salesperson?"

As a result, prospects may mask their emotionally-based fears by reverting to factors like offer, price or timing that can serve as intellectual alibis in helping prospects justify to themselves a decision on whether to take the meeting. So in the approach and dialogue steps in the buying process, salespeople must be adept enough just to gain a toehold.

In doing so, they won't want to come across as a beggar though. To do so would emotionally undermine their ability to establish value because they will be seen as *wanting* instead of *providing*. Thus the successful salesperson will be relaxed, confident, upbeat—and discerning. More specifically, they will also want to guard their own time and energy by making both a rational and an emotional assessment in initiating the buying

In the Approach and Dialogue steps, be careful not to plead for the sale.
As soon as that happens, a salesperson goes from *provider* to *beggar*.

process. The overall goal must be to discern the prospect's ability and willingness to pay. Just as the prospects want to know about the company that stands behind the salesperson, so must the salesperson know what resources the prospect has available to draw on.

Ability to pay is more straightforward, at least to some degree a rational matter of budgetary resources and authority to spend them. But willingness to pay is at once both very emotional as well as often quite oblique. Of aid to the salesperson trying to make this assessment is to cast the five steps of the buying process in terms of the Great Chain of Buying and its two cycles: the Cycle of Satisfaction versus the Cycle of Opportunity. (See Figure 7.4.)

Fig. 7.4 The Great Chain of Buying: Stages and Pertinent Emotions

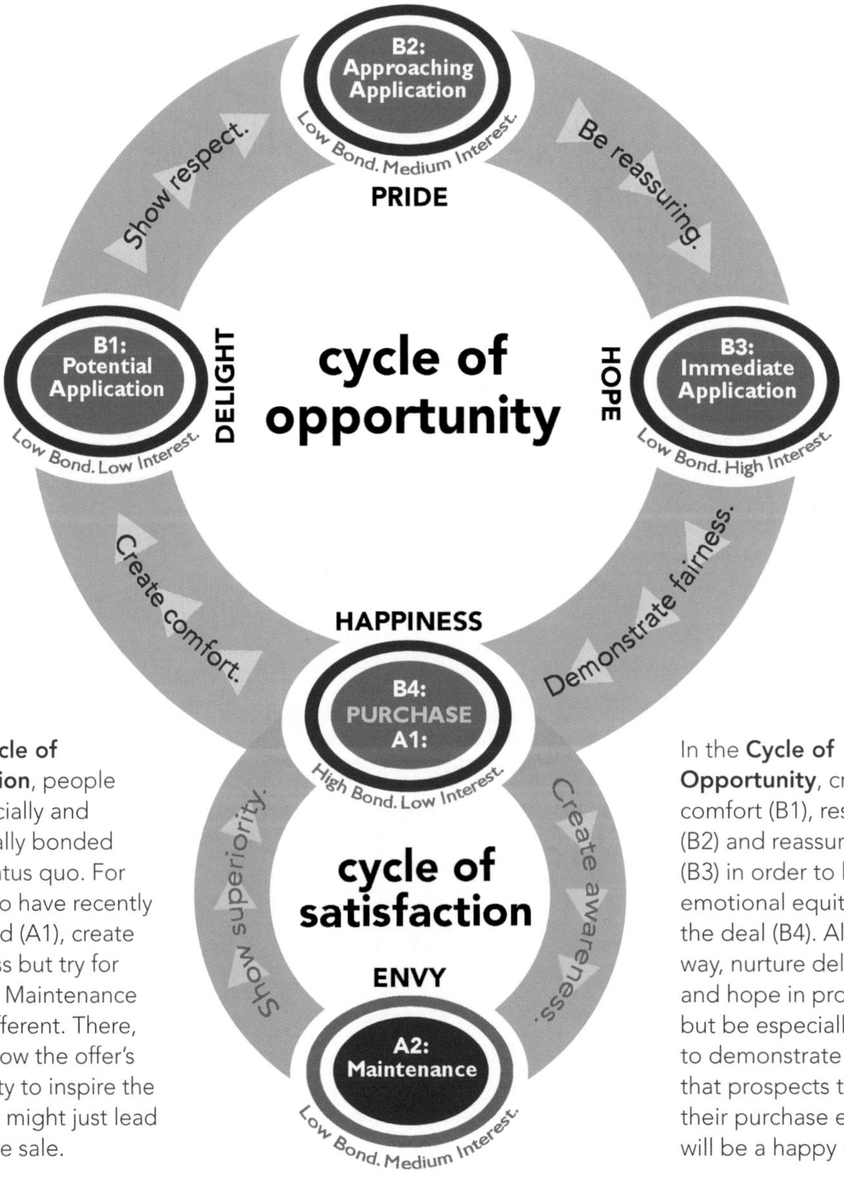

In the **Cycle of Satisfaction**, people are financially and emotionally bonded to the status quo. For those who have recently purchased (A1), create awareness but try for no more. Maintenance (A2) is different. There, gently show the offer's superiority to inspire the envy that might just lead to a future sale.

In the **Cycle of Opportunity**, create comfort (B1), respect (B2) and reassurance (B3) in order to leverage emotional equity and close the deal (B4). Along the way, nurture delight, pride and hope in prospects, but be especially careful to demonstrate fairness so that prospects trust that their purchase experience will be a happy one.

To understand the Great Chain of Buying, let's take a closer look.

First, what exactly is the Great Chain of Buying? It refers to the fact that everything that's for sale has a chain of greater or shorter length and heavier or lighter emotional weight. For example, a motor vehicle has a buying chain that's both longer and typically of greater emotional weight than does a banana, which gets purchased more frequently and involves less financial as well as emotional significance than purchasing one's next motor vehicle.

In other words, every offer has its own unique chain. But at the same time, every offer is identical in that salespeople must understand the prospect's potential relationship to the offer they're selling within the context of the Chain's two subsidiary cycles.

Of these, the **Cycle of Satisfaction** is short and in general terms isn't viable for new sales because prospects either feel good about what they have bought or want to feel good about it, so as not to doubt their purchase decision. Emotionally, the distinction hardly matters. The bottom line is that these prospects won't be inclined to consider a new offer because they're emotionally invested in what they've already chosen. To tell them they've made the wrong choice is tantamount to threatening their self-identity (*I'm a loser*) and undermining their status in the eyes of others, so don't go there.

That being said, there are two stages to the Cycle of Satisfaction and they involve slightly different emotional realities. Here the **Purchase** stage (point A1) indicates that prospects have just recently bought an offer and so there's little to no chance that dissatisfaction has emerged yet. As a result, a salesperson can really only present the alternative offer, as an act of creating awareness, because emotionally there is no viable strategy other than to be generous and congratulate those prospects on finding happiness with an offer that works for them. In that way, the salesperson is being a friend and may accrue emotional equity for the future.

Only slightly more promising in terms of sales potential is point A2 in the Cycle of Satisfaction. The difference here at the **Maintenance** stage is that some time has passed since the purchase. So while these prospects remain happy about their choice, they might be less emotionally committed to it because they have come to realize its limitations on their own.

A salesperson shouldn't induce disappointment. At the maintenance point in the Cycle of Satisfaction, the most a salesperson should be trying to achieve emotionally is to create a slight degree of envy in these prospects, who may sense that the salesperson's new, alternative offer could be superior. A hard sell shouldn't be attempted, however. Otherwise, the emotional outcome will be that the salesperson will have painted him or herself as manipulative (destroying trust) and as the bearer of the bad news that these prospects previously made a poor purchase decision (creating the sadness of buyer's regret). That's a dead end because people will avoid pain whenever possible.

In contrast, the **Cycle of Opportunity** is longer but far more promising in terms of the ability of the salesperson to emotionally connect on terms favorable to building a relationship and enacting new sales. Here the cycle consists of four points, based on the degree to which a purchase decision is imminent.

In this case, the end point, B4, is again the purchase stage. Once it's made, the question becomes whether the prospect turned buyer is satisfied with the purchase. If so, those prospects start to travel within the Cycle of Satisfaction. Salespeople who can take a prospect there have an excellent chance of getting repeat sales if they continue to attend to the relationship. If satisfaction isn't rendered, however, then the prospect reenters the Cycle of Opportunity. Unfortunately, however, that opportunity will most likely exist for a different salesperson.

Prior to purchase, these are the other three stages in the Cycle of Opportunity:

() **Potential Application**—On the left at point B1, prospects have either no immediate need and/or haven't yet separated themselves emotionally from an offer that didn't fully satisfy them. Either way, their goal is to feel comfortable during the approach step. An emotionally savvy salesperson will recognize that prospects at this point in the cycle are limited opportunities for now. Emotionally, the most that should be attempted is to inspire either *delight* in what the new, alternative offer can achieve or *relief* that a viable alternative exists.

() **Approaching Application**—At point B2, prospects are emotionally prepared to go beyond the approach step and onto the dialogue step. They may need or want a new solution in the not-to-distant future, but they're not there yet. For now, what they want more than the offer the salesperson is selling is to be shown respect. In turn, they may then develop respect for the salesperson who is investing time and effort in getting to know them, thereby building the relationship, rather than simply trying to make a quick sale. Emotionally, the key here is to play to the prospect's sense of *pride*.

() **Immediate Application**—With a pressing need or interest (B3), prospects can be taken right through the approach and dialogue steps on the way to the presentation. That's not to say the salesperson isn't an important focal point or that comfort and respect don't have to be established. Those factors matter. At the same time, however, prospects will be open to learning more readily about the offer. Assurance that the salesperson, company and the offer all check out well and are consistently aligned will protect the *hope* prospects are inclined to feel.

Including **Purchase** (B4), where prospects' faith in fairness is paramount while negotiating the factors of price, timing and other terms in order to preserve a feeling of yearning to acquire, those are the four stages of the Cycle of Opportunity. Note how those four stages also relate to the four first steps in the buying process. That's the overall picture. But since the focus right now is on the approach and dialogue steps, two additional considerations should be introduced before moving on to the presentation step.

The first is the importance of asking questions. Not only does an emotionally savvy salesperson use questions to readily discern where prospects are really at emotionally, that person will also use questions to unearth each prospect's pain. In revealing the problems inherent in the status quo, prospects become more likely to be emotionally alert to the possibility of finding a new, more fulfilling solution seemingly on their own. In short, good questions move prospects through the

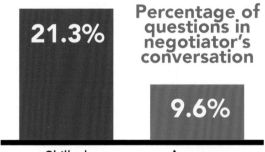

21.3%

Percentage of questions in negotiator's conversation

9.6%

Skilled Negotiators | Average Negotiators

Fig. 7.5 The Power of Asking Questions
It's almost too late to ask questions at the point of negotiating a sale: the earlier, the better. Research indicates that good deal makers ask over twice as many questions as their less effective counterparts.
(Rackham, *Major Account Sales Strategy*, McGraw-Hill Companies 1989)

Cycle of Opportunity more quickly and accurately, as a latent desire becomes a vivid possibility waiting to be enacted.

Secondly, the speed at which prospects move through the Cycle of Opportunity will likewise be influenced by whether the emotionally savvy salesperson gets prospects to focus on their needs or their wants during the approach and dialogue steps. What's the difference between a need and a want? The first is more rational. The second is pure emotion. Guess which one prospects will pay more for? Yes, satisfying wants that involve aspirations.

Needs	Wants
VS.	
Air	Blue Skies
Apartment	Mansion

Fig. 7.6 Needs and Wants: Not the Same
What's the difference between needs and wants? Emotion. Which is more appealing: a shaker of salt or the lightly salted edge of a chilled margarita glass?

The bottom line during the approach and dialogue steps is to set up the first part of the formula that applies to the whole buying process:

Lead with wants.
Follow with value.
Close with price.

Whatever happens during the first two steps of the buying process, the emotionally savvy salesperson will remember one other truth: never try to create a need. Why? Because it takes forever. Prospects know their own circumstances best. Don't try force-feeding them because that's not what we do to friends when building a relationship.

Now that we've discussed the Cycle of Opportunity, including in relation to wants, let's focus next on establishing value during the presentation step.

The Presentation Step in the Buying Process
*The key to a successful presentation isn't the offer;
it's the relationship building that's involved.*

Good dialogue sets the stage for step three, the presentation, enabling the emotionally savvy salesperson to understand the prospect across the table before the formal presentation begins. Interactive inquiry is crucial because the biggest mistake most salespeople make during their presentations is that they fail to keep the audience fully in mind. As a result, the prospects the salesperson hopes to influence and persuade during the presentation may emotionally float away instead, feeling as if they're receiving a generic pitch not tailored to them.

When that happens, the salesperson is forgetting that the specifics of the offer tend to be overshadowed by other factors. The most notable of these is still the salesperson and whether the prospect feels emotionally compatible and at ease with that person.

To put the presentation itself in context, consider the six principles of influence outlined by the psychologist R. B. Cialdini (O'Shaughnessy). Of them, four are emotional in nature and already in play before the formal presentation begins. Here's the first of these four:

- **Liking:** Prospects will initially focus on whether they enjoy the salesperson's presence, whether they feel that they'll like whom they're with. Over subsequent meetings, if interactions have been supportive and pleasant, familiarity will grow and the degree of liking will increase. But up front and at first, prospects are alert—even wary—and must be put at ease. Likeability is especially pertinent during the approach step, when establishing comfort for the prospect is vital.

The other three emotional influencers are compatibility, reciprocity and consistency. While emergent during the approach step, they mostly come into focus for prospects during the dialogue step. They consist of:

- **Compatibility:** Training programs that tell salespeople to "mirror" and "match" the prospect's body language are half right. Ultimately, even more important is identifying and respecting the prospect's belief system, because nothing is more deeply emotional than a person's worldview. Reflecting a prospect's beliefs respectfully is decisive, because people are comfortable with and like those who are like them.

- **Reciprocity:** Both liking and compatibility can be reinforced through favors or small signs of courtesy that invite reciprocity from prospects. Not only do people feel socially obligated to return favors, doing so makes them feel good. Mutual generosity adds "glue" to the budding relationship.

- **Consistency:** Consistency matters because during the first few encounters a prospect is still trying to figure out who the salesperson really is as a person. A consistent manner will help increase comfort in the belief that the personality on display will stay the same once the deal is signed and support services may be required. Consistency demonstrates integrity. As such, it also sets up the quality of assurance that will make the presentation itself far more effective.

Commercial copy:
"Hi! I'm Doug Harrison. My wife Suzanna and I started The SCOOTER Store because we believe that everyone has the right to enjoy life to the fullest."

What's analogous to a salesperson making an in-person pitch? A company spokesperson appearing in a direct response TV commercial. In such formats, body language that supports the message is imperative.

In work we did for The SCOOTER Store, the goal was to analyze viewer responses to commercials from America's leading supplier of scooters and power chairs for people of limited mobility. On camera at left is founder and CEO Doug Harrison aptly using his smile to project the enjoyment his company aims to bring customers by restoring their mobility and independence.

Sales presentations and delivery styles can likewise be critiqued, using facial coding to identify which phrases and visual aids best help to achieve emotional buy-in from prospects.

As for the presentation itself, let's refer to it as just a step in the greater process of enabling the prospect to cross the Bridge of Consideration (Fig. 7.7). That metaphor is meant to emphasize that the formal presentation involving the offer is, indeed, vital—the ostensible reason for the meeting—and yet really only a moment in time, a means to the end of getting the prospect comfortable enough to take the risk of leaving "solid land" to cross over into trying something new. In other words, the presentation is a point of transition between having earlier concentrated on building up emotional equity with the prospect and now seeking to supply the prospect with intellectual alibis as well.

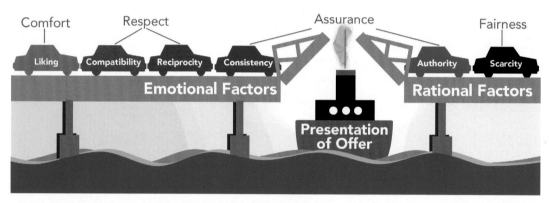

Fig. 7.7 The Bridge of Consideration and Influence Factors
The Bridge of Consideration involves crossing from emotional factors to rational factors by way of the presentation. In order to successfully do so, a salesperson must adequately address all six influence factors (represented as cars) and manage to appeal to the emotional needs of the prospect (shown in red above the cars). If the salesperson can maintain emotional awareness throughout the whole process and make the prospect feel safe, he or she will gain a loyal customer.

If done well, the presentation incorporates learnings from the approach and dialogue steps and prepares the prospect for the negotiation step to follow. In particular, what a salesperson should do to ensure safe passage over the Bridge is to establish value (which is emotional) by placing the offer within the larger context of the buyer/seller relationship. Why? Because value isn't in the offer as rationally defined. Instead, value resides in what the offer means to the prospect *internally*.

To protect customer-centric value and bolster the long-term customer relationship, the astute salesperson will stay focused on the prospect during the presentation. Doing so reduces errors in three ways:

- It minimizes the chance that prospects will tune out emotionally because the interaction continues to emphasize their wants and WIIFM (what's in it for me).

- It makes it less likely that the offer will seem like a "stretch" for prospects, since their needs and ability to pay will have been kept in mind.

- It helps to avoid negativity concerning rival offers, which will increase comfort levels. A long-term, viable relationship is based on positives. Going negative is a disconnect because it threatens to undermine the tone of respectfulness ideally created during the dialogue step.

Stay focused on the prospect's needs and wants

Remember that telling entails describing tangible features. It's overly rational. Selling entails touching the prospect's inner self with an offer's emotional benefits and doing so in personal terms.

Still to come on the far side of the Bridge are Cialdini's other two influencers: authority and scarcity. They are both more rationally-oriented and yet, in truth, the rational never truly separates from the emotional. That reality becomes evident in the end goal of sales: getting prospects to have true belief in the offer, something that is partly rational (involving justification) and partly emotional (since it can entail accepting reasons on faith).

The rational influence factor that helps achieve true belief is authority. Salespeople who can establish the offer's quality tap into people's innate sense of respect for and acceptance of authority. The experts among us command obedience, but the emotionally intelligent way to do so is by recognizing that legitimacy flows from trustworthiness. While they emerge as crucial on opposite sides of the presentation, before and after, consistency and authority help to establish the emotional goal of assurance.

The other rational factor is scarcity, which, like authority, comes with a rational veneer. "Limited availability" is the cry and it plays on people's instinctive desire to taste the forbidden fruit or to hoard what seems scarce. A salesperson can bolster the value of the offer by citing its unique, hard-to-get-elsewhere quality. Scarcity can be hinted at during the presentation step, but where it really comes into play is during the negotiation step to be discussed next.

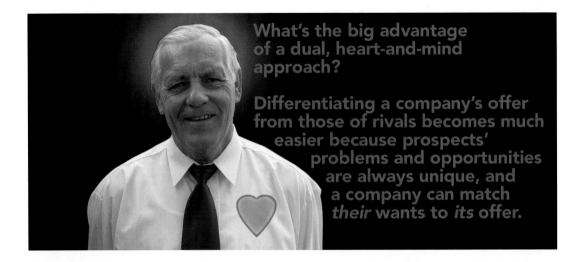

What's the big advantage of a dual, heart-and-mind approach?

Differentiating a company's offer from those of rivals becomes much easier because prospects' problems and opportunities are always unique, and a company can match *their* wants to *its* offer.

The Negotiation Step in the Buying Process
The deep-seated explanations for prospect resistance are always emotional in nature.

So far we have covered the approach and dialogue steps (about leading with wants while establishing comfort and respect) and the presentation step (about following with emotional and rational value while providing assurance). Now it's time to address the negotiation step, which is about closing with price while ensuring a sense of fairness.

At each of those steps, the salesperson remains the key focal point: the prospect's potential partner in what is meant to be an emotionally-oriented, sales relationship model. But in moving from presentation to negotiation, the offer itself now gets subsumed by a focus on terms like price and timing. The emergence of these traditionally rational terms might suggest that the typical sales force training approach is correct in emphasizing, first, getting to know the offer (as opposed to getting to know the prospect) so salespeople can explain it most persuasively; and second, techniques for closing the deal in order to take the order.

Why to avoid discussing price too early in the buying process: price only has to be heard for the offer to be pigeon-holed; value has to be assessed.

But salespeople will be effective to the extent they realize that the longer the buying process stays primarily in the sensory and emotional parts of the brain, the better, and here's why. As discussed earlier in this book, most of people's thought processes and communication are rooted in the intuitive, subconscious, non-verbal realm in which the two oldest parts of the mind specialize ("*What*"). Thus the *heart* of the matter is truly the heart of the matter. The longer and more often the salesperson gets close to prospects *emotionally*, the greater the extent to which a connection can be formed.

Moreover, to the extent that negotiation is really about trying to make something (a sale) happen, remember that only the sensory and emotional parts of the brain drive muscle activity. As a result, if a salesperson hears "No" from the prospect when the time comes to discuss a potential purchase, the wise move is to look for the emotional reason likely to underlie much of that rejection. Three key explanations for buyer resistance will then emerge:

- The first is that the salesperson has failed to establish his or her own personal value in terms of the qualities of liking, compatibility, reciprocity and consistency that enable the prospect to feel comfort, respect and assurance.

- The second is that the salesperson has failed to establish the value of the offer in emotional terms. An offer detailed in rational terms alone is much less likely to induce buy-in because its functional superiority may not exist or be sufficiently easy enough to communicate so as to motivate a switch from the status quo.

- Finally, the third explanation is, ironically enough, price and timing. These focal points may seem to be entirely rational in nature. But in reality they often get imbued with emotion based on whether or not they feel fair to prospects.

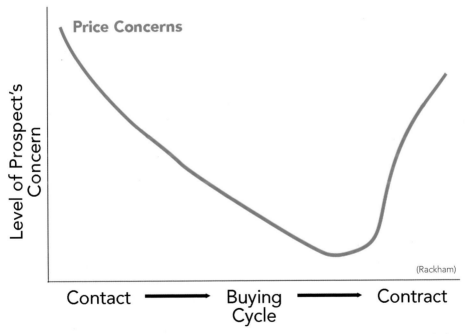

Graph used with permission from Huthwaite® and is not to be reproduced. For more information, visit www.huthwaite.com.

Fig. 7.8 Money Matters When the Offer Matters

Negotiating about price means value has been established and the prospect is interested in the terms of the offer. Serious negotiations then come down to three conditions: the size of the need/want, the fit of the offer to the solution, and the strength of the salesperson's relationship with the prospect.

In all of this, pricing is the single most complicated factor not yet discussed. So let's explore it in greater depth.

Yes, the idea that the salesperson should seek to close by discussing price might seem to be strange. Not only does it raise the specter of giving a discount, it would also seem as if a prospect without funds clearly means the end of the road. But if the salesperson has done his or her job right, then an answer like "Not in the budget" or "Can't afford it" doesn't have to signal that no working relationship is possible. After all, if the original meeting wasn't cut short after a true inability to pay now or in the foreseeable future was diagnosed, then presumably the dialogue went on because both the salesperson and prospect feel the relationship is worthwhile and has potential. Indeed, the opportunity may be just over the horizon. So a salesperson should be happy to close with price. As Figure 7.8 shows, price concerns arise again when a deal is imminent.

So an initial "no" related to price shouldn't necessarily be a big concern. It may be merely the prospect seeking enough of a price break to justify the purchase to a boss or to feel like a smart haggler. Moreover, remember that over 80% of directly stated objections are price related. At the same time, however, research indicates that about half to two-thirds of sales supposedly lost because of "price" were lost largely due to another factor (Rackham).

That makes sense, since complaints about price provide a respectable, rational, intellectual alibi way to express resistance based on emotionally oriented factors like doubt about value or a fear of consequences based on an offer too unfamiliar to put the prospect at ease. In those cases, for prospects to say "It's too expensive" *avoids* acknowledging the underlying feelings involved. And thus that response is an entirely human, emotionally-encoded reaction to the pressure of being sold to by a relative stranger.

Assuming a real opportunity exists, what's the smartest emotional means of handling "No"? It's certainly not to attack fear head-on using facts. That approach serves up a double whammy: increasing the prospect's worry that the salesperson is a predator while also driving fear ever

Hope means showing prospects that they can do more, be more and have more by acquiring the offer. On the other hand, fear is about making sure prospects don't forget the emotional pain and cost of their current predicament.

deeper underground. The bottom line? Fear can't be eased logically. Instead, an emotionally savvy salesperson should try to earn and retain the prospect's trust. In other words, personal brand equity is really the key because reasons don't persuade—people do.

In preparing for entry into the buying process, one initiative salespeople should undertake is to examine both their own personal brand equity as well as their individual equity in relation to the company's brand equity. As suggested in Chapter 4 on branding, which salespeople should also read, such a step entails understanding especially the character traits and the image associations most likely to accrue in prospects' minds over time. For instance, salespeople should ask themselves: "What traits stand out about me and how do they manifest themselves?" Moreover, "Are the traits and associations being communicated show consistency between me, the company and what the offer is about in emotional terms?"

Then during the buying process—and especially amid negotiations that have proven to be difficult—emotionally savvy salespeople have two approaches to rely on. The first place they can guide prospects toward is hope: the dream of being more, having more, or doing more.

But since people tend to hear bad news more loudly than good news, the second place to go is probably even more important: by keeping prospects focused on the emotional cost of the problem they have, salespeople can re-establish the value of the solution. Then—since we don't rush our friends—they should sit back. Salespeople tend to like the chase. But in this case, they should stop. Prospects must be given the time to *feel* for themselves the dire necessity of the change being offered.

Interwoven Rewards:
creating a "we" mentality

Synopsis: Much depends on how the context for the buyer/seller interaction is set up by the company. Management should protect the opportunity for repeat sales by making sure salespeople are motivated to look out for the prospect even after the sale is made. To that end, this section focuses on the follow-up to a sale, when the salesperson and the supporting staff must stay committed. How to make sure that happens? In part, the answer lies in financial benefits structured to reward teamwork and customer satisfaction.

Key take-aways:
- Sales forces interact best with the company when they don't get too isolated.
- Incentives should reward proven loyalty to customers and colleagues alike.

The Follow-Up Step in the Buying Process
Sales forces interact best with the company when they don't get too isolated.

A common mindset in sales force management is to think of the salesperson as a conquering hero, who wins the war but doesn't have to worry about the peace because the money's been made. The problem with this scenario is that nobody else really wants the salesperson to be victorious—certainly not prospects turned customers, and in truth, perhaps not even general employees or fellow sales force members at the salesperson's own company.

Emotion and Motivations

What makes **envy** the dominant emotion in regard to the follow-up step, and especially in terms of compensation, is more a matter of relationships within the company. Fellow salespeople and support staff may feel envious on seeing others do better financially, thereby harming teamwork. Colleagues and customers alike, however, will find their expansive desire to **bond** with the salespeople they know transformed into an instinct to **defend** their own interests if they sense an "I've got mine" attitude.

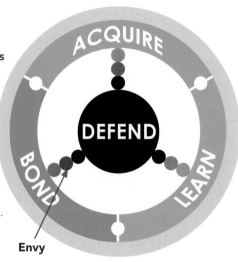

Envy

Externally, the reason is simple: the salespeople who "win" and make a show of their success offend customers who fear it means they've been conquered and may be abandoned. Nobody likes to feel as if he or she has been manipulated for monetary reward. Internally, there's also trouble. That's because money really does motivate people. Our need to acquire is driven by our fears about survival. Leading and less successful salespeople eye one another warily, concerned about the modern day equivalent of survival: status. As a result, envy may surface as the dominant emotion within the sales force.

Moreover, for the company staff that already thinks salespeople get overpaid and are granted too much independence, envy may also become chronic if the conquering hero routine continues and is reinforced. These workers probably believe that the offer actually sells itself. Or they may not emotionally accept salespeople, seeing them instead as the equivalent of mercenaries to be merely tolerated instead of valued.

The end result of this tension is that *everyone* ends up worse off, including the customers, whose paperwork and follow-up requests require the interaction of staffers and salespeople. The net emotional outcome of resentful customers and envious co-workers means nobody is on the same page. Then customer support, as part of the follow-up during the equally vital fifth step of the buying process, crumbles.

Lower follow-up standards than those already practiced are not advisable. Consider survey results regarding the top five frustrations people have with salespeople. The first three are poor communication skills, lack of knowledge of the customer's company, and overly-aggressive selling. But the fourth and fifth greatest aggravations both involve the crucial follow-up step: slow delivery or failure to deliver fully on what was promised (Davis).

Nobody likes the successful salesperson who gloats from the top of his or her commission pile.

To examine the impact of daily sales force management practices, let's skip over retention and motivation strategies for now and focus on how the sales force is coached. The sales force leadership must remember that their subordinates are looking to see if leadership walks the talk. A sales director or manager who has encouraged the sales force to get closer to both potential and repeatable customers out in the field but does nothing to foster good will between the sales force and the rest of the company back in the home office creates an obvious disconnect.

As Figure 7.9 shows, that's the situation a homebuilding company in the Philadelphia area faced, as confirmed by Sensory Logic's sales force interviews. Diagnosed and confirmed through facial coding, the situation became clear to all involved. With crucial information in hand, the company was then able to move forward by stopping the flow of mixed messages.

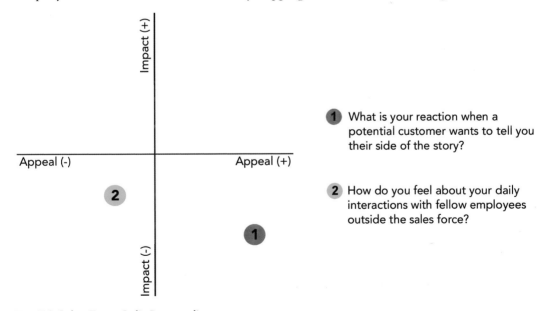

Fig. 7.9 Sales Team Split Personality
Being encouraged to be closer to prospects (Q1 results) while being kept isolated from and therefore at odds with the rest of the company (Q2 results) isn't a viable strategy. A sales force should intuitively want all the allies it can muster. Good sales force management involves implementing policies that show empathy for prospects while getting the sales force on the same page with supporting staff.

Retention and Motivation Practices
Incentives should reward proven loyalty to customers and colleagues alike.

In regard to sales force management, motivation and retention practices should also adhere to the fundamental truth that emotions matter. Thus the basis on which performance is judged should look beyond sales volume alone toward efforts made to inspire feelings of loyalty among customers and comradery among co-workers. The sales force leadership should reconsider rewarding sales team members only with monetary bonuses in order to inspire potentially greater feelings of loyalty to the company.

Let's start with performance evaluation criteria. As Figure 7.10 indicates, the typical salesperson checks out the moment the sale is complete, figuring the deal is done. But that's not how it feels for the customer. They're now committed and seeking support because, as Figure 7.11 indicates, they're often left struggling to learn how to use what they bought.

Some salespeople will always be careful to attend to the customer's post-sale needs because therein lies the opportunity for repeat sales. But consider a salesperson about to leave the sales team or who knows the customer probably won't buy again. Then there's a good chance that he or she might just ignore the obligation to follow-up.

Given the adverse, long-term impact that poor support is likely to have on the company's reputation, something more is needed to ensure that post-sale support is enacted. That extra step involves job evaluations and incentives based on multiple factors. Individual sales volume will of course be part of any evaluation, but it's also worth considering giving weight to the degree to which the salesperson interacts well with post-sale customers and fellow employees.

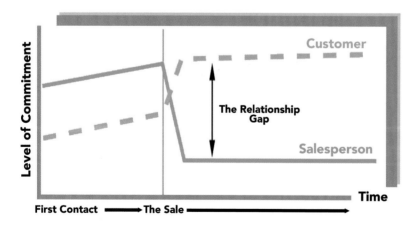

Fig. 7.10 The Potential Relationship Gap
Carole King sings, "Will you still love me tomorrow?" In a similar vein the prospect wants to know, "Will the salesperson still care after the sale is made?" Good salespeople know that they fulfill a customer service role if they want repeat sales (Owen 2004).

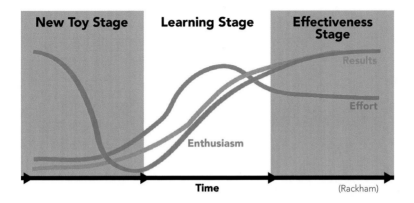

New Toy Stage   Learning Stage   Effectiveness Stage

Results

Effort

Enthusiasm

Time   (Rackham)

Graph used with permission from Huthwaite® and is not to be reproduced. For more information, visit www.huthwaite.com.

Fig. 7.11 Stages of Motivation and Implementation
As this charts shows, it is important to help buyers out. As they move past initial enthusiasm and into the nitty-gritty stages of actual knowledge and use, their amount of effort will yield less results than anticipated—leading to a drop in enthusiasm for the offer and purchase (salesperson included). On the other hand, as the buyers' results improve, enthusiasm resumes.

As to just what kind of non-monetary incentive or bonus a salesperson might receive for superior performance, one idea is a tangible reward like a desirable high-tech device or a vacation package. At present, cash rewards are probably more prevalent than tangible bonuses. But tangibles have psychological merit, as they provide the opportunity to incentivize a salesperson in a way that's more emotionally engaging than cash (Jeffrey). The reason that "cash is king" is because it's highly mobile and allows the person who's rewarded to spend it as he or she pleases. But those same qualities make cash incentives facile and more susceptible to supporting the here-and-gone, predator/prey mentality that can prove to be disastrous in selling situations.

In contrast, a tangible reward has the advantage of creating a long-term affinity. For instance, every time a salesperson uses the awarded device or reminisces about a particular vacation, emotions will be rekindled. Such reinforcement is less likely to happen if the reward was cash, which might have been spent paying off a credit card bill or used in other ways that leave no traces.

As Figure 7.12 demonstrates, tangible incentives can be competitive with monetary rewards. In this case, one involving a major technology company's sales force, Sensory Logic determined that bikes and camcorders were either ahead of or as well received as cash. Moreover, based on our emotional analysis, tangible rewards seem to be more socially acceptable than cash in terms of public discussion among the sales team, thus downplaying the kind of corrosive envy that undermines relationships. Most people don't like to brag or enter discussions about money and salary. As a result, tangible rewards do double duty. They keep the heart warm over the long term and have more discreet social reinforcement value than does cash, which tends to generate and support a mercenary mentality.

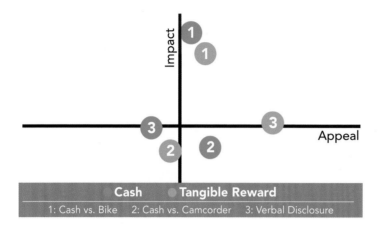

Fig. 7.12 Emotional Response: Cash vs. Prize

In this test, two items were pre-selected as benchmarks. The emotional verdict favored the bike but not the camcorder being presented. These results surely had to do with personal interest in the reward and could be improved on in a real life situation where a catalogue of choices would be made available. In comparison, the greater social comfort involved in telling a colleague about a tangible reward made it the emotional winner hands-down over cash.

However salespeople are rewarded, it is important to choose and distribute rewards so that two results predominate. The first is that salespeople are reminded that past sales, and current work that builds on past sales relationships, are important to management. (In this way, the salesperson's customers should feel supported and valued.) The second is that the sales team remains a team, with members who are emotionally connected instead of divided by corrosive envy.

Conclusion

Prospects follow their gut instincts. Just as emotion comes before reason, feelings about the status of the relationship with the seller come before paying attention to the quality of the offer. Inevitably, belief in the offer follows from trust in the seller. So to be effective, sales force directors, managers and their sales teams must accomplish the following:

- Move beyond the common orientation that implicitly and unknowingly treats salespeople as heroes and casts the prospect as prey to be subdued through aggressive, rational arguments. Emotionally smart hires will be attuned to taking a truly relationship-based approach to sales.

- Make the buying process about the prospect at every stage, from approach through negotiation and follow-up. So salespeople should take the time to ask questions and clue prospects into the degree of pain they're feeling with the status quo, making a change to the new offer easy to consider. Then provide post-sale assurances that the purchase was wise, including documentation of good news concerning the offer and its implementation, to help alleviate any unresolved fears and cement the bond between buyer and seller. These steps will allow the salesperson to influence future decision criteria.

- Avoid buyer regret by addressing prospects' needs post-sale. Also be proactive about dissipating inter-company and inter-sales force envy before it becomes corrosive. Both initiatives will be more likely to happen if the right coaching and reward structures are in place. Ideally, bonuses should be determined by calculating not just complete sales but also the degree to which satisfaction exists in the hearts of customers.

An Action Plan

To make sure that sales force efforts are emotionally healthy, here are a few things to check when assessing effectiveness:

☐ Hire salespeople who can provide consistency not just in giving the pitch the same way, but who can also match the offer and their style of presenting themselves with the company's preferred image. They should know that knowledge about what they're selling isn't a substitute for learning their prospects' feelings.

☐ Train the sales force to recognize and connect rational explanations (the intellectual alibis) to what are essentially emotional motivations for purchase. A well-constructed pitch balances practical needs with emotional wants.

☐ Develop two emotional templates. The first involves the qualities any new job candidate must meet. The second concerns the emotions that prospects will probably experience. Besides pocketbook issues, what emotional factors influence the way various prospects respond? Identifying that framework will make it easier to handle resistance to purchase

☐ Verify that the sales force believes in what it's selling so that prospects believe too.

☐ Strive to build trust between management and the sales team as well as within the sales team itself. Otherwise, it's difficult to maintain a spirit of optimism and prospects will sense a lack of hope, which could be fatal to winning them over. The sales force members should enjoy a positive group identity that makes them feel like they belong to something that will nurture and protect them.

8 customer satisfaction

Were you satisfied?

Yes.

That about sums up the extent of most customer satisfaction surveys.

Unfortunately, this simple yes or no method doesn't provide much insight into what can be done to emotionally bond with customers.

OVERVIEW

How truly satisfied are "satisfied" customers? As chairman of the National Automobile Dealers Association, Alan Starling described the feedback system used by automakers as "broken" and in dire need of fixing. No wonder the number of companies tracking customer satisfaction dropped by 26% during the late 1990s (McEwen). And yet according to the Conference Board, the single biggest concern for CEOs is retaining their existing customers (Applebaum). So the practice of relying only on "lip-service" responses needs to change. Protecting one's revenue stream is too important *not* to get to the heart of the matter. A more sensitive approach makes sense because what is loyalty, after all, if not an emotion? To help companies better gauge and reinforce customer satisfaction, this chapter will focus on:

- **Respectfulness:** People prefer to do business with companies that make shopping and customer service experiences more convenient—for consumers. Showing respect means operating so people can see that a company values their time and energy. Eliminating inconvenience whenever possible enables customers to feel like they are being honored instead of ignored, trapped or rebuffed. Respect starts with acknowledgment, as in being noticed. But it really means the right to achieve one's goals on one's own terms and as efficiently as possible.

- **Engagement:** Because a desire for excitement animates the heart, curiosity is a huge part of why people like to shop. To satisfy people's urge to explore, merchants can gain an edge by playing to the senses. That involves creating an emotional connection by studying shoppers' experiences, identifying sweet-spot opportunities and eliminating sore spots. Meanwhile, customer service departments can do their part by ensuring that people get the opportunity to tell their tales of woe—but only once—to somebody qualified to provide a satisfying resolution.

- **Reassurance:** Shopping lets people see how well they fashionably fit in, making just the right choices at the right prices. To make retail and e-tail more than just a price war—and to make stores and websites more than just battle grounds—merchants must help customers experience a sense of community. Then shoppers can vicariously belong to the social groups to which they aspire as well as interact and support each other with advice. But support alone doesn't eliminate the need for help from customer service representatives who are able to provide real assistance.

Two big drivers of customer satisfaction are experiences related to shopping and customer service. This chapter will address the emotional aspects of both so that companies can boost loyalty.

Now let's look more closely at how buying the offer and getting service related to it can lead to satisfaction, starting with what happens when consumers initiate these activities.

Respectfulness:
enabling efficiency

Synopsis: Nobody likes to be disregarded. Yet companies too often seem to be treating customers that way by failing to eliminate bottlenecks and facilitate a sense of control. This section will address the emotional cost of neglecting to give customers satisfactory access to service, followed by analysis of the underlying psychological reasons why delays affect human nature so severely.

Key take-aways:
- With customer service, what's really at stake is a person's sense of self-worth.
- A feeling of loss underlies customers' distaste for having inefficiency imposed on them.

"Can You Hear Me Now?"
With customer service, what's really at stake is a person's sense of self-worth.

There are two good reasons for opening a discussion of customer satisfaction with customer service. First, of all the marketing mediums nothing else is more emotional for the consumer or more dangerous for the company than customer service. That's because service comes closest to affecting the customer's inner self.

After all, what concerns people most deeply? Hint: it's not the company they've bought from or even the offer purchased. Rather, it's their sense of personal worth and security. In a service situation, the company has customers' full attention because they've bought and are now typically trying to rectify a problem in order to salvage not only the purchase but, ultimately, to defend their belief that they made an informed, sensible purchase decision that benefits them.

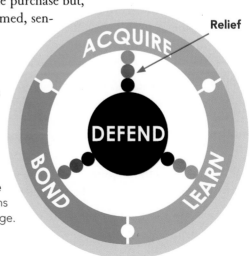

Emotion and Motivations

For weary or frustrated consumers, the context is as crucial as what gets bought—making **relief** the crucial emotional outcome. The difficulties consumers experience shopping or initiating customer service requests makes them want to **defend** their limited supply of energy and attention. But as the real purpose of shopping and service is to **acquire** something, and remain satisfied with it, defend remains relevant right through the customer service stage.

"A lot of companies fall into the trap of believing that some new customer-service technology will take cost and management burden away and will eliminate the need to have very talented people on the phones and in their retail outlets."

—Dan Leemon, former Chief Strategy Officer, Charles Schwab

In other words, respectfulness from a company helps to protect customers' own self-respect.

Second, because shopping and customer service are typically self-initiated activities, they invite expectations of having it your way. However, as we'll soon see, those expectations often run directly counter to the experiences people have shopping or seeking service.

As a result, Verizon's famous catch phrase—"Can you hear me now?"—is unfortunately an apt place to start in establishing why the respectfulness opportunity is so important. What the phrase highlights, in essence, is a lone individual trying to reach somebody else in real-time, using technology meant to facilitate, not hinder, the communications process. As Verizon's phrase implicitly acknowledges, however, the reality is that technology doesn't always live up to its promise. Disappointment, even outright rage, can result.

Based on Verizon's catch phrase, people's attempts to contact a company by phone for service provides a natural segue into talking about, first, simply being acknowledged. There is no doubt many among us who have been tempted to spew forth an irate equivalent of "Why can't you hear me *now*?" after having heard a message like "We apologize for the delay that you are experiencing due to unusually heavy call volumes. Your call is very important to us. Someone will be with you momentarily."

For financial reasons, adequate staffing to handle all service calls doesn't seem to be in the cards. The expense would simply be too great. At least that's the official, rational explanation. But just how reasonable is it? Research indicates that it's five times as expensive to gain a new customer as it is to retain a current one (Desatnick). Moreover, not only will 80% of a company's dissatisfied customers do business with it again if the company can solve their problems quickly, they will also spend three times as much as other customers (Desatnick; Gitomer).

So getting off on the wrong foot by failing to have attentive and available staff doesn't seem to be a patently sound business argument. Yes, protecting profitability by holding down costs is valid. But to date, the trade-off involved in terms of possibly sacrificing customer satisfaction has been a strategic operating decision companies have made without the benefit of complete information. Surely it's worthwhile to know how customers feel about being forced to wait. Yet, until now only think-your-feeling measurement tools like surveys have been available to help inform business leaders as to the possible depth of the downside of making customers wait.

In short, one has to wonder: what's the trade-off in terms of dollars lost through negativity generated? To learn the emotional cost to companies of being disrespectful of their customers' time and efforts, Sensory Logic conducted a test to learn the extent of people's displeasure with not getting their service needs immediately handled.

Figure 8.1 shows the results for various types of customer service delays, where waiting runs contrary to consumers' desire to have it their way immediately. The types of delays we tested for consisted of: 1) an in-person customer service desk (simulation of an airport delay, e.g., subjects were shown a videotape of people left waiting in line to get a question answered), 2) a call center help desk audio recording with either background music or 3) a company's promotional "spiel" played at discreet intervals and, finally, 4) a website that subjects were forced to wait to download.

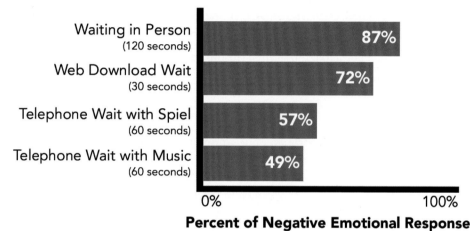

Fig. 8.1 Oh, How We Hate to Wait
Sensory Logic ran simulations to see how people responded to being forced to wait. The above chart shows the results. Obviously, people are most offended when being forced to wait in-person. But none of the results supports the practice of keeping people "on hold." Only the wait with music option neutralized people enough to bring as many smiles to their faces as it did negative feelings like disgust and anger.

Obviously, any kind of wait rankles people. Yes, hearing some music while waiting for help is better than hearing a spiel in terms of reducing negativity. But all delays sent people into a foul emotional state, except for the music option that at least makes a nod at designing the experience to be emotionally more acceptable. Thus the overwhelming conclusion to be drawn is that it would be worthwhile for companies to invest more resources in handling wait times. They can do so with more staffing or, at a minimum, through even moderately pleasant distractions.

Why Delays and Inconvenience Are So Harmful
A feeling of loss underlies customers' distaste for having inefficiency imposed on them.

Now that we can quantify the negative emotion felt as a result of waiting, the question then becomes: why is this negativity present? Or to frame it more positively, what must companies do to overcome such negativity so that the activities of buying an offer and getting service related to it create instances of customer satisfaction?

From a psychological and emotional perspective, there are three key underlying reasons why delays and inconvenience matter so much to people and are, therefore, in need of being resolved by companies. From the consumer's point of view, they consist of:

- **Loss of control:** being forced to wait or otherwise suffer inconvenience against their will means that consumers have relinquished control.

- **Doubt:** delays and inconvenience lead to inefficiency that makes consumers wonder if the company is a failure in general.

- **Avoidance:** difficulty interacting with a company can create the suspicion that consumers are being avoided, especially when technology seems to serve as more of a shield than a bridge.

Let's briefly look at each of those three reasons separately, related to shopping, service, or both depending on relevancy.

Loss of Control

A desire to exert greater control over one's immediate environment is an innate human priority (Pooler). It's not hard to understand why. Without control people feel less secure and more vulnerable and, therefore, experience fear that is ultimately related to survival instincts. This control/fear syndrome readily applies both to shopping and service situations, though in opposite ways.

Why do people shop? Yes, for the functional benefits, of course: clothes to keep them warm, food to sustain them, et cetera. But another reason, pertinent to the problem of inconvenience, is in

Consumers want a shopping experience to be like on-demand TV: when they want it, on their terms and under their control.

order to exercise control. As a self-initiated activity from which the other party, i.e., the merchant, can realize a financial benefit, consumers expect the clerks and the company in general to affirm their importance. In other words, the act of shopping gives people enjoyment and they expect a degree of deference to be shown by company representatives trying to satisfy shoppers' needs and wants. A chance to be in power and make decisions speaks to a desire to control one's own destiny, which is among the psychological forces driving the shopping experience.

In contrast, customer service situations aren't about exercising control but, rather, trying to regain it. What customer hasn't felt vulnerable, knowing he or she has spent the money and now hopes the company—a much larger entity—will still care about making the deal come out right?

Doubt

People naturally like to ally themselves with winners while avoiding losers. The same rule of thumb applies to shoppers, who would rather frequent companies that have their act together. Again, it's a matter of feeling respected and responding in kind. After all, consumers don't have to put up with inferior performers.

How important is ease of access and convenience in general? Consider a pair of research findings, which together cover both retail and e-tail:

- In regard to traditional, brick-and-mortar retailing, a survey found that 64% of consumers say they will leave a store if checking out takes too long and 70% say they make a point to shop at stores that don't waste their time (Ander).

- In regard to e-tailing, a study found that less than 40% of shoppers consider the finding-and-buying process easy (28% consider it tough), resulting in over 60% of all virtual shopping carts being abandoned (Kotkin).

These statistics help validate two of the five key positioning options retail experts Ander and Stern propose in their book, *Winning at Retail*. All five of those options are listed in Figure

Position	Rationalized	Emotional Goal
Quickest	Most Efficiency	Provide Relief
Easiest	Fewest Hassles	Provide Relief
Hottest	Newest Fashions	Create Delight
Biggest	Largest Offering	Eliminate Fear
Cheapest	Lowest Prices	Eliminate Fear

Fig. 8.2 Five Positioning Strategies Relevant to Shoppers
The positioning options described here are those of Ander and Stern, with the rational component implicit in their descriptions of each option. But the final, feeling category—the emotional goal or benefit available through the various options—is my own addition.

8.2. But the two relevant in regard to avoiding delays and inconvenience are *quickest* and *easiest*. Quickest is about timing and speed. At a deeper level, it is about avoiding the feeling of having been trapped: a claustrophobic sensation that human beings, as animals, instinctively dislike. In contrast, easiest is about not being forced to expend unnecessary energy to secure resources. When consumers are after the easiest way to get what they want, they are not necessarily looking to avoid traps so much as hassles they can do without.

As animals, humans instinctively dislike the feeling of being trapped.

Avoidance

Consumers also naturally want to do business with respectful companies that help them, rather than avoid them or practice indifference by failing to make customer satisfaction central to their plans. The role that technology plays is a big factor. In a study funded by the Society of Consumer Affairs Professionals (SOCAP), 80% of the people surveyed agreed with the statement "I'm frequently frustrated by the way companies use technology to avoid talking to me" (Broetzmann).

The bottom line in customer service is that consumers want to talk to a live body in real time because their essential dilemma doesn't involve an offer but, rather, their inner self.

In the end, the biggest problem in customer service isn't customers who give a company a hard time. It's those who abandon contact altogether, who give up and claim "I'm not getting what I want; I'm done." In the short-run, losing complaining customers might not seem so bad. But brand equity will take a nose dive if enough customers jump ship. Lack of satisfaction harms the degree to which shoppers will consider buying from a company again, thereby rendering high awareness of a branded offer essentially irrelevant.

In summary, regarding the initial, approach stage of both shopping and customer service, companies should remember to safeguard respectfulness because their relationships to customers are only partly economic in nature. A company's efforts to contain costs are sure to backfire to the extent that they undermine a consumer's emotional desire for hassle-free experiences from access to checkout, in the case of shopping, and for more personalized interaction in the case of customer service. What do consumers want at this stage? To protect their time, their energy and their egos for the crucial engagement stage to follow.

Engagement:
bringing back delight

Synopsis: Playing to people's innate desire for discovery and pleasure is fine, but then that desire has to be fulfilled. In the first half of this section, the focus is on how companies can get high-quality attention from retail shoppers by creating a sensory-rich store environment while in e-tail an engrossing plot is the key. The second half of this section is devoted to the service equivalent of pleasure: not so much getting the problem solved but, rather, acknowledging and respecting the plight of the customer as a human being caught up in a problem.

> **Key take-aways:**
> - The essence of therapeutic shopping is immersion in the experience.
> - Great service means validating that the customer with a problem is important.

Choreographing Retail and E-tail
The essence of therapeutic shopping is immersion in the experience.

During their heyday from the 1860s to 1960s, department stores were glorious urban "cathedrals of commerce." But with the rise of mass-discounters and big box category

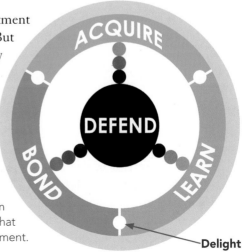

Emotion and Motivations
The emotion to elicit is **delight**. For shoppers, it's done by creating experiences that balance comfort and allure. In customer service situations, it's done by connecting customers with caring and capable staff. Stores and even websites should be seen as sensory opportunities that consumers want to **learn** about and, if enjoyed, create a desire to **bond** with the merchant. In customer service, customers want to bond to the extent that service staff is interested in their predicament.

Delight

Acerbated by the increased presence of e-commerce, the question has become: "How to put the twinkle back into shoppers' eyes?" The key is to make sure they are emotionally engaged and pleased by offline experiences that surpass the advantages that shopping online provides.

killers, shoppers typically endure no-frills warehouses of commerce instead. Why the shift? The likely socio-economic reasons include a shrinking middle class (hence a rise in cost-consciousness) and new forms of entertainment like TV, VCRs, DVDs, the Internet, et cetera, that have made shopping pale as an alternative.

But whatever the explanation, the result is that the struggle to attract shoppers and to make shopping fun has reached near-crisis proportions for both traditional merchants and those selling over the Internet. Their customer satisfaction conundrum: how to get the twinkle back into shoppers' eyes.

Of the five key positioning strategies outlined by Ander and Stern, creating emotional engagement pertains to consumers seeking the hottest offers from the hottest places to shop. *Hottest* can be too narrowly interpreted as referring only to the newest fashions, but it is really much broader than that. Successfully capturing consumers who want the hottest is about attracting not merely their attention, but attaining quality attention. And doing so will be based on shoppers' experiences: first of the store's or website's general environment, then of the offer as specifically merchandised. In all, those experiences should ideally generate emotional warmth—most notably the blend of surprise and happiness that leads to delight.

In the old days, a store's display windows were the primary way to engage shoppers. But now the big box retailers have typically dropped them altogether, relegating this means of igniting an initial spark to the interior of malls and a few pedestrian-friendly retail settings like the stores on New York City's Fifth Avenue and on Michigan Avenue's "Miracle Mile" in Chicago.

In the "old days," good display windows were like free theatre, bringing imagination into play in a way that car culture has all but obliterated.

In place of enticing window displays, brick-and-mortar retailers rely heavily not only on advertising (Sunday circulars are the new window displays), but also on the entry area and the atmosphere inside. Thirty years ago, Philip Kotler recognized the power of deliberately designed environments and coined the term "atmospherics" to describe a store's ability to entice and influ-

**Fig. 8.3 If They Don't Look at It,
They Won't Buy It**
What's the epitome of consumers wanting
convenience? The menu board in a quick-service
restaurant. In Sensory Logic's study for a company
evaluating the success of adding a café to its
convenience store operations, we found an
inadequate degree of visual gaze attention being
given to the café's menu board (see the minimal
results to the right). What would be the upside of
making some changes? A study commissioned
by Coca-Cola found that, when mixed right,
information, pictures and prices are the key
elements on a menu board, with the inclusion
of a photograph of branded cups, for example,
capable of lifting beverage sales by nearly 10%
(Crawford).

ence shoppers' buying decisions. As Kotler noted, people respond to an entire experience when shopping, not just to individual offers in a store's mix. Moreover, sensory atmospheric details serve as clues that talk to shoppers in exactly the silent, non-verbal language that facial expressions do, which is fitting since those clues both elicit and convey emotions.

Of course, during the three decades since Kotler first emphasized atmospherics, much has changed. For one thing, the amount of retail space has tripled (to 21 square feet of space per person in the U.S.), while retail sales per square foot have dropped by nearly 25% (Ander). For another, e-commerce has exploded. By 2010, one estimate is that at least 30% of all retail sales will be influenced by evaluations formed online while reviewing a company's website (Clancy).

E-tail's growth has brought with it a focus on encouraging engagement through five main elements, all of which involve the plot of drawing the visitor in (Davenport):

- **Interactivity** means participation. Comment and response features provide one common approach to encouraging interaction. Allowing visitors to a site to vote or rank offers is another.

- **Competitions** such as games or quizzes take time and get site visitors involved.

- **High-production values** help turn e-tail's sight-and-sound atmospherics limitation into an advantage. For instance, Zappos.com makes browsing its online shoe catalog easy, with a multi-view feature that lets visitors see any pair of shoes from all angles.

- Finally, while **entertainment** more or less speaks for itself, **narrative** is a special form of it. The co-creation of advertising by consumers submitting amateur videos is likely to be the next prominent form that will spill into e-tail. People can submit branded, offer-related "stories" that utilize text, video, photos, questions and advice, which can then be posted to a website.

Science has now shown that "retail therapy" is a matter of shoppers feeling "high." That happens naturally when the chemical dopamine is released in the brain because the person is experiencing something new and exciting.

At the same time, however, the importance of atmospherics in regard to traditional retailing has grown, creating increased competition. Now more than ever, merchants need to know whether their stores are eliciting the kind of favorable emotional responses that facial coding can measure. That's because the right store environment becomes a strategic advantage, especially when compared to e-tail, as merchants have the opportunity to engage shoppers by creating a sensory buffet that leads to immersive, emotionally enriching experiences.

Justification for making the effort and expenditure can be found in the payoff of shoppers making impulse purchases. Science has now shown that "retail therapy" is a matter of shoppers feeling "high," which happens naturally when the chemical dopamine is released in the brain because the person is experiencing something new and engrossing. What merchant doesn't want to provide therapeutic retail shopping sessions with exciting items available in a stimulating environment?

Nor does that therapy have to wait until consumers enter the setting. As evidence of the fact that entrances have real potential, consider the research Sensory Logic did for a high-end restaurant franchise (Fig. 8.4). We assessed the emotional reaction of subjects to different areas and features of the restaurant. In this case, we actually found the entrance area to be best, overall, at generating a positive emotional response. A distinct logo on the awning over the door and tastefully handled signage proved to be very appealing.

By contrast, once they got indoors the subjects found the main act—the dining room—less to their liking. Individual features, such as the lighting and art, worked well. But all in all, the dining room didn't exhibit the literal warmth of the adjoining, open-view kitchen very well, causing the subjects to feel a distinct lack of coziness. In short, they *admired* the setting (and management confessed to us that being admired was the designer's goal). But that kind of emotional response wasn't enough. The designer's creation was leaving consumers feeling uneasy—and so the management ultimately felt uneasy, too, since the bottom line was spotty.

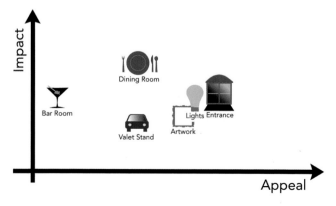

Fig. 8.4 Facial Coding Results for Upscale Restaurant Design

Sensory Logic's study of emotional response to different areas of a restaurant revealed some interesting outcomes. The entrance was received well with positive Appeal and Impact responses. But further inside the restaurant, more negative feelings emerged. Management later confessed: the designer was designing for himself, instead of suiting their customers.

For atmospherics to succeed, companies should design *everything*—especially the subtler aspects of the shopper's experience—according to the shopper's emotional needs and wants. In short, make it not only quick and easy but also make it fun. In doing so, retailers enjoy the advantage of engaging a broader sensory bandwidth than do e-tailers and should therefore leverage the natural sensory logic of see, touch, buy, own. It's eternal, innate logic that works again and again, making buyer and seller alike that much happier.

The "Me-Story" of Customer Service
Great service means validating that the customer with a problem is important.

After finding a live body ready and willing to help, what do customers want? They want to find pleasure in telling their stories, of course. And there's always a story. There's a pre-story about the customer's expectations of the company and then there's the current me-story, meaning the story that spells out the customer's reasons for seeking vindication.

Vindication is important because, in terms of what customer service really provides, there are just two categories: what customers want and what customers don't want. They come to customer service wishing to get what they want and seeking assurance that they won't get what they don't want. As it turns out, vindication is really about validation.

What conclusions and feelings don't customers want to internalize? *"I've been cheated. I'm insignificant and easily ignored. I never get things right."* Any of those toxic responses fit the don't-want category. In contrast, wants go something like this: "That was easy. Yeah! I got what I needed. People can be so helpful. I'm glad to find I wasn't crazy. Now I understand." Those responses show how delight can be part of the customer service experience: let the customer's "me" win (and do so graciously).

After all, disgruntled customers represent a wonderful relationship-building opportunity because then a company has their full attention—a rarity in today's marketplace. And best yet, moving a customer from negativity to affinity isn't all that hard.

Consider a study Sensory Logic did evaluating shoppers' experiences at a big-box retailer, including the effect of employee behaviors on customer satisfaction. In this case, the study didn't focus on customer service representatives per se but on retail sales employees and their interactions with customers. To help us do our work, the client agreed to let us

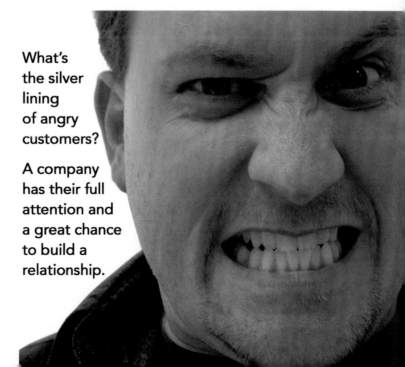

What's the silver lining of angry customers?

A company has their full attention and a great chance to build a relationship.

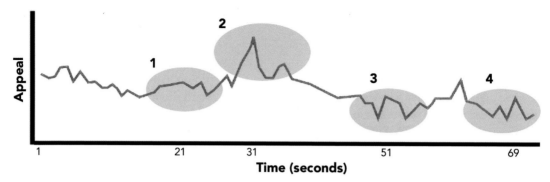

Fig. 8.5 Consumer Reactions to Poor Customer Service

The chart shows on a real-time basis the average emotional Appeal response of subjects to viewing a 73-second video segment of a checkout clerk barely paying attention to the customer facing her at the cash register. Four time groups stand out within the results:

- Group 1: the clerk is getting change with her back to the waiting customer. Appeal falls accordingly at second 26.
- Group 2: the only major Appeal rise as the clerk acknowledges the customer's presence through interaction.
- Group 3: Appeal level drops as the clerk ignores the customer in favor of chatting with a co-worker while waiting for the receipt to print.
- Group 4: shows the response to the clerk handing over the receipt and saying, "Have a good day." As the Appeal results show, by this time the customer simply doesn't believe the clerk cares.

use a concealed video camera so that we could secure spontaneous, natural film footage. Then we showed video segments to subjects to learn their emotional responses to both the store environment and various service situations.

In the results shown in Figure 8.5, the footage involved a checkout clerk handling one particular customer. What the second-by-second results show is both obvious and illuminating. More intent on talking to a co-worker than to a paying customer, the clerk violates the cardinal me-story rule: she fails to accentuate the customer's "me." As might be expected, subjects' collective emotional response to the indifference displayed by the clerk was a huge thumbs-down.

To avoid those kinds of situations, what can companies do? Training all frontline personnel in how to read customers' faces is surely not financially feasible. But supervisors might be trained in top-level facial coding and sales associates could be shown customers' reactions to situations similar to those captured in the example just given in order to sensitize them to the impact their behavior can have on customers. Moreover, everyone on staff could benefit from emotional awareness training. Just to understand that customers want to tell their emotional me-story first, before they're ready to accept rational, operational support, could be helpful. Meanwhile, for those customer service representatives on the phone, identifying and thereby reacting quicker and better to customers' emotional states through the assessment of vocal intonation will improve outcomes (Fig. 8.6).

"Service is a feeling. Don't give any feelings to others you wouldn't want to feel."

—Jeffrey Gitomer

	Fear	Anger	Sadness	Happiness	Disgust
Pitch	High	High	Low	High	Low
Rate	Fast	Quiet	Slow	Varies	Slow
Range	Wide	Wide	Narrow	Wide	Wide
Articulation	Precise	Tense	Slurring	Normal	Normal

Fig. 8.6 Translating Vocal Intonations into Emotions

How customers speak reflects how they feel. This chart shows what certain speech patterns reveal about a customer's likely emotional state.

Reassurance:
proving oneself right

Synopsis: The topic here is providing ways to connect either with other consumers or with the company itself. As this section will first address, shopping is informed by consumers' instinct to belong. It's a social activity, a way to gain a sense of community. Second, shopping and service overlap in consumers' desire not to end up feeling like they bought foolishly. Consumers must feel like they have a supportive network to draw on for confirmation about their purchase decisions.

Key take-aways:

- Shopping smart involves proving to the tribe that one has the right to belong.

- Good customer service requires overcoming the fears of everyone involved.

Emotion and Motivations

The operative emotion here is **fear**. The risk of being off-the-mark, socially or financially, is rooted in consumers' desire to be ahead of the pack, but not so far ahead that they are in jeopardy. With customer service, consumers wonder whether company representatives will approach the discussion as friend or foe. The resulting motivations are to **bond**—to affirm one's identity vis-à-vis others—while still wanting to get the good deal that signifies superior ability to **acquire**.

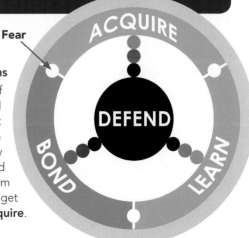

Honoring the Savvy Shopper
Shopping smart involves proving to the tribe that one has the right to belong.

Just as control and curiosity are central to the aspects of shopping already discussed, ability is the key to the remaining aspect. More specifically, ability covers two related yet slightly separate applications in regard to retail and e-tail. The first is that shoppers want to demonstrate their ability to navigate style—by being able to bolster their own unique identity while still being adept enough to fit in with their desired social groups. Second, shoppers also want to demonstrate their ability to secure goods on terms, including price, that give them a chance to practice and prove their "hunting" skills.

In terms of the five key positioning strategies outlined by Ander and Stern, the goal of being savvy, whether socially or financially, pertains to the two remaining options: *biggest* or *cheapest*. That's because wanting the biggest selection, for example, implies that shoppers have seen what's out there and won't be caught on the down-and-out, socially or stylistically. Wanting the cheapest deal? That's code for wanting the right offer at the right price from the right place.

Now let's look at how the twin abilities of knowing how to navigate style and securing good terms function in retail practice, starting with style in relation to wanting to belong. Why do group dynamics matter so much? Surely, the reason is that through affiliating with others, con-

Why do group dynamics matter so much?
Because through affiliating with others, we gain a sense of security.

sumers gain a sense of security (Pooler). So it should be no surprise that both retail and e-tail involve resolving shoppers' fears that they might be vulnerable and alone.

Of the two versions of shopping, brick-and-mortar has the traditional advantage of letting shoppers literally see for themselves how well they might be doing in terms of their purchases, making social acceptance more viable. In other words, they can look at their fellow shoppers in a store and observe for themselves the offers and styles in vogue and whether the stores they're frequenting attract the kind of people they aspire to associate with.

In that regard, stores with the biggest selections have at once both an advantage and disadvantage when it comes to satisfying a shopper's urge to belong. A large selection provides comfort. It implicitly tells the shopper: you're going to be wisely informed because you will have seen all the merchandise options. That's the advantage. But the disadvantage is that, in a marketplace where shoppers strive to feel special while also fitting in with their own unique groups, biggest can be socially empty. In effect, if everybody goes there, nobody goes there.

So, unless a store can also deliver on the social group shoppers want to identify with—in other words, the people option—it will miss out and default to being merely a pricing option. As a result, boutiques that

Additional Positioning Mixtures

Other formulas are possible, of course. For instance, biggest can combine with another of the positioning options—hottest—in a paradoxically smaller, yet ultra-trendy boutique type store that sifts through mountains of product, essentially performing the searching process for its customers. That type of approach can weaken a big box store's advantage because, when successful, the boutique only offers the socially or stylistically appropriate options for its devoted "tribe." Likewise, savvy could also involve a store with both the hottest and the easiest form of accessing merchandise, thus smart in terms of saving one's time. In the end, any store or website can satisfy most if not all of the major five positionings, thereby enhancing its odds of success so long as its identity and value proposition doesn't blur by trying to do too much.

address niche markets will often have an edge when it comes to fulfilling a shopper's desire for a sense of community.

Meanwhile, without any fellow shoppers in sight, e-tail has needed to be more imaginative in order to fulfill on the urge to belong. How has that been accomplished? The answer is in part by providing an ever increasing amount of personalized customization so that consumers feel acknowledged not just by name but also by their procedure and content preferences. The other part is that e-tail has taken the lead over brick-and-mortar retailers by allowing more opportunities for the co-creation of content. By enabling users to add content to a site, e-tailers create the possibility for consumers to feed off the additions of others, thereby building and experiencing community via the art of sharing.

Why is that approach so emotionally smart and so appealing to the savvy shopper? The answer is that websites are emotionally alive to the extent that consumers feel that the sites are responsive and are like a home base when they're looking to connect with others.

The old model was for companies to provide content as an assumed, fixed value. But in today's business climate, it's not the content but the context that matters. The abundance of choices now available in the marketplace makes *how* a particular offer is used, and by whom, far more important than what that offer actually is (Grantham). In other words, value isn't a given but, rather, is created in the eyes of the beholder during the transaction process.

Now that's all very good, you might say, but why should merchants bother addressing the urge to belong? Well, otherwise what's left to provide the savvy shopper other than going the cheapest route? In that case ensuring satisfaction becomes a matter of delivering bargains. And without any more emotional buy-in from customers than that, being the source of whatever's cheapest becomes a tough positioning for all but the largest and most disciplined of merchants.

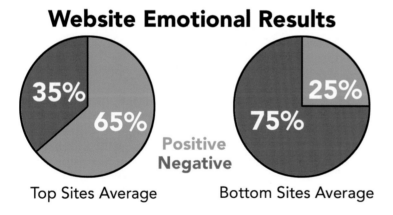

Website Emotional Results

35% 65%   Positive 25% 75%
                      Negative

Top Sites Average   Bottom Sites Average

Fig. 8.7 Surfing the Web for a Gnarly Page
This example shows the emotional results from some research Sensory Logic did for a financial services company looking to change the homepage of its website. Among the four options being considered, whether subjects could relate to the people portrayed on screen proved to be the biggest variable. But in rational terms that difference wasn't apparent. Individually, none of the possible choices had a positive verbal response below 60%. When we looked at the top two options averaged and the bottom two options averaged, however, it became clear that the rational responses given by the subjects didn't match up with the vast disparity in how they felt about the web pages and whether they had anything in common with the people being depicted there.

Establishing Better Customer Service
Good customer service requires overcoming the fears of everyone involved.

As it turns out, the fear that motivates shoppers to both fit in socially and secure bargains so they appear smart applies to customer service as well. At a basic level, customer service is really all about the fears of three different entities: the customer, the service representative and the company at large. Here's what that statement means, one entity at a time.

Why do people need customer service? Truth be told, customers actually try to avoid having to deal with customer service. In fact, they may not feel like the two words go together. After all, people usually go to customer service when they've run into problem situations in which they, the customers, feel like they haven't received real service or else have bought something that wasn't of value. The reason customers resort to customer service is almost always problem related and human nature is geared toward trying to avoid problems.

Meanwhile, customer service representatives are likely to be equally fearful. They know the people calling or coming in think they have made a mistake. They know that those seeking customer service are probably feeling nervous about not getting what they expected and are, therefore, worried about starting from an inferior position. So what do consumers do? They

As the look of ire on this customer service rep's face portrays, customer service at its most basic level is about fear.

For reps, it's fear of the customer.

For the customer, it's fear of the rep and the company at large.

over-compensate. They hide their fear through aggressive behavior and sometimes the nervous representative goes there first.

Likewise, customer service is something companies also seek to avoid. For companies, customer service isn't a profit center; it's a cost center. Thus the goal becomes containing the cost of customer service in order to protect profit margin. Most companies view it that way. They rarely, if ever, see customer service as an emotional opportunity to safeguard or even enhance value.

What's the way out of this destructive dynamic? Three major improvements can and should be made to demonstrate a company's ability to deliver satisfaction in terms of customer service.

First, *change hiring and retention practices.* It's hard for customers to feel well supported when the customer service departments they're interacting with suffer so much turnover that it seems as if nobody knows what anybody's doing. Fortunately, a solution exists. The employees most likely to be effective brand ambassadors already occupy other positions in the company. Internal transfers will work out best for two reasons: internal people already know the company and, as veterans, they will also be more invested in its performance. Yes, staffing at least some positions with veterans instead of rookies will cost more. And the same is true of doing more to retain good employees. But the company will come out ahead in the long run, especially if it fills customer service positions with employees chosen for the job because they demonstrate an active interest in connecting with customers emotionally.

Think customer service isn't viewed as a monetary black hole by companies? Notice the similarities between the two operations pictured here...

Second, *make customer "satisfaction" surveys more meaningful and insightful.* While the typical surveys may measure the more rationally oriented, functional aspects of customer service, they are woefully inadequate at gauging the emotionally charged me-story aspects of the customer service relationship. A decent half-step solution would be something like Gallup has done, shifting to more emotionally-oriented satisfaction survey questions (Applebaum). Even better would be to occasionally tap the emotional wells of customers using a more innately emotional tool like facial coding. If that's not going to be funded, at least make sure the first question asked addresses the issue or problem most customers would have so they can quickly have their say. (A short, short, short form that's *easy* works best.)

Finally, *rethink customer service to see it as a valuable offer in its own right.* Bolstered by knowledgeable, committed employees and research that really grasps the situation, customer service departments would be better able to proactively design and deliver superior service experiences. The financial benefit is real. After all, research suggests that great customer service enables companies to enjoy a 10% growth in their annual profit rates, in contrast to only 1% for those with merely adequate service (Desatnick).

Great customer service adds value to consumer purchases. Every understanding and on-emotion solution ultimately improves the company's bottom line through greater customer loyalty.

There's no reason why the goal couldn't be to make customers who experienced customer service happier than those who did not. To that end, the question becomes: what does great service look like? Here are three examples by which to answer that question.

The first example involves Amazon.com, which treats customer service more like a research and development lab (Fishman). Every customer contact, i.e., complaint, is monitored as another opportunity for improvement. In fact, one team does nothing but anticipate problems and develop solutions while other service department members are part of every new launch.

A second example is that niche businesses are emerging out of the service problems that larger "soft-goods" retailers haven't been able to solve. These home-based businesses lure away the upscale merchants' most profitable customers simply by offering stellar, high-touch service through direct sales. For example, former personal shoppers at upscale department stores are now helping former department store clientele buy clothes by showcasing lines of merchandise in non-retail settings. A hallmark of this kind of service is that consultants track purchases and know style, color and size preferences, sometimes even delivering new items to a client's home "on approval." This kind of attention and emotionally satisfying service have helped direct sales grow 79% during the past decade (Kaplan).

Finally, a third example is the retail model offered by Apple, recently chosen by the readers of *DDI* magazine as retailer of the year (not bad for a company with zero retail presence half a decade ago). Yes, the ethereal white décor makes the merchandise seem heaven-sent. But the real stroke of brilliance was transforming the customer service desk into a "genius bar," which casts the entire issue of customer problems in a more positive light (Sway).

"What companies really need to measure is emotional attachment —their real bond with customers."

—Paul Wigham
former CMO, Wal-Mart

Conclusion

The psychological reality of shopping and customer service is that the "average" consumer doesn't exist. Each consumer's plea is always: understand me. To be effective, retailers, e-tailers and customer service providers must accomplish the following:

- Create easier access. Emotionally, the key is to welcome people.

- Reward curiosity. Connect with consumers through engaging atmospherics and empathetic interactivity so as to provide delight.

- Provide support. Help consumers feel secure by connecting them to their fellow shoppers or "super agent" service veterans.

An Action Plan

To ensure that the retail, e-tail and customer service experiences delivered to consumers are emotionally healthy, here are a few things to check when assessing emotional effectiveness:

- ☐ Develop a strategy to increase shoppers' average lengths of stay in the company's stores or on its website (without frustrating them). To that end, try to separate shoppers' emotional experiences from their utility-driven activities of looking for what they came for. The more a positive emotional experience predominates, the more likely they will add purchases to the list with which they started.

- ☐ Prepare the store or site for different kinds of visitors. In doing so, provide a variety of emotional hooks for the target market. What are the shoppers after? Is it quality? Price? A deal? The satisfaction of comparison shopping to prove they're savvy? Have something for every key profile.

- ☐ Focus on the shoppers' emotional experiences when they interact with the company and seek to remove or alleviate the barriers and frustrations they experience. Specifically, make it a priority to identify and remove barriers that elicit strong negative emotional responses. Similarly, watch out for service occasions in which customers feel as though they're being led or pushed through a series of activities. If customers react negatively, a company should change what it's doing.

- ☐ Do an emotional profile of both the offer and customer service experience to ensure they align. Ideally, service should be integrated into the offer and isn't merely tacked on.

- ☐ Make sure the service is no-fault to avoid evoking emotions such as fear and anger. Always remember that the optimal outcome is that both the person giving service and the person receiving service feel like winners. To that end, the service should be real and involve genuine concern about the outcome for the customer.

PART **TH3EE**

WorkplaceApplications

9 leadership

The company's "us" is composed of employees who bet their livelihoods on the idea that the house (the company) will win and enrich them also. A great leader has the qualities of a winner willing to share the glory.

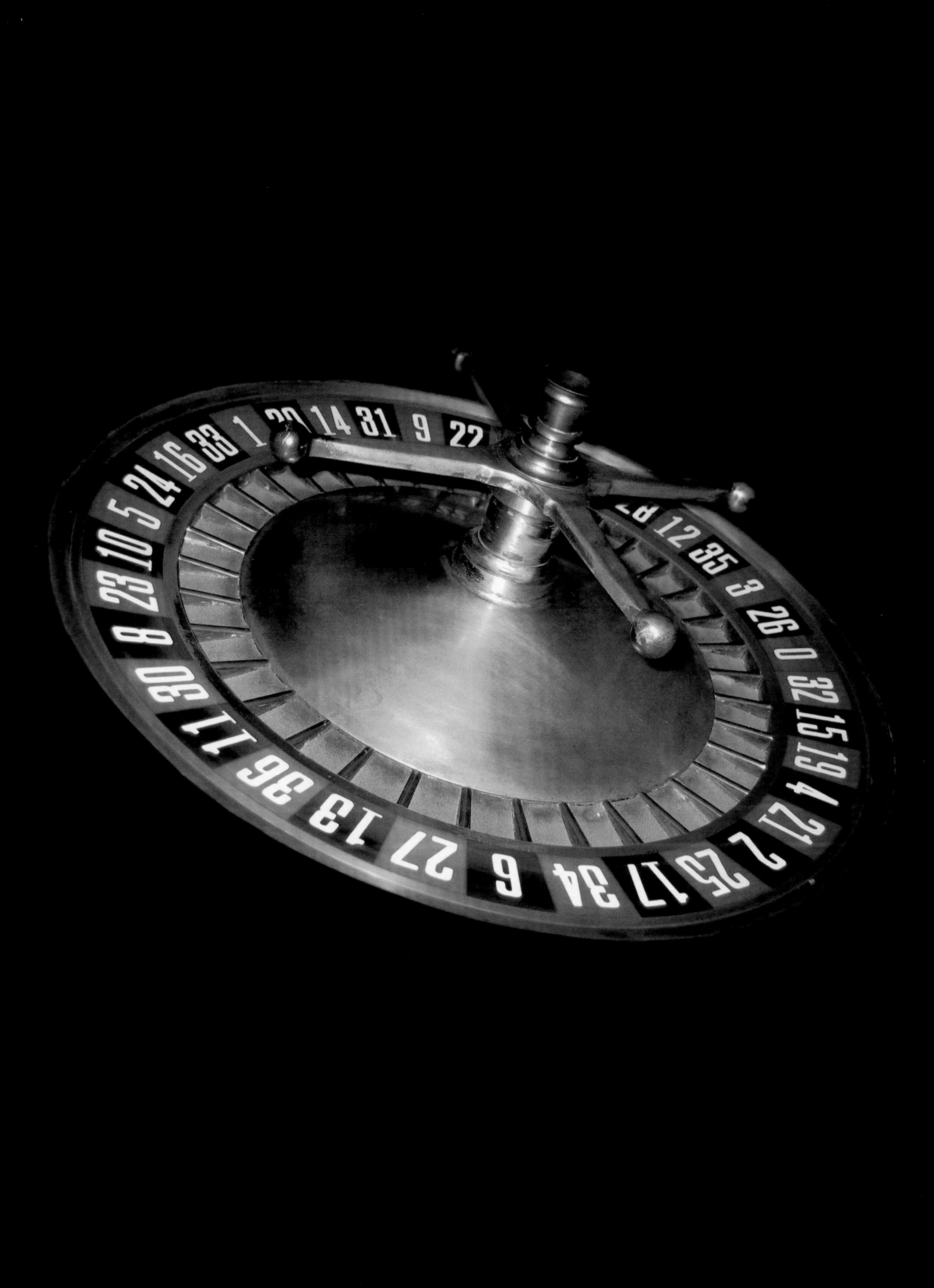

OVERVIEW

When *The Wall Street Journal* runs extensive, front-page coverage about executives exercising stock options on dates that "luckily" lead to windfall personal profits (Forelle), you can bet that people notice. And they take special notice of cases like that of one executive, whose chances of having such fortuitous timing in exercising his options year after year was calculated by the newspaper's analyst to be *one* in 300 billion. Was it "blind luck," as the executive said (before resigning)? There's reason to doubt it, thereby reducing trust and making leadership a tougher, more urgent task. To help executives connect emotionally with employees, this chapter will focus on:

- **The Greater Good:** In joining an "us," employees don't surrender their "me." Instead, they subsume it, believing that the greater "us" will feed the "me." Therefore, company leaders should ideally be able to establish themselves not only as credible but also unselfish, someone who looks out for the group. That profile gives followers faith that, at the end of the day, there will be something left for them and, indeed, more than they could attain on their own.

- **Clear Vision:** There is a profound difference between leadership that looks ahead versus leadership that simply manages the status quo. As Peter Drucker notes, "Every product and every activity of a business begins to obsolesce as soon as it is started." Therefore, successful leaders have clear visions of the future and respond to change by providing direction in accordance with those visions. Moreover, because the inevitable need for change can be so traumatic to followers, leaders must also have the ability to paint a convincing picture of the future and, in doing so, motivate employees by preparing them for what's coming down the line.

- **Cohesive Culture:** To offset the risk of isolation, successful leaders not only read the situation around them in emotional terms, they also foster a cohesive culture in which employees feel invited to participate and collaborate. To that end, they seek to surround themselves with talent: people as smart or smarter than themselves (both rationally and emotionally), who will be recognized for their abilities and promoted for their good work. The outcome is that the workplace becomes less stressful and more relaxed, with all parts working in sync.

Now let's look more closely at how leadership conveys both competency and caring, starting with how best to demonstrate a sense of togetherness.

The Greater Good:
why character matters

Synopsis: The key here is ensuring that the company's workforce views senior management as worth having faith in and, in best-case scenarios, even magnanimous and generous of spirit. In this section, we'll address how the CEO's character, as communicated to others, will determine the extent of employees' trust and commitment. Specifics to be examined include: first, the need to close the emotional gap between leaders and followers to compensate for the financial gap between them; and second, how the emotions displayed on leaders' faces reveal their core personality traits.

Key take-aways:

- Pay disparities require leaders with emotional savvy to offset the disconnect.
- Trust is based on a leader's honesty and generally pleasing emotional profile.
- In a complex, busy world, projected emotions are rightly taken as substance.

Getting People to Follow
Pay disparities require leaders with emotional savvy to offset the disconnect.

Whether it's political, religious or corporate leadership, the emotional dynamics of being in charge don't change very much. People will become ardent, true followers to the extent that they believe it's safe to do so; that victory is possible, if not outright imminent; and that they will get to share in the

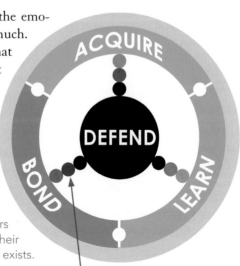

Emotion and Motivations

Alarm, the feeling associated with the risk of imminent danger, is a plausible response to knowing that a powerful leader could choose to act in his or her own interest. Employees see the leadership as embodied by the CEO, so there's an instinctive desire to identify and **bond** with that leader. At the same time, however, people commit their careers and livelihoods to the company, so an instinct to **defend** their own interests also exists.

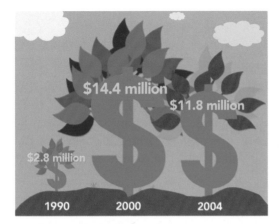

$14.4 million

$11.8 million

$2.8 million

1990   2000   2004

Fig. 9.1 Average CEO Compensation Chart
$27,000. That's what the average worker made in 1990—and what they still make today (adjusted for inflation). But CEO compensation over that same period has been 100 to 400 times higher (Lebaton).

accomplishment and the rewards that come with success. Then a "me" will join the "us" and do so willingly—without coercion, without doubt, without questioning—because that person has forged an emotional bond and made an emotional commitment.

Unfortunately, creating a top-down "us" in the business world has become harder than ever because of two major trends.

The first involves the spotlight CEOs occupy and their related rise in pay. Until the wave of Enron-style scandals somewhat blunted this trend, the leadership type in ascendancy was the superstar CEO who, possessing the stature and political acumen to woo and wow Wall Street analysts, as well as the business media, could keep the all-important stock price from flagging (Khurana). In contrast, the understated, behind-the-scenes leadership celebrated in Jim Collin's best seller *Good to Great* had begun to seem old-fashioned.

The counter-response to the scandals and the whole celebrity CEO phenomenon has been a re-emphasis on the brass-tacks executive at the expense of "the golden child." But either way, the dividend-focused business world has driven compensation to unprecedented levels, putting leaders on an economic plateau far removed from those they lead.

What has the general response been? With recent surveys showing that 90% of institutional investors believe that executives at most U.S. companies are overpaid ("Most"), one can imagine how lower-ranking employees feel. Warren Buffett may not be speaking only for himself when he said: "Too often executive compensation in the U.S. is ridiculously out of line with performance" (Miller). Given the disparities in compensation, how can employees (and investors) not be inclined to feel suspicion and envy—even outrage—as the corner office continues to surpass the cubicle set by ever-widening margins?

Research indicates that in countries with pronounced income spreads, the inequality correlates to lower life expectancy rates, since such stark contrasts introduce stress into people's lives (Klein). In short, envy is divisive. What's the risk being taken by CEOs who have economically distanced themselves too much from the pay scale their average employee can relate to or accept? They've put their ability to forge an internal, emotional "us" in jeopardy.

Even worse is the second trend, the ongoing wave of downsizing, outsourcing and other "adjustments" like the demise of pension plans. In addition to widening the already-mentioned economic divide between top leaders and employees, these moves undermine employees' sense of security and well-being. To cite one figure, it's been estimated that over 10% of all the jobs in America are at risk of being outsourced (Bardhan; Center).

Former GE CEO Jack Welch knew that emotions were a key part of running an innovative and profitable organization. The subtitle of his book affirms this perspective.

Taken together, the two trends endanger the likelihood that employees will see their leaders as invested in a shared outcome and put additional pressure on the leadership to establish an emotionally solvent, personal connection with employees. In other words, the degree to which leaders are economically divorced from their workers places a premium on having the emotional savvy to offset the disconnect.

Therefore, to overcome perceptions of selfish indifference and get people to be emotionally on-board as followers, CEOs and senior leadership in general will have to add another dimension to the four leadership "E's" spelled out by GE's former CEO Jack Welch. What are Welch's four "Es?" They consist of having a competitive *Edge*, being a good *Executor* and being *Energetic* while *Energizing* others (Byrne). What's the new, fifth "E"? *Emotional* intelligence: a competency that two studies by the training firm Hay/McBer have confirmed to be what successful leaders have most in common (Goleman 2000).

Aided by *Emotional Intelligence* author Daniel Goleman, Hay/McBer analyzed the key characteristics that distinguish adroit leaders. What did they find? First, in a study of executives at 15 global companies, only one cognitive, intellectual skill proved to be a good barometer of success: the ability to sift through the big picture for patterns. *All* of the other core competencies involved emotionally-based skills and characteristics like collaboration, political acumen and resiliency.

Meanwhile, in a related study that looked at executives at IBM, Coca-Cola and Pepsico, those people with a high degree of emotional competencies were in the top third of management, as reflected in salary bonuses

"Leadership isn't something you do writing memos, you've got to appeal to people's emotions. They've got to buy in with their hearts and bellies, not just their minds."

—Lou Gerstner
former CEO, IBM

for performance. So pervasive was the profile that it held true in more than 80% of the various divisions within those companies.

Maybe former IBM CEO Lou Gerstner was part of the second study. Even if he wasn't, he clearly appreciates the value of emotions, given his remark that "Leadership isn't something you do writing memos, you've got to appeal to people's emotions. They've got to buy in with their hearts and bellies, not just their minds." In summary, effective leadership depends on getting people emotionally on-board.

The Importance of Hiring Right
Trust is based on a leader's honesty and generally pleasing emotional profile.

What's the message of the Hay/McBer research results? It's that people skills matter. They're not "soft," though they're definitely emotional. Instead, they help a leader to connect with others—not through using emotions to manipulate perceptions, but by using emotional intelligence to understand where people are "coming from."

Corporate Board Member magazine has editorialized, based on Deep Throat's famous advice, "Follow the money," that CEOs should spend 40% of their time on investor relations (Khurana). But the audience that will help make the company's profitability actually possible is the internal "us" of managers and rank-and-file employees, who must be emotionally energized to care.

What specific kinds of emotion-based traits should CEOs have? In perhaps the seminal study in this field, the leadership experts Kouzes and Posner engaged in research involving over 400 case studies and 75,000 people worldwide. What's their conclusion?

The key qualities people value in their leaders are, in order of importance: honesty, being forward-looking and inspiring.

Why is honesty the preeminent attribute employees wish to see in leaders? Employees naturally want to know where a leader stands. So they'll ask themselves, "Can so-and-so be trusted to look out for my security?" This question emerges from survival instincts because, as followers, they rely on a leader's ability to enhance their odds of staying alive and thriving (thus avoiding alarm).

It seems then that a company seeking to hire a leader with whom employees will appropriately bond will look for, among other things, an honest, forward-looking and inspiring person. The large stakes involved in hiring the right person for leadership positions are more evident than ever given the litany of CEOs who have gone from pinstripes to prison stripes. For years now, *Fortune* 500 companies and other small firms have been relying on verbally-based methods, including the excellent but expensive Hogan Assessment Systems survey, to probe the inner emotions of candidates for the job in order to secure the best one (O'Donnell).

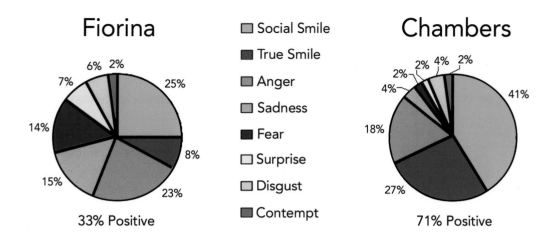

Fig. 9.2 CEO Composure Comparison
We analyzed videotaped interviews of high powered CEOs John Chambers and Carly Fiorina. Over a quarter of Chamber's facial activity involved true smiles—a phenomenally high percentage. In comparison, Fiorina vacillated between social smiles, anger, sadness and fear.

Sensing the importance of a CEO's emotional profile, but looking for a new approach to measure it, an investment firm approached Sensory Logic a couple of years ago with a theory: the personality of the CEO affects the corporate culture, which in turn drives stock performance. Based on this theory, the firm wished to use facial coding as a supplementary means of assessing which companies to invest in. In other words, they were banking on facial coding to help them gauge a CEO's emotional make-up, thereby giving them an edge in identifying sound investing opportunities.

Our first assignment was to analyze the facial expressions of then current Hewlett-Packard CEO Carly Fiorina and Cisco CEO John Chambers. What emerged? Chambers lived up to his billing as "Mr. Sunshine." With expressions indicating a high degree of positive emotion, he was genuinely upbeat and conciliatory. In contrast, Fiorina's expressions indicated largely negative emotions, betraying the signs of a person already under siege. In a world where emotional competency matters, she rubbed a lot of people the wrong way, and presided over a 50% drop in the price of HP's stock during her six years at the helm. (See Figure 9.2 for the comparison.)

The investment firm had its own proprietary system of determining which leaders to support based on eight key traits, with honesty getting a double weight. Emphasizing honesty makes sense for investors assessing a leader, as well as for employees. For most of us in life, honesty comes first: if we don't believe we will get something at least approaching our fair share, then the odds of our hanging in there—emotionally, and not just physically as merely another "warm body" at work—will decline severely.

Related to honesty, Sensory Logic also conducted another, separate study in which we looked at the responses of employees whose companies had recently undergone dramatic organizational changes, such as a merger or acquisition. In that case, we asked among other questions: did em-

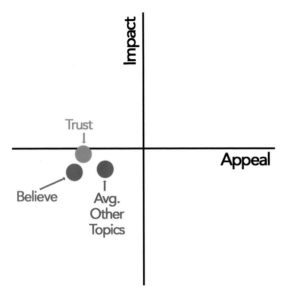

Fig. 9.3 Employees Not On-board
The two questions that revealed the emotional concerns of employees amid change most clearly were, "How much do you now trust the leaders of your company?" and "How much do you believe what you've heard from the company about the change your company recently experienced?" Our research revealed that faith had been broken, imperiling the "we" culture necessary for success.

ployees trust their leaders, and did they believe what their leaders had told them about the changes?

What did our results uncover? (See Figure 9.3 for details.) When subjects were asked the belief question, anxiety in the facial coding activity reached the highest level in the study: 22%. That's illuminating and here's why. Anxiety signals fear and, along with surprise, fear makes up the alarm employees are likely to feel when confronted with reminders that their leaders are powerful enough to brush their concerns aside. Put another way, change may bring with it concern, even suspicion, about whether one's leader will be a faithful guide during the struggle ahead.

In It for the Long Haul
In a complex, busy world, projected emotions are rightly taken as substance.

The investment firm's approach of wanting to analyze emotions through facial expressions was smart. And their emphasis on traits when assessing good leadership was astute.

After all, personality, traits and emotions are closely related concepts (Howard 2000). Personality refers to the set of predictable behaviors by which others recognize us as ourselves. These specific behaviors are often called traits. Repeated, commonly shown emotions are, in turn, a means of assessing traits, which is why, for example, we say so-and-so is a "hot head" when he or she gets angry quickly and often. How do we know that person is angry? The answer is in no small part because of facial muscle activity that reflects and communicates our feelings.

Since the core of an emotion is readiness to act, analyzing a person using facial coding can provide a means of gauging both their core personality and related behavioral tendencies. To that end, I looked at the exhibited personalities of Ken Lay and Martha Stewart for *Fast Company* (McGregor), picking up on the contempt both showed for the proceedings and the fear displayed by Lay. I also critiqued the 2004 presidential debates for *The New York Times* (Tierney), National Public Radio (Feldman) and *BusinessWeek.com* (Dunham) in order to better understand how the public might respond to George W. Bush's smiling smirks and John Kerry's deadpan expressions.

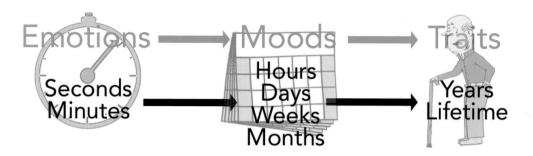

Fig. 9.4 Creation of Personality Traits Over Time
What are traits? They're actually emotions embodied over the long term and, like beliefs, represent the influence of emotions at their most sustained level.

What's the bottom line here? Executives shouldn't underestimate the value of facial expressions in helping them understand how audiences will respond to them. One CEO who understood this value had Sensory Logic review three of his public appearances: two consecutive annual meeting addresses to employees and a one-on-one interview at a business club function. Notable were three findings:

- During the annual meetings, this CEO only showed codeable activity every other minute while on camera: a relatively low degree of expressiveness. In the more intimate club setting, however, the CEO opened up and was more expressive. The implication? The CEO was likely to make a stronger emotional connection with workers in venues like breakfast meetings or smaller, department-size sessions where he might convey his feelings more vividly.

- Previous coaching to encourage this CEO to deliver his message in a more upbeat style was succeeding. The latest employee meeting data was far more positive than the earlier one. The implication? Without undercutting a CEO's integrity, it's possible to train leaders to improve their body language and, thereby, convey more warmth and hope.

- Overall, this CEO was sending mixed signals. The good news was that a complete absence of skepticism verified his authenticity (he never used a social smile to mask a negative comment). His expressions of frustration were also authentic and understandable due to slower than anticipated implementation of new initiatives. The bad news? This CEO could be undercutting his goals by displaying contempt, an emotion that employees could interpret as an inability to please him. The implication? In situations where a positive outcome seems remote, human nature is to give up—thereby robbing companies of the effort they need from employees in order to cope with a changing, competitive marketplace.

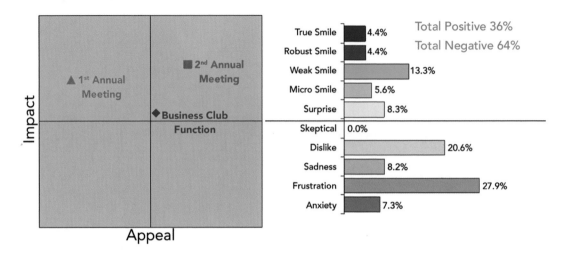

Fig. 9.5 Analysis of CEO's Emotional Display
The left chart shows that the second annual meeting had the most positive result. The right chart shows the average emotions shown by the CEO across three public appearances and defines trouble spots: most of the positive emotion is from less lively forms of smiling, while dislike (including contempt) is prevalent enough to be possibly off-putting to employees.

In the end, leaders aren't leaders just by title or power alone. They must have followers who pledge their loyalty, talent and energy based on the belief that they'll get something back. Therefore, a CEO must protect his or her credibility above all else, because people expect to believe their leaders and want to feel that their leaders care about them. People follow people they like and, without being deemed trustworthy, the probability that employees will truly like an executive and strive on behalf of achieving success for the greater good is close to zero.

"Change is fundamentally about feelings. The new management paradigm says that managing people is managing feelings. The issue isn't whether or not people have 'negative' emotions; it's how to deal with them."

—Jeanie Daniel Druck

Clear Vision:
forward thinking and feeling

Synopsis: The next key criterion for success is reassuring employees that they will be protected by astute, decisive leadership that knows how to keep the company not just abreast but ahead of the curve. Here, the CEO's strategic instincts—as communicated to others—will determine the extent of employees' confidence and support. In this section, we'll analyze how executives must negate stress and reach out to employees in times of change so that their visions are realized rather than resisted.

Key take-aways:

- Looking ahead is about providing hope while also alleviating fear.
- Amid change, leaders must negate the stress that causes productivity to implode.
- Change is aided by identifying and understanding the resistance involved.
- The emotional dynamics should be factored into change management planning.

Aspirations Lead to Inspiration
Looking ahead is about providing hope while also alleviating fear.

Why should the quality of being forward-looking or visionary come in second overall, behind honesty, in Kouzes and Posner's leadership survey results? George Bush (the elder) half-dismissively called this quality "the vision thing," trying to escape comparisons to the Reagan Revolution. So why is it something employees prize? And why might an executive's being forward-looking translate into feelings of confidence in employees?

Emotion and Motivations

A vision for change that affirms for employees that new opportunities are plausibly attainable can inspire **pride**. Given an understanding of why the change is necessary and how it can be reached, employees will want to **learn** more in order to **acquire** wealth and prestige. Of course, the downside is that change enforced without inspiring pride will battle with fear and perhaps lose.

In most basic terms, the answer is at least hinted at by how our brains are hardwired through evolution. Being visionary, forward looking, physically tall and, therefore, *literally* able to see better than others: again, the logical and the biological come together. After all, what would have forward-looking literally meant on the ancient grasslands? What physical characteristic might have been helpful out on the savannah many thousands of years ago? Could it possibly have been being tall so that one could see farther across the horizon—a helpful attribute for hunting wild animals and spotting approaching danger? Couldn't there be something to the joke that diversity in senior management often consists of including a short white guy?

In other words, are we really so sophisticated and advanced as a society? Or is it that we've just held onto that physical attribute—height—as a proxy for another equally desirable quality in our leaders: the ability to envision (see) and enact a better future for all?

Less than 15% of all men in the United States are six feet tall or taller, but in *Fortune* 500 companies 58% of all male CEOs are six feet tall or taller. Even outside the executive suite, each inch of height correlates to $789 more per year in salary (Gladwell).

Instinct suggests that deep down, subconsciously, the first answer is "no" because the second answer is "yes." Height and strength: these are correlatives that indicate the ability to win the battle for resources. That's the game. And it is profoundly emotional in nature for two reasons.

First, a visionary executive who gives employees a cause that distinguishes them from others provides the opportunity for both hope and pride. Many of a company's best workers will be explorers by nature, eager to conquer new lands. Second, being given a sense of direction by such an executive soothes anxiety and brings relief to all employees, who can then focus and get excited about the possibilities ahead.

Nobody saw more clearly the need for executives to be forward looking than the legendary Drucker, who urged companies to embrace "creative destruction" since "today's certainties always become tomorrow's absurdities." Embracing that same spirit is Samsung's CEO Kun-Hee Lee. Yes, he may not be literally tall. But Lee is a giant when it comes to being visionary, having transformed Samsung into the world's fastest growing brand during the past half decade by emphasizing the need to spark people's emotions with elegant, human-centered design (Breen).

Vision, then, is part of being a true leader. But a successful leader must also make vision translate into action by being able to convincingly communicate what direction is being taken and why in order to get employees emotionally on-board. Followers have to accept emotionally, not merely rationally, that it is in their best interest to join in an endeavor. Because the immediate reality of change is often quite negative, the reasons given to accept the change must alleviate concerns and provide relief. Otherwise a sense of hopelessness and toxic fear sets in for employees, a scenario executives must strive to avoid.

Leadership Amid a M&A or Major Reorganization

Amid change, leaders must negate the stress that causes productivity to implode.

Effective leadership is a visionary and process-oriented combination: executives focus on what will be, while their managers receive guidance in order to handle what is. But as statistics show, in times of great organizational change, that combination will get derailed if employee emotions are not also recognized and handled adroitly. Amid change, boosting employee pride is vital because the emotional alternative—engendering fear—is so destructive to a company's productivity and, therefore, ultimately its profitability. It's a causal chain that starts with the announcement (or, usually first, rumor) of change, followed by anxiety, stress and a slump in productivity.

To understand why the sequence gathers such momentum, let's look more closely at how change, fear and business results correlate. The two yardsticks will be physical and financial in nature, starting with the physical.

Boosting employee pride is vital because the emotional alternative of fear destroys productivity and profitability.

As biologically monitored, how does the experience of change affect the body? The technical answer is that people's heart rates, blood sugar levels and cortisol hormone levels all shoot up (Boyatzis 2006). Meanwhile, the underlying, psychological answer is that this trio of physical changes indicates that changes in a person's (work) environment causes the body to go into overdrive in order to cope with adversity. Given that this trio of physical changes corresponds exactly to those that have been measured when people experience the emotion of fear, no wonder the estimate is that only 25% of employees willingly accept change (Bill).

Yes, in the short term those physical adaptations make peak performance possible. They're nature's way of helping people rise to the occasion. But typically organizational changes take time to unfold, and in the process the very same biological tricks-of-the-trade that make peak performance possible start to undo it. For instance, over time high cortisol levels prove to be toxic and capable of dulling the mind's receptive capacity.

In short, biology helps, then hurts. Anxiety starts to eat people up, as lingering change proves to be a major physiological and psychological, body/mind distraction that lowers employee productivity.

Now for the financial yardstick to bring that point home. For starters, let's note that fear is powerful enough that no amount of corporate planning has ever proven equal to that emotion. It's been estimated that organizational change can cause a decline in work productivity *at levels approaching 75%* (Childre). More specifically in regard to financial outcomes, the dismal track record for merger and acquisition activity can be found by examining Figure 9.6 (Carleton).

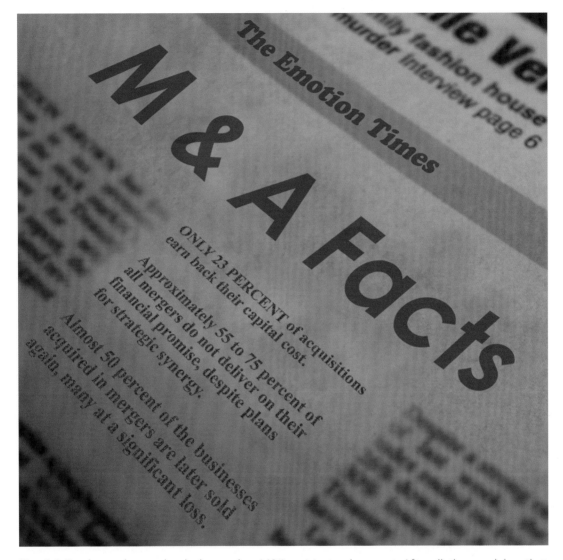

The Emotion Times

M & A Facts

ONLY 23 PERCENT of acquisitions earn back their capital cost.

Approximately 55 to 75 percent of all mergers do not deliver on their financial promise, despite plans for strategic synergy.

Almost 50 percent of the businesses acquired in mergers are later sold again, many at a significant loss.

Fig. 9.6 For those who put the deals together, M&A activity can be sweet. After all, the pendulum that swings between advocating "synergy" or a "pure play" to undo a failure involves heavy commissions. But for the employees of the affected companies, dread not glee is the far more common emotional response.

Obviously, something other than pure rationality drives executives to initiate mergers and acquisitions given such poor success rates. The answer is that CEOs are under pressure to show rising stock prices, and that the emotionally-driven concern of swallowing to avoid being swallowed by another company runs strong (Ravindran).

But how does it feel to be an employee amid change, even change as relatively simple as an internal re-structuring? The emotional reality: it's scary. Fear replaces happiness, which can be in short supply as change causes concern about who will win and survive and who will lose and go under.

Think of the movie *Jaws*, specifically the scene in which the mayor urges residents and tourists alike to get back into the water because "It's safe." Nobody leaves the shore. Inherent to any significant change in any company is a signal to employees that there's a corporate shark circling, with the likelihood of *blood in the water* imminent. All employees will feel emotionally and perhaps even physically vulnerable—given the stress involved—because it's easy for them to imagine that the blood could be their own.

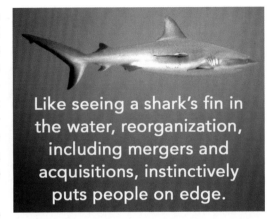

Like seeing a shark's fin in the water, reorganization, including mergers and acquisitions, instinctively puts people on edge.

To avoid company-wide paralysis, executives must take the lead to quell the fear that sets the causal chain of fear leading to lost productivity in motion. Moreover, they must do so as quickly as possible—before the physical toll of stress so saps the workforce that a corresponding decline in the company's financial performance follows.

Employee Response to Change
Change is aided by identifying and understanding the resistance involved.

Curious to follow up on the estimate that only about 25% of employees willingly accept change, Sensory Logic studied the emotional response of employees at companies amid dramatic organizational changes and found the estimate to be, if anything, a little too optimistic based on our research findings.

Among other questions, we asked, "What degree of resistance do you expect leadership to face from remaining employees?" The subjects gave the issue a verbal rating that tied for the most positive, which would indicate little resistance. But the emotional acceptance tied for second lowest in the study. In other words, a large say/feel gap was exposed—with what employees said versus felt being dramatically different (Fig. 9.8).

Combining the acceptance estimate of 25% with our own results of 14%, it's no surprise that the number of organizational transformations that work is no higher than 30% (Carr). With such a low success rate, a new approach must be found.

The place to start is by establishing a firm understanding of why people emotionally resist organizational change. Figure 9.7 details seven reasons why employees become emotionally resistant to change in the workplace. A tool like facial coding could be a crucial advantage in situations where leaders are trying to identify and understand the nature and depth of the resistance they might be encountering in their efforts to move the company forward.

As part of that analysis, it's worth remembering that there are really four types of workers. First up are the winners—those employees most likely to benefit from organizational change and

Fig. 9.7 The Seven Reasons Behind Emotional Resistance
One or more of these reasons may come into play for employees actively or passive-aggressively resisting a change brought about by a company's senior management (Jarrett).

7 reasons for emotional resistance

Insecurity
Economic concern about job security is obviously the place to start. People wonder if they will be able to make ends meet. They feel vulnerable and, therefore, anxious about entering the unknown.

Powerlessness
Not only does change bring chaos, it also can create or reinforce the realization in employees that they lack control. Their influence may wane or the access they previously enjoyed to somebody with power may go away. In large scale change, the events are bigger than the people involved and may cause them to retreat or otherwise collapse in on themselves.

Dread
Somewhere deep in the psyche in response to organizational change is dread. It comes in response to knowing that the final change in life is death. Being reminded of the ephemeral nature of existence generates some of the subtlest and yet most profound anxiety in employees during a time of company change.

Betrayal
Employees have emotionally formed a pact with the status quo, sometimes fully, sometimes half-heartedly. But at whatever level, they feel attached to the familiar. Now they may say to themselves, "I didn't ask for this. I thought things were going so well. Who let us down?"

Exhaustion
Change requires effort, and especially when sapped by the nerves of waiting for "the other shoe to drop" any extra push might be hard to give. Expending energy to understand and adjust, first to the disruption and loss of comfort, then to the new, simply isn't welcome.

Defeat
Bad news falls on deaf ears as survival instincts will tend to shut it out. Employees may feel as if the change is a result of failure, theirs or the company's, with the stigma of losing attached. The sentiment: "We had to do this because we're not good enough."

Injustice
With most change, there are clear winners and losers. Given human nature, employees may feel passing sorrow for unknown "losers" while being consumed by jealously for the winners. Grievances will grow if employees don't perceive much of an advantage for them personally.

Resistance of Remaining Employees

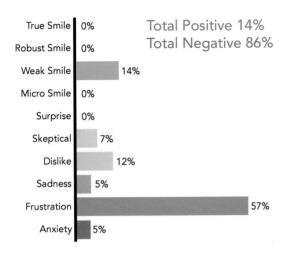

True Smile	0%
Robust Smile	0%
Weak Smile	14%
Micro Smile	0%
Surprise	0%
Skeptical	7%
Dislike	12%
Sadness	5%
Frustration	57%
Anxiety	5%

Total Positive 14%
Total Negative 86%

Fig. 9.8 Employee Emotional Resistance
Given that these emotions were elicited from employees in response to a question about the degree of resistance leaders should expect from remaining employees, things certainly could have looked better for senior management. Clearly, people have a tendency to dig in their heels when confronted by change.

to feel pride at the prospect of an enhanced company identity—for whom some of those seven reasons may come into play. But those reasons will be felt far more strongly by other employees. In addition to the winners, there are three other defacto worker groups that emerge during change:

- **The Switchers:** These high-achievers can readily go elsewhere and may not have the patience for the turmoil and paralysis that comes with change—especially if this change seems wrong-headed to them.

- **The Survivors:** Employees who will do anything to hold on, for reasons varying from trying to protect a pension to lacking the energy or talent to go elsewhere.

- **The Losers:** Those badly affected by the change may turn into the walking dead because of a loss of hope combined with increased fear or even anger. They can harm the winners, motivate the switchers to go and make the survivors even more bitter. Therefore, this group must be removed from the company ranks as quickly as possible to avoid infecting others with their negativity.

Proactive Executive Response
The emotional dynamics should be factored into change management planning.

To bring about progress during major organizational change, executives must plan in financial, legal, operational *and* emotional terms. Now, including the last part might seem obvious. But during the planning stage prior to implementation, the odds are that companies locked in rational mindsets will not have devoted much time or thought to the emotional dynamics of change.

In part, that's because of lacking enough time to do it all. But in all honesty there are other factors involved, too. For one thing, outside resources like lawyers and consultants aren't likely to have a good feel for the company's internal dynamics. For another, neither they nor senior management may have much aptitude or stomach to contemplate in human terms the possibly wrenching changes involved.

As a result, a company's senior management may focus on the logistics of change and be blind to the human dimension and inevitable emotional fallout that accompanies the announcement of a merger, acquisition or reorganization. Furthermore, as noted by Carey and Ogden in *The Human Side of M+A*, not only are these transactions often done in haste, they are also done "without the required know-how to assess the people and to get a clear window into the organization."

Focusing only on the logistical issues of a merger or acquisition can cause the human element to remain blurred in the background.

Given the likelihood—even certainty—of employees giving lip service answers to survey questions related to change, facial coding can be of decisive help. In Sensory Logic's study of the emotional response of employees in companies amid dramatic organizational changes, we knew that one key to assessing employee response would be determining if their feelings of being part of a winning team surpassed the uncertainty that comes with the change.

What's the good news here? The employees we studied had a sense of being victorious and proud amid change, which overshadowed the ambiguity of the situation. When asked, "Does the change feel like a win, loss or draw for your company?" the subjects showed a 30% higher degree of positive response than they had to the question: "Has the uncertainty that came with change bothered you?" (Fig. 9.9). In contrast, the verbal self-report ratings responses for the two questions were a tie.

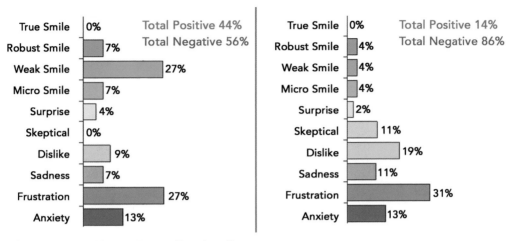

Change as Win, Loss or Draw

True Smile	0%
Robust Smile	7%
Weak Smile	27%
Micro Smile	7%
Surprise	4%
Skeptical	0%
Dislike	9%
Sadness	7%
Frustration	27%
Anxiety	13%

Total Positive 44%
Total Negative 56%

Uncertainty of Change Bothersome

True Smile	0%
Robust Smile	4%
Weak Smile	4%
Micro Smile	4%
Surprise	2%
Skeptical	11%
Dislike	19%
Sadness	11%
Frustration	31%
Anxiety	13%

Total Positive 14%
Total Negative 86%

Fig. 9.9 Victory vs. Uncertainty. . .Emotionally

Two keys to navigating change successfully are not to let employees feel like losers or to drag out the pain of uncertainty. These results show a split verdict. Despite a negative total of 56% for the win/loss/draw topic to the left, the companies in this study were actually doing fairly well establishing hope for new opportunities. However, those same companies were not doing a good job moving employees through the uncertainty that comes with the change (evident in the very high negative total of 86% for the topic to the right).

Without a doubt, more reliable insights into employee feelings can aid executive planning. To quote Carey and Ogden again: "Most mergers—even those that are ultimately less successful—sounded good on paper. Yet in many cases, the highly variable human element—the softer side of the deal that is not as obvious or easy to quantify—was not accounted for."

Even without benefiting from the scientific rigor of facial coding, however, executives must do better during the planning stage. Incompleteness is the primary problem. Too often, the planning remains exclusively rational and lacks input from people more intimately aware of the feelings and attitudes within the company ranks. Adding middle-managers and seasoned employees to the planning mix will broaden the company's knowledge of the emotional environment in which the change will take place.

Next, in preparing the case for change, senior management must identify the various rationales they might use to explain the change to employees. They can then test drive the persuasiveness of those rationales by gauging the likely emotional acceptance of them by employees. This step is crucial. Executives who aren't in touch with the emotional pulse of the company, but still seek change, will find themselves in a predicament equivalent to driving a car with the emergency brake on.

The most important rationale to identify and communicate successfully to employees will be the risks of sticking with the status quo. People's emotional desire for security will motivate them to accept change if they understand the consequences for failing to change. At the same time, however, hard truths should be delivered softly so that people don't panic, freeze or surrender. Simply saying, "It's safe to go back in the water," isn't good enough. The picture of the future has to be vividly clear and exciting—stressing the company's move into a superior position vis-à-vis the competition, if it's to be successful in retaining the switchers.

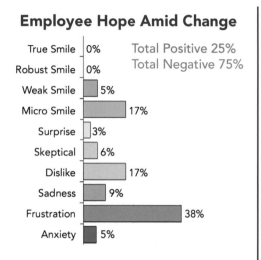

Employee Hope Amid Change

True Smile	0%
Robust Smile	0%
Weak Smile	5%
Micro Smile	17%
Surprise	3%
Skeptical	6%
Dislike	17%
Sadness	9%
Frustration	38%
Anxiety	5%

Total Positive 25%
Total Negative 75%

Meshing of Company Cultures

True Smile	0%
Robust Smile	0%
Weak Smile	7%
Micro Smile	0%
Surprise	2%
Skeptical	13%
Dislike	7%
Sadness	13%
Frustration	49%
Anxiety	9%

Total Positive 9%
Total Negative 91%

Fig. 9.10 Protecting Hope and Struggling to Mesh Cultures
The left chart shows the limited emotional "hope" of employees at companies undergoing M&A activity. The chart on the right shows the response of those employees to the meshing of corporate cultures. Clearly, companies could use some more help to ensure that productivity improves rather than sags under the weight of negative emotions. But emotions can't be managed if they can't first be measured. Quantifying employee emotional responses during change can inform leaders of the type and extent of intervention required.

In officially communicating the case for change—in front of employees and not through e-mail, memos or a video—executives must explain credibly how change will deliver more benefits to employees than the emotional turmoil incurred. To make the case clear, leadership should focus on emotional benefits such as a sense of victory, greater job security or a fresh new direction, along with a clear synopsis of facts and data. Rational analysis alone doesn't motivate employees. They must grasp a "truth" that touches their feelings. The delivered message should therefore be simple, heartfelt and aligned with the current emotional climate within the company.

Moreover, in their delivery executives should be careful about their non-verbal signals because people dance to music—not words—in regard to what they accept most deeply. As the sensory and emotional parts of the brain preceded the rational brain, where verbal abilities reside, employees will trust the CEO's body language more intuitively than anything that gets said.

Finally, in selling and enacting change senior management must account for the fact that there are, of course, always two channels of communication in a company: the official channel and the grapevine. Leaders must leverage the former but be wise to the realities of the latter, which, contrary to its reputation, research has found to be 75% to 90% *accurate* (Conniff). In enacting change, leaders would be wise to remember the physiological data pointing out how anxiety eats people up over time. As a result, there's real value in getting big changes over quickly—before the emotional and financial trajectories dovetail downward.

Cohesive Culture:
bringing everyone along

Synopsis: The other mark of a great CEO is the ability to build a company in which employees feel they will be invited to participate, collaborate and be recognized for achievement in ways that promote good work. As this section shows, this attribute is a matter of establishing the right emotional tone first. Then it's a matter of building a leadership team whose emotional intelligence makes it possible to foster an entire corporate culture capable of inspiring employees to give their best effort.

Key take-aways:
- The CEO's personality looms large in a company but works best close up.
- A beneficent CEO is inclusive and able to draw on the talents of female leaders.

Creating Good Will
The CEO's personality looms large in a company but works best close up.

The third key leadership quality in Kouzes and Posner's worldwide survey is an executive's ability to inspire. As with honesty and being forward-looking or visionary, valuing inspiration makes sense. Honesty comes first because employees need to know whether they trust their leaders enough to follow them. Being forward-looking comes next because employees feel more secure knowing the direction they will be heading (provided that they're convinced it will lead to a good outcome).

Then to round out the list, there's being inspiring. Now the question becomes: do employees feel motivated enough by leaders to adhere to the direction that's been set and the pace being asked of them?

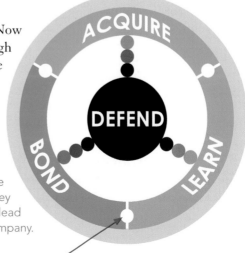

Emotion and Motivations

A good leader makes everybody believe they can get ahead, thereby fostering the comfort and confidence that are the underpinnings of **hope**. Employees will look to the leader, and also to one another, to **learn** the appropriate behavior for the culture they're part of. If they like what they see and feel, then the desire to **bond** will manifest itself and lead to a more cohesive, dynamic company.

Hope

The emotional climate within a company may account for as much as 30% of its performance.

Furthermore, over 50% of that climate gets predominately established by the CEO.

The term that sometimes gets applied here is "charisma," though that term is misleading. Being inspiring doesn't involve a magical, magnetic charm but, rather, a leader's ability to inspire good will and hope. Closer to the mark is the argument made by Daniel Goleman, Richard Boyatzis and Annie McKee in *Primal Leadership*. They write that, above all else, executives must "prime good feeling in those they lead," because *"resonance*—a reservoir of positivism that frees the best in people"—is what's required to make a vision come true. In other words, the sooner executives embrace the fact that they should focus on emotional uplift, the sooner their plans will be realized.

To support their argument, Goleman and company cite numerous examples, including:

- A study of 62 CEOs and their top management teams that correlated positive emotional outlooks and interaction with superior business results.

- A study of 19 CEOs and their direct reports at insurance companies, where the emotional climate accurately predicted high versus low profits and growth.

What's the authors' overall conclusion, based on a score of case studies? The emotional climate within a company may account for as much as 30% of its performance. Furthermore, over 50% of that climate gets predominately established by the CEO.

Perhaps more riveting than a pile of statistics is to provide a single dramatic instance. Let's look at the success of General Electric's former CEO Jack Welch (Byrne). His nickname, "Neutron Jack," came from the way he focused on downsizing by sacking weaker performers. But in contrast to former Hewlitt-Packard CEO Carly Fiorina, another hard-driving executive, Welch proved to be far more adept at keeping more people emotionally on-board and helping GE reap the resulting financial benefits.

What's the difference between the two leaders? In a nutshell, it's probably Welch's love of interacting with employees. Already famous for spending half his time on people issues, Welch took the extra step of devoting hours to being in "the Pit" at the GE training center at Croton-on-Hudson.

There Welch demonstrated accessibility in his management development courses. Seeing his personality and leadership style up close, people could judge for themselves the man who took GE's market value from $12 billion in 1981 to around $300 billion almost two decades later. Welch understood that spending time with employees face-to-face in the Pit and in other everyday interactions within the company could really work wonders. A corollary to Welch's success is that to emotionally connect with employees, a leader must both exude and generate an element of enjoyment.

In contrast, consider the cautionary tale of an isolated CEO, whose new vision for the company was at risk of losing employee support. Sensory Logic became aware of this situation when asked to perform research involving two different positioning statements, each consisting of three one-word descriptors. The goal was to learn which statement (the CEO's preferred version or an alternative) would be best accepted by employees (Fig. 9.11).

What were the results? The CEO's key descriptive term came in *last* among the six terms.

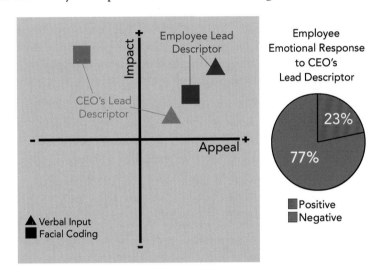

Fig. 9.11 Employee Emotional Buy-in

Facial Coding revealed true buy-in that verbal input alone was not able to measure. Without a more incisive tool, the company could have taken the wrong path. Not only was the CEO on a different page than his employees regarding which brand positioning statement they would favor, his favorite descriptor generated a positive emotional response of only 23%.

What was his reaction to this news? Rather than defensively dismiss the findings, the CEO magnanimously accepted the alternative brand positioning statement developed by his staff. In that way, he provided the company's employees with a positioning statement they could believe in and act on as part of an effort to update the company's image to better fit a changing business-to-business marketplace. All in all, he knew that without employee support and emotional buy-in, his strategy was dead on arrival.

Leading, But Not Alone
A beneficent CEO is inclusive and able to draw on the talents of female leaders.

In truth, as top dog the CEO inevitably sets the emotional tone for the company. Or perhaps I should say top *ape*, since research involving primates demonstrates that it's laughably obvious how much others in the tribe look to the alpha leader for guidance (Conniff). Why should it be surprising then that in a variety of settings—from speeches to press conferences, negotiations or testifying in court—the character and temperament on display in CEOs' faces can help predict the outcomes.

That being said, CEOs can't—and in effect won't—build hope and cohesive corporate cultures on their own. They need good, emotionally intelligent members of senior management to round out the top team. Here's where the willingness of a corporate leader to share the glory can really pay dividends. After all, what aspiring, talented junior-level executives wouldn't be tempted to join a company whose CEO feels secure enough and generous enough to allow them to exercise their abilities and reap the rewards?

To create a positive, unified culture, a leader must commit rationally to being emotionally vulnerable. As a result, emotionally savvy leaders won't be afraid of being usurped because they realize that they and the company at large will benefit from not hindering the professional growth of others.

What we are ultimately talking about here is nurturing, instead of holding people back. It's about motivating people to want to do their best because they're grateful to the CEO for being a servant leader (Greenleaf), the kind of person who helps others achieve their potential because everybody benefits in the end.

Now, given their acknowledged skills at emotionally-oriented core capabilities like relationship-based communication and collaboration—among other things—shouldn't women get more of an opportunity to lead? To prove the point, consider these findings:

- As summarized by Douglas Elix, head of IBM's Global Services Division, women are often superior at thinking through decisions, and they tend to interact more collaboratively and seek less personal glory. Instead of being internally focused, women are often more driven by "what they can do for the company" (Sharpe).

- Elix's view is seconded by Professor Rosabeth Moss Kanter, author of the twenty-year-old management staple *Men and Women of the Corporation*. Her research has found

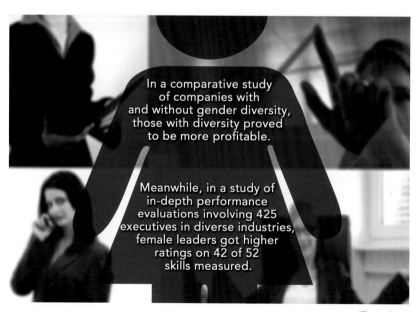

In a comparative study of companies with and without gender diversity, those with diversity proved to be more profitable.

Meanwhile, in a study of in-depth performance evaluations involving 425 executives in diverse industries, female leaders got higher ratings on 42 of 52 skills measured.

(Sharpe)

that "women get high ratings on exactly those skills needed to succeed in the global Information Age, where teamwork and partnering are so important" (Sharpe).

Yet there are remarkably few women in senior leadership positions, thereby curtailing the opportunity for them to help make their companies' cultures more emotionally inviting and capable of bringing out the best in people.

Just how few? In 2005 women held just 16.4% of *Fortune* 500 corporate office jobs requiring board approval—a measly increase of 0.7% from the level documented in 2002. As of 2005, women also comprised only 6.4% of the top five earners among corporate officers. Women of color were represented even more poorly. They held but 1.7% of the corporate officer spots and were 1% of the *Fortune* 500 top earners (Hymowitz).

Those low numbers can't be because there aren't any openings or available candidates. Gallup reports that, for instance, during the first four months of 2005, 441 CEOs of companies of varying sizes left their jobs (Gerber).

Potentially ready to move up, women comprise 49% of those in the professional and managerial ranks. Nor does that number alone give full justice to the talent pool available. Get ready for two more statistics. Consider the fact that not only are 40% of all small businesses in America women-owned, they also employ 35% more people than the entire *Fortune* 500 does worldwide (Barletta). Often feeling stymied and sidelined without profit-and-loss responsibilities, women in the U.S. are launching small businesses at more than twice the rate of men (Hymowitz).

Finally, the low number of women in senior leadership positions also can't be because the status quo is working so well that their skills and emotional intelligence aren't required. One dirty little secret about senior management is that companies are often saddled with unhappy, unproductive leadership. *USA Today* reports that only 49% of top executives are engaged by their jobs. On the other hand, 9% of top executives are actively *disengaged* (Jones 2005).

Women get high ratings on exactly those skills needed to succeed in the global Information Age, where teamwork and partnering are so important.

Furthermore another study shows that 40% of all newly promoted executives and managers fail within the first 18 months of their promotion because they don't build strong teams or reach out to colleagues and peers (De Koning 2005). What are the odds that the majority of the leaders who struggle to involve others are men? Pretty high, given the earlier statistics indicating the greater likelihood that women will be collaborative in nature, demonstrating emotional intelligence in the process.

Surely, a better way forward exists. CEOs need good teams supporting them, people who can communicate and emotionally connect.

So why not give women, proven to be highly skilled in both of those skill sets, the chance to exercise them? The essential masculine code of the strong, silent type calling the shots downplays the emotional factor. In contrast, women tend to be more conversant and emotive and, indeed,

Sensory Logic's research results indicate that they are more emotionally expressive, on average, than men are.

Our research also shows how important women's less combative, less winner-take-all approach can be in fostering a cohesive culture. What I remember most from conducting an interview with two male employees at a recently acquired company in Denver was the *yelp* of one employee when he realized the other employee—from the acquiring company—saw the Denver operation as a conquered entity. Not surprisingly, in our study of companies amid change the difficulty of meshing cultures exhibited the lowest percentage of positive facial coding results (Fig. 9.10).

Given the emotional intelligence women bring to the job, companies would be wise to promote more women into top-level positions. After all, to compete in the global marketplace they need a diverse leadership team that can relate well—with emotional sensitivity—to diverse employees and customers alike.

Conclusion

Leadership must always remember two realities that showcase the importance of emotions. The first is that it's the human side of business that consumes most of the operating costs. So a failure to be emotionally adept is very counterproductive, even suicidal. Second, it's the employees at a company who turn the CEO's dream of progress into more than just a strategic plan by becoming emotionally committed to that plan. To be effective executives must, therefore, accomplish the following:

- Create faith in a "greater we" by establishing themselves as real people, rather than merely as the holders of big titles, big offices and big salaries. Part of the reason why it's important to be more personal is that nowadays leaders must also establish themselves as honest. Only then can they generate the emotional momentum necessary to push through change.

- Have a vision that instills pride in employees. Otherwise, the hidden costs of negative feelings such as envy or fear can undo a company during a period of change because emotions are highly contagious. Remember that emotions are, indeed, a hyper-effective means of communicating without words. So disengagement by employees is a leading emotional indicator that executives aren't doing their job well.

- Use face time to make the journey of an unknown future, due to corporate change, emotionally acceptable to employees by being willing to meet in person and ask for and accept advice. Unless very poorly handled, those meetings will reap emotional benefits because, in general, greater familiarity leads to greater appeal.

An Action Plan

To make sure the leadership style on display is emotionally healthy, here are a few things to check when assessing effectiveness:

- ☐ Do employees and investors believe the leaderships' goals and interests align with their own? Do customers believe that the company and, therefore, its leadership has their best interests at heart? The psychological equivalent of the Bermuda Triangle, in which ships disappear from sight, is the emotion *fear*, the motivation to *defend* and the actions of *avoidance* and *denial*. Using a scientific, objective tool like facial coding ensures that a company's executives truly know where they stand with key audiences.

- ☐ Leaders with a mission must appear to be confident, unafraid and the equal or superior of every other leader in companies similar to their own. People being people, employees will inevitably make comparisons. So it's best to be seen as top dog (or ape) through body language that conveys assurance but stops short of arrogance, because if caring isn't projected by leaders, their employees won't buy-in.

- ☐ Deliver bad news early and clearly (without using legalese or financialese). When employees and investors receive bad news later rather than sooner, they will feel betrayed. Be timely when delivering news; get it out there before people make up their minds emotionally about what they're going to hear.

- ☐ Senior leadership should appear to have unity within its ranks, and any newly hired leader should be justified to employees in an emotionally relevant way. In other words, employees need to easily answer the question: why was this person the best choice to safeguard everybody's interests? Never forget to offer hope about how employees' lives will improve as a result of initiatives or changes.

- ☐ Develop communication plans that identify formal and informal points of contact within the company. Emphasize the latter in order to learn more—especially during a time of change when sincere as well as frequent opportunities for employee input and feedback are necessary. Senior leaders with training in facial coding will be able to understand how employees feel before, during and after a change by reading their spontaneous expressions during small group or one-on-one meetings.

10 employee management

To create the foundation for a great workforce, companies first have to identify and hire emotionally adept individuals.

Then they must build on that potential through emotional engagement and training.

OVERVIEW

Managing employees is the single most emotional element in the business world. It's a real life, working relationship between a boss and the staff in which the interaction is ongoing and sometimes intense. Crunch-time crises will happen, and misunderstandings or disagreements will creep into the daily relationship—affecting morale and trust. Inevitably emotionally-charged "moments of truth" will come to dominate the relationship, subtly overshadowing rational components like company goals and specific work assignments. To help managers and staff enhance their working relationships, this chapter will focus on:

- **Compatibility:** Gauging the emotional aptitude of job candidates for the roles and companies they're looking to fill and join is crucial. Knowing credentials and skills isn't enough. What's missing? The seemingly intangible factors like personality, energy level and interactive abilities. Assessing those "soft" factors is less rational, requiring emotional tools that will enable companies to determine a candidate's real fit and potential value in a job. Only then can companies form a more realistic understanding of the candidate's compatibility with the manager and the organization at large.

- **Reciprocating Trust:** There's nothing flashy about making a manager/employee relationship work. It depends on both sides being able to feel that the other party is looking out for one's own best interests. A strong connection only happens when there's an aura of respect and trust—in a word, authenticity. The two parties don't always have to like each other, but they must be able to share both rational and emotionally-oriented information to avoid lapsing into the paralysis that comes with mutual alienation. To overcome situations in which employees feel like their efforts aren't supported and managers feel like they're not getting what they need, the emotional equivalent of an "open door" policy should be in effect.

- **Mission Critical:** Authenticity is tied, in turn, to employees being able to enjoy the work at hand because it's meaningful. Feed the heart, feed the spirit and the company's bottom line will be fed. What's required here is a mission-critical sensibility, not in the sense of requiring nerve-wracking deadlines but, rather, by helping employees avoid stagnation. Managers can gain emotional leverage by letting the staff plug in and prove their capabilities. Often the best way to do this is to organize employees into effective, emotionally satisfying teams.

Now let's look more closely at how to build stronger work relationships, starting with getting the right person on-board.

Compatibility:
identifying what works

Synopsis: Trying to change people verges on the impossible. The wiser route is to identify their patterns and tendencies—their emotional profile—in the interview process, so that the right personnel gets put into the right positions. To aid in that outcome, this section opens by examining flaws in the interview process and why new hires go wrong. Next, it looks at the role of emotional intelligence in selecting new hires who work well with their bosses and colleagues. The section then concludes with a discussion of personality types and how generational diversity is making workforce compatibility a tougher challenge.

Key take-aways:

- Rational hiring criteria miss the large role emotion plays in the outcome.

- Compatibility is rooted in gut-level judgments like comfort and credibility.

- Long term, emotions show up most in character traits and belief systems.

- New, shared experiences help overcome generational conflicts.

Interviewing: the Age-Old Dance
Rational hiring criteria miss the large role emotion plays in the outcome.

Any relationship, professional or otherwise, is built on the character traits that individuals bring to the party. How are companies doing in their search for suitable talent? In truth not very well, as the following statistics make clear.

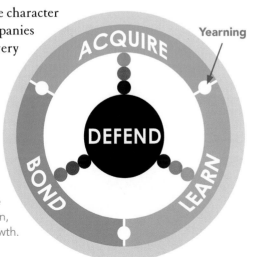

Emotion and Motivations

A mixture of happiness and sadness, **yearning** is the key emotion here as job candidates try to discern how they may end up feeling about the available position. They seek happiness, but may also suffer doubts based on previous work experiences. In motivational terms, from the job candidate's perspective the pertinent drivers are to **acquire** and **learn**. Potential employees seek to acquire power and status through an entirely new job or promotion, thereby simultaneously gaining opportunities for growth.

A study has found that nearly 50% of new hires will fail within eighteen months. Poor interpersonal skills are primarily the reason. To be specific, of those who fail 26% will do so because they can't accept feedback, 23% because they aren't able to understand and manage their emotions, 17% because they lack motivation, and 15% because they have the wrong temperament for the job. Way down in fifth place among the reasons why so many new hires don't succeed is a lack of the necessary technical skills, at 11% ("Poor").

How can companies improve on these kinds of results? The feeding of résumés into a machine coded to look for certain key terms, qualifiers, et cetera, may serve as an adequate tool in screening for certain more technical, rationally-oriented skills. But another step is needed in the process to lift the success rate for new hires, given the importance of emotions in general and, specifically, the degree to which interpersonal skills are lacking.

What could that step be? If not the outright use of facial coding to help evaluate the personalities of candidates, then at least interview inquiries or exercises geared toward ensuring emotional compatibility is in order.

Any hiring process exclusively focused on rational skill sets will clearly have blind spots. What the people conducting the interviews may not acknowledge, however, is that any job interview is inherently emotional in nature. How could it be otherwise? The people doing the hiring are human beings, with their own preferences and biases, their own way of filtering the information they're hearing from candidates. The question isn't whether the hiring process will be influenced by people's emotions or not. Instead, it's whether the individuals involved in the job interviews will realize and accept the role of emotions in the process and do something to wisely incorporate that reality into the proceedings.

To that end, remember that people do business with people they like. We like and often hire someone with whom we can easily relate. Meaning, we tend to hire ourselves. So a company runs

We tend to do business with people whom we like. people like us who share our beliefs. In effect, we tend to hire ourselves.

the risk of lacking diversity with regard to race, gender and age as well as subtler factors like work style. This emotionally driven, often unacknowledged inclination can reinforce a company's narrow perspective—and that's just one of the holes in the usual, supposedly rational hiring model.

Here are the others:

Talent gets overrated in relation to character: A company needs to know what's going on inside the job candidate to know whether things will work out in the long run. Talent is a great advantage. But since research indicates that an inability to manage emotions or accept feedback combine to account for 49% of the reasons why new hires fail, an emotionally savvy route to screen for those factors should also be part of the mix.

A candidate's interactive skills (or lack thereof) are simply overlooked: People are social animals and business requires people getting along with other people. One survey found that *only 40%* of employees were deemed able to work well with others (Harris).

People spin, deflect, hint and hold back: Skills and levels of experience listed on résumés tend to be inflated, despite the irony that they may not be central to what determines success on the job. Oftentimes, candidates will say what they know they're expected to say to land the opening. Therefore, assessing their non-verbal signals becomes the avenue to securing greater veracity.

Why are these issues so prevalent? One veteran of the personnel placement industry has used his experience to outline his top ten hiring "hot buttons." Seven of the ten are emotionally oriented: initiative, self-confidence, leadership, compatibility (personality and behaviors), attitude, social skills and integrity (Straits). These are the types of qualities that companies too often do a

Sophie **deflects**, **hints** and **holds back** on her resumé...

Hmm...
Burger Quick drive-thru worker
or COMMUNICATIONS MANAGER FOR
A NATIONAL
CHAIN RESTAURANT!!!

Hire for Emotional Intelligence
Compatibility is rooted in gut-level judgments like comfort and credibility.

In their book *What Happy Companies Know*, Baker, Greenberg and Hemingway observe that companies can improve the hiring process by screening for both intellectual *and* emotional intelligence. The authors define the latter as actively managing both "thoughts and feelings to bring out the best . . . abilities and to create positive interactions with other people."

But how can companies identify and screen for emotionally smart people?

The obvious way is certainly to do a gut check assessing one's comfort level with, and trust of, the job candidate—a route companies rely on much more often than they might realize. Research has found that interviewers typically make their decisions quite early in the interview process,

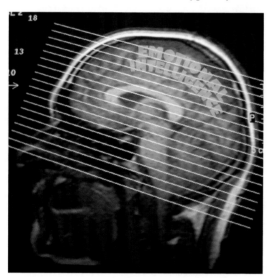

If only it was as simple as scanning a person's brain to determine emotional aptitude. But for now, at least, it isn't, so other steps must be taken.

typically within the first four minutes (Arvey). But for interviewers either unsure of their gut instincts or inclined to override them using a surfeit of rationally-oriented facts, a safeguard might be prudent.

The key is to focus on how candidates unknowingly disclose a wealth of emotionally-based insights regarding their character traits, interest in the job and so forth throughout the interview process. Using a tool like facial coding can help hiring managers scientifically reinforce their snap decisions when interviews are short. Likewise, it can help them truly evaluate longer interviews and keep them from turning into rote exercises in which checking for qualifications may not reveal the true personality of the candidate sitting across the table. For example, facial coding can help a company identify potential red-flag emotions in candidates (e.g., contempt or fear) as well as more desirable responses (e.g., happiness and pride).

We're talking Facial coding 101. As discussed earlier in this book, that approach would involve interviewers learning how to read and distinguish Ekman's set of core emotions on at least a superficial level. At a more sophisticated level, a company like Sensory Logic, with an expertise in facial coding, could work with companies to code all potential hires for sensitive positions based on an assessment of their responses to a set of predetermined, baseline questions.

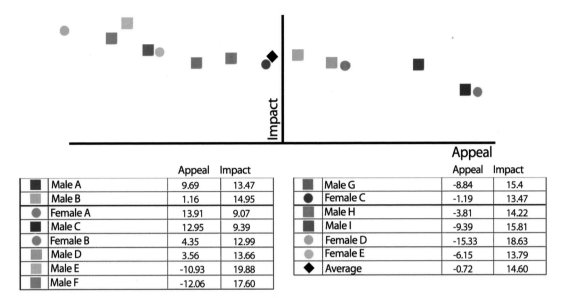

		Appeal	Impact
■	Male A	9.69	13.47
■	Male B	1.16	14.95
●	Female A	13.91	9.07
■	Male C	12.95	9.39
●	Female B	4.35	12.99
■	Male D	3.56	13.66
■	Male E	-10.93	19.88
■	Male F	-12.06	17.60

		Appeal	Impact
■	Male G	-8.84	15.4
●	Female C	-1.19	13.47
■	Male H	-3.81	14.22
■	Male I	-9.39	15.81
●	Female D	-15.33	18.63
●	Female E	-6.15	13.79
◆	Average	-0.72	14.60

Fig. 10.1 Facial Coding Results for Casting Call
Audience reactions to potential spokespeople are analogous to an interviewer's responses to potential employees. In other situations, an alternative approach is to analyze a job candidate's expressions to learn what they reveal about that person's personality and suitability for the job.

To see how precise and beneficial facial coding can be in making a hiring decision, consider a slightly tangential though apropos case in which we were asked to help a pharmaceutical company's advertising agency decide which actors to hire for a new ad campaign. The offer was controversial in nature, and the target market feels a clannish loyalty toward fellow members seeking to kick the smoking habit. Therefore, the actors to be chosen not only had to be likeable and have stopping power (e.g., stage presence), they also had to be highly credible as authentic members of the target market.

In this case, the subjects were shown brief, videotaped excerpts of fourteen actors ad libbing about the special nature of the offer. The subjects became, in effect, the hiring managers, and the actors the job candidates. The actors' taped appearances were the equivalent of the answers job candidates give when asked, "Why do you want this job?"

As shown by the results (Fig. 10.1), clear preferences emerged. The subjects recruited to fit the profile of the target market gave less than half the actors a positive response. And of those viewed favorably, the subjects clearly preferred two actors. Only that duo was able to consistently embody a personality that the target market would be likely to accept. How do these results relate to the hiring situation? While comfort isn't everything—remember: hiring who we like can undercut diversity efforts—to do entirely without it won't work, either. More importantly, in this case, emphasis was placed on gauging credibility through facially coded responses to the actors, and without trust there's no viable, long-term working relationship between a boss and employee.

Tools for Gauging an Appropriate Fit

Long term, emotions show up most in character traits and belief systems.

Human resource leaders are becoming increasingly aware of the value of hiring job candidates who are good psychological fits for the company at large and with respect to the specific positions to be filled. The idea of adding emotional assessments as part of the job hiring process is catching on for good reason. Breakthroughs in brain science have shown how central emotions are to people's intuitive, immediate behavior. But in combination with psychology, neurobiology has now also revealed that the impact of emotions is by no means fleeting. Two deeply-entrenched, on-going manifestations of the power of emotions are personality traits and belief systems, both of which are highly relevant to the job candidate evaluation process.

Let's look at personality traits first. These largely fixed, enduring characteristics will come into play across a wide-ranging set of situations should the candidate be hired, effecting productivity and assignment outcomes. Fortunately, much of what is likely to manifest itself on the job can already be apparent during the initial interviews, making wise hiring choices more feasible.

An ideal vehicle for assessing a candidate's personality type is facial coding: emotionally-oriented, scientific and capable of gleaning more than can be readily gathered from the candidate's more conscious, verbally-delivered responses. Barring that route, however, here are other specific tools that also exist to help companies improve their hiring odds.

One is the well-known and often used Myers-Briggs test, but it's so transparent in what it measures that its validity gets undercut in the process. A second option is the Hogan test mentioned in Chapter 9, which is highly acclaimed but expensive. A third option with both critical acclaim and financial feasibility is Costa and McCrae's "Big 5" factor model (Fig. 10.2), which arose from the rigorous computer modeling of over 4,500 factors related to personality traits (Howard 2000). Unlike Myers-Briggs' four-factor model, Costa and McCrae's version of assessing personality includes neuroticism—the second most heavily documented personality dimension.

A number of tests are available for measuring the Big 5, including the International Personality Item Pool (which is in the public domain) and the NEO PI-R, a 240-item inventory (packaged as a commercial offer). These could be given not only to the job candidate but also to the manager involved to ensure compatibility.

The other deeply-entrenched emotional variable human resource leaders and hiring managers should address are the belief systems embraced by all parties involved. Talk concerning the candidate's need to acclimate to the corporate culture can be vague. Of greater, more actionable help in engineering a good fit between the company and a potential employee is identifying what values the company cherishes, then learning whether those same values matter to the candidate. Besides using facial coding to make an assessment of emotional buy-in to those values, the authors of *What Happy Companies Know* point to Endo Pharmaceuticals and the public relations firm Waggener Edstrom as examples of companies adept at making a values linkage part of their hiring process.

The Big 5 Factor Model

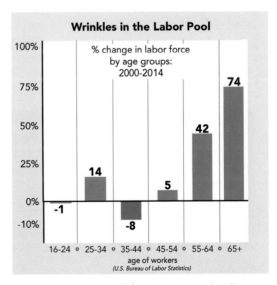

Extraversion
A significant, pronounced tendency to engage with the world. Extroverts are talkative, high-energy and assertive. Natural sales people.

Agreeableness
A concern with cooperation and social connectivity. Agreeable people are sympathetic, kind and affectionate; good customer service qualities.

Conscientiousness
An ability to be self-disciplined and thorough. Conscientious people tend to be organized, thoughtful and are plan-oriented. This makes for great strategists and implementers.

Openness
A creative, imaginative approach to problems and the world. Open individuals have a wide range of interests and are both imaginative and insightful - a profile often found in top-notch creatives.

Neuroticism
A tendency to experience and dwell on negative emotions. Neurotics tend to be tense, moody and anxious. Good leaders in high stress jobs will have low neuroticism.

Fig. 10.2 Costa and McRae's Model of the Key Personality Traits

Generational Diversity
New, shared experiences help overcome generational conflicts.

For a while now, companies have been wrestling with the emotionally-charged topics of gender and racial diversity in the workplace. Slowly coming into sight, however, is another obvious division among employees: relative age (Dychtwald). The labor pool is aging. Although companies continue to downsize and outsource, they will soon face a new dilemma of finding enough skilled workers once the Baby Boomers start to retire en masse.

Age diversity brings with it both of the two, deep-seated emotional elements just discussed: personality traits and belief systems. While the relative mix of the "Big 5" factors

Wrinkles in the Labor Pool

% change in labor force by age groups: 2000-2014

age of workers	% change
16-24	-1
25-34	14
35-44	-8
45-54	5
55-64	42
65+	74

(U.S. Bureau of Labor Statistics)

Clearly, America's workforce is aging—leading to new, emotionally-charged issues that current and future managers will have to resolve (Dychtwald).

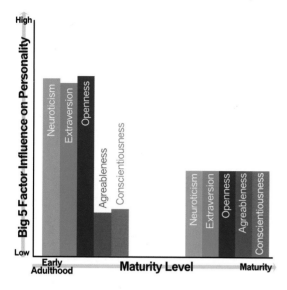

Fig. 10.3 Changes in Personality Due to Maturity

As we grow older, wiser and more experienced, our personality tends to even out. When younger we tend to be more outgoing and open to new ideas—but also more concerned with setbacks and challenging the world. Over time, we begin to find our place in the grand scheme of things and develop a more even outlook (Howard 2000). Companies benefit from having employees at all stages of life, so as to have a richer range of dispositions.

is likely to remain stable in a person over time, they do tend to fluctuate based on maturity (Fig. 10.3).

In contrast, the dynamics of belief systems involve interpersonal rather than intrapersonal differences over time. With an unprecedented four generations of workers—Traditionalists, Baby Boomers, Gen-Xers and the Millennials—great potential exists for emotional, value-based conflicts. After all, employees now have frames of reference stretching from the Dust Bowl to the iPod. If some portion of a company's employees don't feel respected and understood, then the whole effort to be effective in the workplace is at risk because being emotionally in sync is vital to the enterprise.

The solution is to recognize that different frames of reference involve different experiences that reinforce generational conflicts. While employees' belief systems won't readily change, what is possible is to ensure that colleagues from different eras find themselves integrated into collaborative team efforts. Then new, common ground experiences can supplement—and at times perhaps even supersede—the memories of other experiences that separate the generations.

the workplace now consists of four generations of experiences and different ways of comprehending the world around us.

Is it important to make that kind of effort? Absolutely. Only 51% of employees believe different generations work well together. More critically, 19% of employees report experiencing frequent intergenerational miscommunication (Cummins). Clearly, there's plenty of room for improvement. Hiring employees with greater emotional aptitude will make the issues involving an age gap that much easier to navigate. That's because they'll be able to read and respond to the emotions of others not only more quickly, but also with greater ability.

Reciprocating Trust:
avoid disconnects

Synopsis: Contempt kills relationships. Fortunately, managers and employees can develop a good, sustainable working relationship with rapport built on mutual trust and respect. In the pages to follow, we'll confirm how emotional the workplace really is. Then we'll look at why the bulk of formal training doesn't work and why manager-led training is superior. Finally, the link is made between constructive performance reviews and improvements in morale and retention that lead to greater productivity and lower turn-over costs.

Key take-aways:
- Alleviating employee concerns makes the working relationship feel right.
- Knowledge-based training ignores how emotionally-driven idea retention is.
- A constructive job review is really about developing a path for self-growth.
- The more emotional morale issues become, the more hidden they're likely to be.

Emotion and Motivations
A mixture of anger and sadness, **sullenness** is the key emotion here because the danger of the manager/employee relationship breaking down is high. That fate can be avoided through a shared sense of mission, with pride of sharing in a great outcome the better emotional result. But managers must be able to protect against the sadness of resignation and the anger that arises from wishing to control the process. Both sides have a tendency to **defend** their own emotional interests, with the drive to **bond** sure to suffer unless the relationship can become and remain robust..

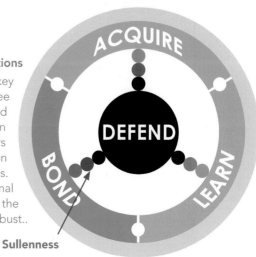

Sullenness

The Emotional Stakes Involved
Alleviating employee concerns makes the working relationship feel right.

Once the new hire is in place, the question becomes: how best to ensure that the manager/employee relationship develops and sustains itself effectively? As background, consider an exhaustive study conducted by Gallup involving over 80,000 managers in over 400 companies (Buckingham). Winnowing down to those questions that best diagnosed the core elements required to attract, focus and retain valuable employees, Gallup cast aside many wrong-headed—and yes, wrong-*hearted*—notions about how success is achieved.

Out the window went the criteria used in the annual study, "The Hundred Best Companies to Work For." Why? Though factors like on-site daycare facilities, vacation time, profit-sharing and training are important, those benefits failed to address the pivotal importance of a good manager/employee working relationship in regard to its impact on employee performance.

Likewise, good pay didn't prove to be crucial. Nor did the organizational structure. Nor did the efforts of senior management. Those things matter, but don't prove to be the critical, causal factors leading to superior employee performance. Instead, the quality of the interaction with a manager and whether the worker had a positive emotional regard for the manager were the keys to loyalty and success. That's because, as stated in Buckingham and Coffman's *First, Break All the Rules*, "people leave managers, not companies." Put another way, employees stick with somebody who alleviates their concerns and respects and values their efforts.

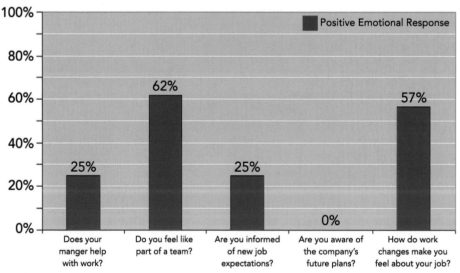

Fig. 10.4 Fast-Food Workforce's Endorsement of Managerial Style
In a study Sensory Logic performed, the two highest positive responses also had the highest Emotional Response Rate levels. We concluded that the workers at this particular company truly feel like part of a team and appreciate changes that seem to improve their daily work. But the low degree of positive response to the other three questions point to a lack of communication and interaction between managers and employees.

In short, Gallup learned that emotions matter. Without a strong tie to the manager, employees lose heart and give up, resulting in plummeting productivity.

Nobody knows the importance of morale better than middle managers. The push to realize ever greater productivity makes them both the object and agency of change. Under stress to perform, they're probably the first to understand that pursuing low wages and low prices is a race to the bottom that only one company per sector can win. For everyone else, the goal instead must be to craft a functional corporate culture and, on a daily basis, foster successful manager/employee relationships. Putting those elements in place brings out the best in workers so that the company can, in turn, provide its customers with offers and service that give it a fighting chance.

To that end, only part of providing good value can realistically come from hard knowledge. The rest will have to be facilitated by better emotional interactions that capitalize on the fact that, as noted at the start of this chapter, managing employees is the single most emotional element in the business world. Without good attention to the emotional dynamics of that working relationship, where is the "steam" of unresolved stress likely to go? Into undermining the manager/employee bond, that's where.

Proof of the inevitably high emotional stakes involved in the manager/employee relationship was what Sensory Logic took away from a study of a fast-food company (Fig. 10.4). We normally see Emotional Response Rate levels around the 40% mark for projects involving offer design, advertising, et cetera. But in this case, where we were testing for employee satisfaction, the average was 50%.

Fortunately, the two inquiries that netted the most emotional responsiveness (that employees felt part of a team and that they felt the changes underway were beneficial) also had the most positive emotional outcomes. Therefore, employee concerns were being addressed and alleviated. But the next three issues that got employees worked up the most were about what they felt wasn't going well: 1) controlling the work flow, 2) knowing what their roles were, and 3) knowing more about the company's future plans. Since these are areas where employees felt the greatest concern, they are also the problem areas in which we recommended management could and should make improvements.

Post-Hire: Training and Coaching
Knowledge-based training ignores how emotionally-driven idea retention is.

Ultimately, in bottom-line terms, employee management is about creating a working relationship in which performance thrives. It's no surprise that a recent survey sponsored by the International Association for Human Resource Information Management found that 96% of the respondents cited "performance" as their top priority. To achieve that goal, those same respondents cited "learning management" (by which they meant linking training and on-the-job knowledge to performance) as their next highest priority.

On first blush, that sounds good and certainly logical. After all, better output through knowing more makes sense. What won't work, however, is the usual, rationally-oriented training and "knowledge" development that fails to engage employee hearts as well as their minds since survey results suggest that this approach isn't cutting it. Only a little more than 10% of the survey respondents saw their companies as presently "well aligned" with respect to skills, abilities and goals. Meanwhile, other findings estimate the amount of training information that gets retained and put into actual use at barely 10% (Baldwin).

That low estimate sounds plausible. For starters, classrooms are rarely places that make people comfortable. Trainees tend to fall into three groups: vacationers (time away from the office), prisoners ("Do I have to be here?") and the eager beavers who actually liked going to school as a kid.

There are three types of trainees...

Vacationers   Prisoners   Eager Beavers

But there's a much more profound reason why formal training can only do so much, and it returns us to brain science. Remember that people are "hardwired" through evolution to *feel before they think*. That's why any formal training that emphasizes rational thought over feelings isn't a substitute for providing more emotionally intimate, one-on-one orientation and coaching. After all, as is true of all memory formation, idea retention during training is primarily a function of striking an emotional chord. To be especially effective, alternative training:

- Must come from a source to which employees will be emotionally alert. In other words, their bosses. Given the heightened relevancy of that connection, employees will really pay attention and take the opportunity to learn.

- Must come from a source the employees respect. Again, this means their bosses—but only if those bosses can gain and sustain their confidence, which can be accomplished through proving real knowledge of both the "facts" and of the needs, wants and beliefs of the audience with whom they're sharing insights.

- Must come from a source with which the employees feel comfortable. Emotionally tone-deaf managers who "know their stuff" but aren't aware of the little, non-verbal signals they're sending may win the battle of minds but will likely lose the war involving hearts.

To that end, managers will find the advice of Nigel Nicholson in a *Harvard Business Review* article about the implications of evolutionary psychology for management practices worth remembering. Evolutionary psychology draws on academic fields like cognitive science, evolutionary biology, genetics and neuropsychology in order to foster a better understanding of the basic human condition.

As discussed in Chapter 1, neurogenesis means that new neurons and new mental connections form throughout our lifetimes. Nicholson's key point is that this plasticity or opportunity for growth and change in individuals must be balanced with the understanding that there are distinct limits to just how much basic human nature can be remolded. Therefore, emotionally wise managers won't despair and forfeit their desire for improvements.

But at the same time they won't set themselves up for disappointment by failing to recognize these truths:

- People usually think most creatively when they feel safe. They're unlikely to absorb something new if on edge.

- People have a tendency to be overconfident in their abilities, and may underestimate the difficulties they face.

As a result managers can make employees aware of their mental blind spots, but must do so gingerly because experiencing a sense of failure (bad news) won't make employees feel very safe or supported. A difficult balancing act arises because employees will resist change unless personally dissatisfied with their performance, yet they may not be capable of acting on what they've heard from a manager if they're not confident.

In other words, the difficulty involved in simultaneously maintaining employees' sense of safety while also getting them to pursue improvements in performance explains why managers who aren't emotionally skilled often falter. By psychologist Richard Boyatzis's calculation, only about 12% of managers are really good at their jobs and the primary reason that percentage isn't higher is because most managers lack emotional smarts.

Is there hope for the almost 90% of managers who aren't especially emotionally literate? Yes, awareness and practice will help. Even tiny steps like reducing the number of non-verbal micro-inequities that happen will be a benefit (Rawe). For example, managers may need to be reminded that using their BlackBerries while supposedly listening respectfully to the advice of a direct report isn't a good idea.

Checking your BlackBerry during supposedly important conversations with staff!

On a larger scale, there should be other resources for managers who struggle to deliver both knowledge and rapport at the same time. For example, one of the really progressive programs belongs to Caterpillar Inc., whose Cat U has been honored as one of the best training programs by the American Society for Training & Development, the Corporate University Exchange and the International Quality and Productivity Center. What makes Cat U so great?

- It's an on-going program integrated into daily business practice (rather than being another flavor-of-the-month exercise).

- The knowledge network the program draws on is broad and flexible. It includes trained program facilitators, advisory board members who serve as strategic partners and, most importantly, access to experts from across the company.

- The program is flexible not just in personnel but also in regard to timing. The coaching is available on short notice, and the collaborative sessions enable those who participate to post questions and share presentations to gain quick input (Caterpillar Inc.).

Feedback and Performance Appraisals
A constructive job review is really about developing a path for self-growth.

If there's ever a point in the year when it all comes together—the employee's, the manager's and, by extension, even the company's hopes and concerns—it's the periodic performance review (White; de Koning 2004). Talk about an emotionally-loaded situation. To avoid having lingering sullenness as an emotional outcome, especially on the part of the appraised employee, the following checklist of objectives should be pursued through careful planning and execution:

Clear Goals: Too often the periodic review is a subjective discussion that doesn't feel fair to those on the receiving end. Employees are unable to anticipate how their managers view their performances and they approach the reviews with a defensive mindset.

To counteract that possibility, even likelihood, the review should be based as much as possible on quantifiable outcome-based metrics tied to sales, customer loyalty, financial returns, quality measurements, complaint levels, et cetera. Identifying the right outcomes and balancing them so as to not skew employee focus is obviously challenging. Done well, performance reviews become a positive developmental activity so long as the goals are

Vague and fuzzy goals bad.
Clear goals good.

clear, long term and reasonably broad and expansive, allowing the employee to feel that pride and hope are plausible. Those goals should map out the path for the employee's self-growth. Avoid narrow, short-term goals that seem to be selfish in nature. In those cases, managers who are merely trying to feather their own caps before moving on to new assignments damage the integrity of the entire performance review process.

Authentic Buy-in: Emotions turn on and propel action when people sense relevancy. So employees should be authentically empowered to take ownership of goals, rather than feel like they are just handoffs from management. At the start of a review period (but separate from the previous performance review meeting), managers and their employees should sit down to discuss performance expectations and agree on specific targets and desired outcomes. Done well, those one-on-one sessions will lead to employees believing that the goals to be pursued are legitimate, real and worthy of their efforts.

Credible, Complete Assessments: While it should go without saying that managers will have a broad understanding of their employees' actual performance levels, too often that isn't the case. Distracted and harried managers risk appearing clueless at review time. Those managers don't know themselves how the employee performed and may fail to incorporate insights from that worker's peers, clients or other managers, all of whose input can help them arrive at a big-picture view.

At performance reviews, informed managers will then be better prepared to offer specific examples of behaviors (good and bad) that are impacting performance metrics. Specific examples are crucial for employees if they are to learn in ways that "break the mold." The mind must be able to *envision* what the boss is talking about for the heart to follow. When done right, the review process gains credibility and emotional responses (both positive and negative) can be better anticipated and managed.

Clear Developmental Path: Engaged employees are interested in improving their skills and advancing their careers. The goals cited earlier must be strategic, not merely small tactical steps that won't take an employee anywhere long term. Too often, managers neglect to help out, creating the disappointment that leads to employee sullenness. Whether as part of periodic performance reviews or separate meetings, managers and their employees should discuss strengths and areas for improvement. Then they should jointly create developmental action plans that will enable progress, without merely resorting to a list of training classes as a proxy for growth.

Genuine Pay/Performance Link: When the review process is founded on appropriate and meaningful metrics, the link between pay and performance is typically self-evident. Still, even the best system can break down if the company's short-term financial results are seen as an excuse to shortchange an employee's compensation. To avoid that outcome, never forget that employees' rewards (for learning to do their jobs well) shouldn't be adversely effected by the company's woes.

How often does it happen that, when a company cries "no money," the job appraisal is suddenly lower than normal? Then the performance appraisal becomes suspect, creating an emotional disconnect for the employee that is bound to show up in future performance levels. Should that result come as a big surprise? No. The financial *and* emotional bottom line here is that the salaries of good workers aren't the place to fix the company's bottom-line. Period.

Focus on Learning: Another guideline for ensuring constructive performance reviews is to make sure they serve as significant opportunities for learning. What's the big distraction here? It's a bottom-line focus on the question that's inevitable even when not spoken aloud: "How much more money am I going to get?" The problem is that when that question becomes too central, nobody really listens and the performance story is forgotten. Fear and hope get affixed to learning the answer, instead of a more proper emotional focus on creating the yearning to improve.

To prevent the audience from merely waiting for the end of the meeting and the financial answer to be given, the solution is for managers to handle the money distraction on a separate occasion. In performance reviews, focus on creating dialogue that gets workers to really emotionally internalize and accept opportunities for growth.

Engaged Follow-up: Finally, let's touch on the critical need to maintain ongoing dialogue and feedback. Employees should never be surprised by the direction of their periodic reviews. This guideline doesn't mean that they should be constantly micromanaged. Instead, it alludes to the need for managers to stay in steady but not overwhelming contact throughout their working relationships with employees. Then they will have the emotional equity required to endorse or coach behaviors that are contributing either to successes or problems.

That's the long-term picture. In the short term, the approach should be to circle back a couple of days after the review. A follow-up discussion provides an opportunity to affirm the positive take-aways, quell confusion and air any issues if there's a bitter aftertaste from the review. Not to do so is dangerous because negative feelings won't go away and will only fester. For a manager not to be proactive by circling back around isn't rational. Instead, it's behavior driven by fear and avoidance, and it will most likely make the whole review process that much messier and unproductive the next time around.

In summary, the performance review process doesn't have to be an emotional time bomb dreaded by managers and employees alike. When appraisals are handled well, employees feel like they're part of a fair, honest, open system and, therefore, the process has the potential to improve their morale, commitment and effectiveness.

Morale and Retention
The more emotional morale issues become,
the more hidden they're likely to be.

Even the best, most sensitive managers will have a hard time knowing what's really going on at the crucial emotional level in their daily interactions with staff members. After all, little can be learned if training, coaching and appraisals occur too deeply in the shadow of the hierarchal relationship of boss to subordinate that tends to suppress the upward flow of information. Why does that tendency exist? Hardwired into everybody's psyche is the realization that danger may be involved for those in the powerless position.

Therefore, even sincere, good-faith attempts by a manager to learn how it's going for his or her employees are unlikely to result in candor. And the more emotional, often negative, the situation becomes, the more morale is likely to be adversely affected even as the employee goes through the motions of pretending otherwise.

A case in point in regard to hidden, unexpressed feelings is a study Sensory Logic conducted for a major company in the financial services sector. As a follow-up to their usual annual survey of employees, we secured volunteers from a smaller sample of workers. Then we videotaped them so that traditional verbal input could be compared to what they *really* felt, as revealed by their facial expressions, about a select number of the survey topics. Here are the topics chosen:

- **Development:** Opportunities exist for me to learn new skills that can help further my career growth.

- **Support:** My manager makes it possible for me to succeed.

- **Satisfaction:** I'm able to find meaning and a sense of progress as a result of my work assignments and outcomes.

- **Life/Work Balance:** The demands of my job aren't overwhelming my commitments at home and adversely affecting the quality of my life.

For the purposes of this test, all verbal responses to each topic were categorized as essentially positive, neutral or negative. The analysis of the comments was then compared to the facial coding results that quantified the degree of positive emotional response or buy-in to these four assertions in the survey.

What emerged in the results? Not surprisingly given that people's livelihoods could seemingly be vulnerable if evidence of negative attitudes became apparent, what our subset of employees said was often very different from what they felt. As Figure 10.5 shows, verbal responses, regardless of topic, were always at least 50% positive. In contrast, in three of four instances the percentage of positive facial coding activity was less than half of the percentage of positive verbal input. Clearly, a huge gap opened between what employees were verbalizing and how they emotionally responded to the survey's affirmative assertions.

The key lesson for managers here is that morale looks vulnerable. Not only was just one score positive—the one related to future opportunities—the others were very low. Normally, we might see scores as low as 35% to 40% positive when facial coding analysis uncovers resistance. But here the other three scores are all below 30% and low enough to indicate that while the future may hold promise, the emotional reality is that at present workers are struggling to find enjoyment.

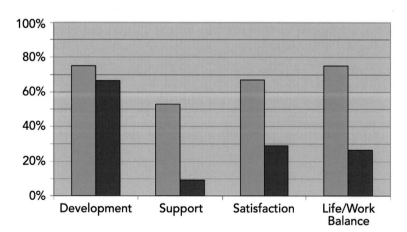

Fig. 10.5 Emotional Addendum to Annual Employee Survey

By contrasting the percentage of positive verbal and emotional responses, Sensory Logic found that employees at the company honestly saw opportunities for advancement, but not much else.

■ Positive Verbal Response ■ Positive Emotional Response

How do companies end up with sullen employees? When workers lose hope. Sullenness results from a combination of rising frustration and sadness (regret and resignation) that simultaneously lowers the energy levels available to deal with work situations. Companies that do not identify and turn that predicament around run the risk of losing morale, then momentum and, finally, employees—especially the top performers with the best prospects for moving on. As noted in Chapter 7, one estimate suggests that every staff turnover costs the affected company at least $60,000 and often much more. That sizeable sum is based on the required training and orientation for the replacement worker, among other factors. So losing all but the most mediocre employees is obviously not the way to go in building a financially and emotionally sound company.

To make the link between emotions, morale and retention statistically clear, note the results from three separate studies (HR Focus; "Workers"; Frost):

- One found that, among employees with intensely negative feelings, 28% are actively looking for new jobs. In contrast, only 6% of those who are happy are on the look-out for other opportunities.

- Another calculated that up to 40% of employees who believe they are being poorly supervised consider departing.

- A third concluded that workers who dislike their bosses are four times more likely to leave the company than those who rate them as excellent.

Without question, managers who can keep employees emotionally on-board are invaluable. To that end, what good workers want is apparent (Fig. 10.6) and tied to all of the core motivations except acquire, indicating that a truly good job isn't just about money.

By being able to evaluate what's wrong, and not just who's wrong, emotionally smart managers improve the odds of creating a productive working relationship in which employees remain open to learning and innovation, rather than succumbing to fear and resignation.

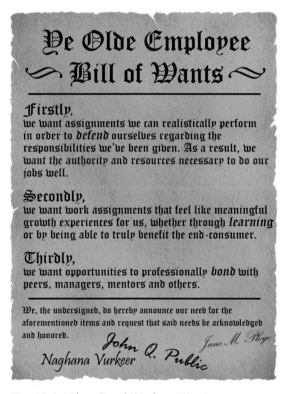

Ye Olde Employee ～ Bill of Wants ～

Firstly,
we want assignments we can realistically perform in order to *defend* ourselves regarding the responsibilities we've been given. As a result, we want the authority and resources necessary to do our jobs well.

Secondly,
we want work assignments that feel like meaningful growth experiences for us, whether through *learning* or by being able to truly benefit the end-consumer.

Thirdly,
we want opportunities to professionally *bond* with peers, managers, mentors and others.

We, the undersigned, do hereby announce our need for the aforementioned items and request that said needs be acknowledged and honored.

John Q. Public
Jane M. Ploye
Naghana Vurkeer

Fig. 10.6 What Good Workers Want.

By providing employees with all three items from the Bill of Wants, companies will get plenty back in return. Emotional engagement makes positive outcomes possible in the workplace. Moreover, study after study confirms that there is a direct link between employee satisfaction and customer satisfaction, and that there exists another series of links between employee satisfaction and higher levels of productivity, profitability and employee retention (Baker; Boyatzis).

Mission Critical:
inspiring a questing mentality

Synopsis: In effect, mission critical refers to eliciting more effort and better outcomes from employees who can find real meaning in their assignments. This section will address the need for nourishing company cultures, whether within the company at large or in smaller, team-based settings in which employees feel the kind of camaraderie that makes greatness possible. The section ends by examining the emotionally-based qualities that enable a team to exceed expectations.

> **Key take-aways:**
> - Employees work better in smaller units and with a healthy dose of encouragement.
> - Great teams enjoy a sense of mission and are able to draw on everyone's talents.

Emotion and Motivations

Pride is the key emotion in play here. It occurs when happy employees feel just enough anger and desire to break through barriers and achieve results. No matter how good the working bond with the boss, employees may experience pride best in peer-based teams more likely to encourage uninhibited action. The primary motivations are the urge to **bond** with co-workers combined with the opportunity to **learn**.

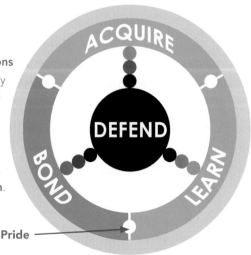

Pride

Getting to the Right Size

Employees work better in smaller units, and with a healthy dose of encouragement.

Everyone at a company is subject to the company's general culture. No manager or employee is immune to its influence. It would be great if most workers regarded their corporate cultures positively but, unfortunately, the statistics aren't promising. As reported in *USA Today* (Jones 2004), a Booz Allen Hamilton survey found that apparently one in three Americans believe they work for a passive-aggressive company, where smiling without actually being in accordance serves as the dysfunctional norm. (Figure 10.6 depicts the survey's full results.)

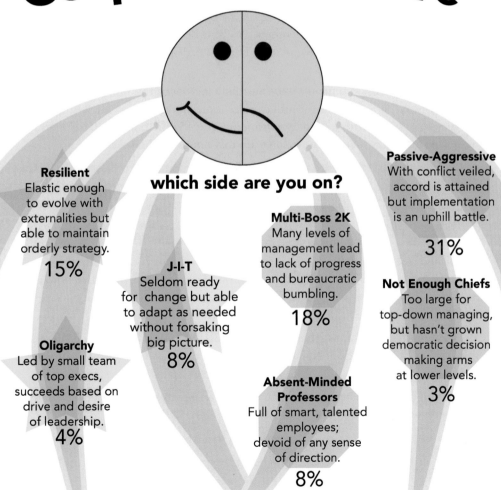

Corporate Culture

which side are you on?

Resilient
Elastic enough to evolve with externalities but able to maintain orderly strategy.
15%

J-I-T
Seldom ready for change but able to adapt as needed without forsaking big picture.
8%

Oligarchy
Led by small team of top execs, succeeds based on drive and desire of leadership.
4%

Multi-Boss 2K
Many levels of management lead to lack of progress and bureaucratic bumbling.
18%

Absent-Minded Professors
Full of smart, talented employees; devoid of any sense of direction.
8%

Passive-Aggressive
With conflict veiled, accord is attained but implementation is an uphill battle.
31%

Not Enough Chiefs
Too large for top-down managing, but hasn't grown democratic decision making arms at lower levels.
3%

Fig. 10.6 Only 27% of American Workers Respect Their Workplace

That picture fits the estimate that there might be *as much as 40%* in "untapped productivity reserves" at the typical company because it's emotionally dysfunctional (Jones). Hamstrung by an unhealthy culture, managers and employees alike begin to feel as if qualities like comfort, excitement and nimbleness are but a distant dream.

How best to find a solution? A constructive approach is to look back at historical human nature to find the way forward. Have people thrived best in groups or alone? What role do emotions play? What group size has traditionally worked well for people? Hint: it isn't the mega-corporations that exist today. In contrast, it's believed that for most of recorded history—99% of it—humans beings lived, hunted, then began farming in small groups of no more than 10 to 50 fellow members (Baker).

From sports teams to military squads, the core unit rarely exceeds a dozen members. It's a size that has traditionally proven to deliver the best opportunity for social and emotional cohesion, thereby creating the best opportunities for positive outcomes. Yes, the whole can be greater than the sum of the parts.

So what's believed to be the ideal team size in the business world? For optimal effectiveness, a team should have no more than six members. As Tom Peters jokes, a team should never, ever be so large that it can't be fed by two big pizzas. The rationale pin-pointing this group size comes from two different angles (Conniff):

- **Every extra person in a group exponentially increases the number of one-on-one relationships.** As a result, larger groups place more emotional and intellectual demands on their members. While a six-person team involves 15 different pairs of relationships, each requiring attention, for a seven-person team that number balloons to 21.

- **A listener should ideally be within five feet of a speaker to hear well.** If there are six inches of shoulder-to-shoulder distance between team members, no more than seven people can sit next to each other in a five-foot diameter circle.

Clearly the second point—being able to hear what's going on—is functionally advantageous. But it's the first point that establishes the core reason why small groups work well. Without a rich sense of undistracted *intimacy*, team members can't bond with one another, feel supported and produce desired results. To accomplish its mission, the co-workers on that team must be able to form good individual relationships so that self-disclosure doesn't seem risky and affirmation takes on a personal glow.

A decade-long study of management teams at Ross Perot's old company, EDS, came away with hard and fast numbers regarding how important emotional support actually is to forming a successful team (Conniff):

- The 15 high-performance teams in the research project averaged 5.6 positive interactions for every negative one.

- In contrast, the 19 lowest-performance teams had a positive/negative ratio of 0.4.

The study also concluded, however, that being too positive can be bad. At more than a five-to-one positive to negative comment ratio, teams get lax and begin to grow ineffective. It's a classic case of cause-and-effect. If emotional support begins to feel inauthentic because every effort gets praised, such empty praise will cause the team's output to suffer.

The Qualities that Drive Great Teams
*Great teams enjoy a sense of mission and are
able to draw on everyone's talents.*

Like its common counterpart (namely the staff or project meetings led by managers organizing the goals of their direct reports), a well-functioning, specially convened team should stick to a pair of basic rules.

First, to get the best from people, members—and especially team leaders—must avoid embarrassing others. Remember that many people fear public speaking more than practically anything else. Therefore, public humiliation of any kind will undermine that person's ability to function in the group. Fear always comes before the opportunity for pride. One study found that an amazing 28% of employees said they typically feel uncomfortable in meetings (MacIntyre), which means that open, full participation won't be easily coaxed from them.

Yes, their reason for discomfort is fear of being put "on the spot" during a discussion. But they could feel uneasy for perhaps an even more justifiable reason: boredom. Meetings should always have genuine purposes and end with clear calls to action. A meeting is a story: it should have a beginning, a middle and an end.

Unfortunately, most meetings have beginnings that drag on and on. So a second basic rule is that if no clear, decisive action will be taken as a result of the meeting, don't meet. Boredom is an emotional cancer that leaves department staff members and specially convened teams both mentally and emotionally bed-ridden.

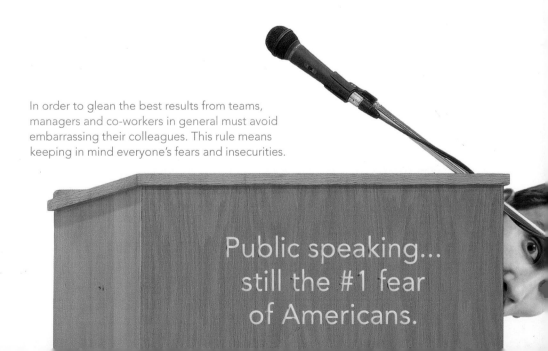

In order to glean the best results from teams, managers and co-workers in general must avoid embarrassing their colleagues. This rule means keeping in mind everyone's fears and insecurities.

Public speaking...
still the #1 fear
of Americans.

Fig. 10.7 Company Culture Claims vs. Practice
The subjects emotionally endorsed the idea that the company has a "we" mentality. But the degree to which it is all encompassing comes into doubt because of weaker responses to specific issues involving how people at the company interact.

"Are your colleagues aware of when they create a problem?"

"Is there a 'we' mentality at the company?"

"Do you feel supported in seizing business opportunities?"

"Are you comfortable proactively handling problems?"

"Are decisions communicated prior to implementation?"

"Is the company doing better at pleasing customers?"

Those are just ground rules, however, to be followed so as not to inhibit potential. Of greater interest is to learn what really makes a team a great team. The question is intriguing, and the answer is primarily emotional in nature.

A case in point is consulting work that Sensory Logic did for a company seeking greater cohesiveness within its ranks. For a group of directors and their staffs, we conducted a study involving half a dozen questions that could serve as a springboard for discussions about how best to improve working dynamics. As is evident from the results in Figure 10.7, everybody involved was emotionally on-board with the general belief that the company was characterized by a "we" mentality.

But that was more at the conceptual level. When the questions got down to specifics, the picture changed. Then the subject's emotional responses revealed that, while specific problems were handled proactively and well, larger, company-size initiatives were falling by the wayside. For instance, the subjects felt assured that customer needs were being addressed. They didn't have the same emotional confidence, though, regarding their own needs when it came to cooperation, communication and pursuing business growth opportunities.

Great teams—which is what this small company's management group aspired to be—take care to get the essentials right. Let's review what they are (Bennis).

The first essential has to be the composition of the team. Talent matters. But just as important to the successful functioning of a team is that its members fit together well, emotionally and in terms of personalities. Don't impair a team from the get-go by establishing the wrong emotional mix. Here are three routinely ignored selection criteria:

- **The right level of status diversity:** team members should be relatively equal in status within the company, since lower-downs usually defer to higher-ups. Mixing status can rob the team of intellectual input and emotional commitment.

- **Gender parity:** there needs to be a good mix of men and women so that the team can benefit from the different emotional skills typical of each gender.
- **Personality diversity:** there can't be too many A-types in the group since they will tend to struggle with each other instead of with the issues the team was formed to address. A critical mass of B-types can serve as a good counterweight to the A-types' influence.

The second essential, team size, we've already addressed.

The third essential is that the team must have a true leader. Often times a leader is imposed on a team. But a great team doesn't gain its leader that way. A great team is emotionally wise enough to recognize that the drive to lead is inborn. It also knows that the drive and ability to lead can depend on (a) circumstances, (b) a would-be leader's location in his or her professional life cycle, (c) the way the team's project fits with a potential leader's interests, and (d) the way the project suits the company's needs. For instance, at IDEO, where innovation rules (they lead the list of offer-design firms year after year), employees choose their teams and then the teams choose their own leaders. From such spontaneity can grow the kind of results a great team dreams of delivering.

Speaking of dreams, that's the fourth essential. Great teams enjoy a real sense of mission. They have a purpose and often an "enemy" that helps to mobilize their energies. This enemy could be a rival company, whose offer a team regards as inferior and yet is currently dominating the marketplace. Or this enemy could even be the company bureaucracy in which the great team operates, struggling to prove its potential as an "underdog."

The fifth essential is that, when blessed with a mission, a great team knows how to swing into action. It knows how to leverage everybody and every resource on the team so that dreams can emerge fully realized. To that end, a successful team will deliver a what's-in-it-for-me (WIIFM) to each and every team member. The team will also let everyone feel as though he or she is in it together and can influence the outcome. Great teams are their own reward, and everyone on them has a job suitable to his or her abilities.

Finally and perhaps most crucially, a great team is so emotionally fueled that it lives on hope, not reality as narrowly defined by a set of deliverables. In other words, the members of a great team find satisfaction throughout the process—not just in completing it—because the experience itself is intellectually and emotionally rewarding. Yes, great teams ship—they deliver—but they do so by meeting standards that exist in their hearts, not on slips of paper. The contract they really have is with themselves.

To avoid violating this list of essentials, there is, finally, one crucial anti-rule regarding teams: don't ever form one if it's merely a cover-up for not taking real action and seeing changes through. The vitality of great teams is dependent on their authenticity. Cease to make them a vehicle for fresh, truly open thinking and actionable outcomes, and management poisons the emotional groundwater that makes them such a valuable addition to a company.

Now, how these great teams relate to the company sponsoring them is always a bit tricky. A team sponsor who can guard and defend the great team's unique culture—its assumptions, values and beliefs—while also acquiring the support of a cross-section of the company is vital. What gets born in a silo will die there, too. Great teams seek a trade-off between being independent and yet having their efforts be appreciated and incorporated into the company's plans.

Ultimately, companies that tap into a great team's inspirational, emotionally-fueled potential day by day—and make it possible—will get the results they long to have. In increasingly flat companies where self-directed work is likely to become the norm, instilling pride isn't some "nice to have" platitude. Instead, pride, hope and emotional engagement, in general, have become a business necessity in order to be highly productive and competitively viable.

Conclusion

Positive, constructive employee management is the heart of most successful businesses. Unfortunately, in the day-to-day distractions of running a business, the emotional components of employee management often get overlooked. To be effective and robust, management must accomplish the following:

- Make the right hires. Companies that know themselves and understand the types of people who will flourish within their ranks are more likely to make the right hiring decisions. The opportunity open to any and all companies is understanding its own emotional components, and then taking into account the job candidates' personalities, values and interactive abilities.

- Build rapport. Because the manager/employee honeymoon is fleeting, it's important to establish good habits early. The key one: given a choice between under-communicating and over-communicating, always select the latter. That's especially true when appraisals and other forms of feedback or coaching become necessary due to setbacks. In those instances, rapport helps provide the emotional equity that sees the working relationship through.

- Don't pen people in, otherwise they will emotionally wilt. Good employees will want room to operate (while still having their managers or team leaders establishing realistic boundaries). Rhetoric about empowering people, coupled with lots of limitations, is asking for an outcome that doesn't exist in nature. It's like trying to breed a cross between a lion and a sheep.

An Action Plan

To make sure that the company's employee management is emotionally healthy, here are a few things to check when assessing effectiveness:

❑ Hire people using a process in which multiple employees meet the job candidate in as casual and social an environment as possible. Build in opportunities for storytelling, both by candidates who can reveal themselves in action and by company representatives prepared to be candid. This way, both sides can address not just the rationally-oriented skills required for the job but also the personality and values best suited for the situation. (In regards to fit, cancel the interview if the manager the candidate would be working for can't make it to the session.)

❑ Ensure that everyone feels welcome and the company's commitment to diversity feels believable and not just like window dressing. Nobody can perform well if they're not emotionally comfortable and at ease. In today's society, the company should be growing more, not less, diverse by race, gender and sexual orientation.

❑ The processes by which the company operates should feel fair and legitimate, not rigged. They should also feel human and personal rather than seemingly being delivered in a unidirectional, cold, distant voice.

❑ The company should be sensitive to the way employees' emotional needs vary as they go through their life cycles of service at the company. New hires will be more anxious about unknowns, while younger-but-established workers will look for expansive futures and veterans will seek both steady situations and new challenges.

afterword

So what now? What does the future hold for emotions?
The science-fiction crowd may not be far off. As technology
progresses in its ability to replicate human characteristics,
we may be standing on the precipice of emotionally
aware robots that respond to their owners' feelings.

The Irish poet William Butler Yeats believed that history doesn't repeat itself so much as form a spiral staircase, with repetition but at an ever higher level. In that case, it shouldn't be surprising that back in the 18th century Adam Smith created not only the "dismal science" of economics but also took a pioneering role in the "sentimental science" of psychology. Today, Smith's twin study of money matters and emotions looks ever more prescient. His two favorite disciplines are intersecting again but at a much higher, more sophisticated level than ever before thanks to the on-going, futuristic force of technology.

Some of that technology involves the *f*MRI brain scans that have been providing striking evidence about the essential role that emotions play in the decision-making process. At other times, however, technology goes beyond confirming the importance of emotions to exploring new possibilities.

For instance, consider the techno toys joining our world. A relatively simple example is Play-mates Toys' invention, "Amazing Amanda," a baby doll capable of showing a small range of feelings that her face emotes electronically while she speaks (Marriott).

At the same time, functional, semi-emotionally-literate robots have begun to appear. After fluffy little robots called "Furbies," came Sony's AIBO Entertainment Robot (Norman). With the programmed capacity for the six core emotions of facial coding—happiness, sadness, anger, surprise, fear and dislike (disgust)—Sony's Robot adapts its emotional state and behavior based on external stimuli, just like human beings do in real life.

Our lives are being "wired" in all sorts of ways, so it is inevitable that emotions have become part of the changes afoot. Indeed, robots replacing humans and capable of doing everything people do—only better, including showing emotions, responding emotionally and even reading the emotions of others—is what many artificial intelligence initiatives are really all about.

Writing for *Scientific American*, Microsoft's chairman Bill Gates provocatively titled his article, "A Robot in Every Home," then backed it up with the estimate that nearly 10 million personal robots will soon be in use. By 2025, the personal robot industry is expected to be worth over $50 billion in annual sales, as robots keep tabs on home security, do domestic tasks and care for the bedridden elderly, among other forms of assistance to their owners.

Even without the use of robots, the confluence of economics and emotions originated by Adam Smith is well on its way to reaching new and higher formats.

Video games are a major sector already, with characters engaged in highly animated movements and displaying a large variety of facial expressions. Perhaps these games, as well as company websites and even camera-enabled cell phones, may soon bring us interactions in which our feelings are read, then reflected or responded to accordingly, in an attempt to heighten our enjoyment or directly modify our purchase decisions.

Does that sound too futuristic? Then consider the fact that the business of emotion detection, using speech analytics, is already a $400 million industry (Shin). What is being done through tracking volume, pitch and the categorization of transcribed words and phrases will sooner rather than later become a reality in regard to facial coding, too.

Ekman's FACS system was created based on individual facial muscle movements, which makes it ideal for computer generation; it is a codified system to accurately and completely represent physiological actions. This ability has allowed game engines, such as Half Life, to model realistic facial movements that transfer across any model for certain actions. As games are capable of rendering graphics more realistically, the need for realistic actions becomes even more pronounced. The realistic rendering of human appearance without the realistic modeling of human behavior creates a completely unbelievable representation. The most well-known occurrence of this lapse is probably *Final Fantasy,* a movie beautifully rendered in exquisite detail, but which lacks believable interaction, thus preventing viewers from reaching the point where they can suspend their disbelief of the situation.

In short, programming machines to display or interpret emotions is going to transform both the marketplace and the workplace, enabling companies to get closer to consumers and re-invent offices and factories in ways that were never imaginable until now.

Why Emotions Win Every Time

In the end, it's really quite simple: to achieve success, companies must follow nature. Given that emotions process sensory input in one-fifth the time that our conscious, cognitive brain takes, reason will always depend on emotion to define what is vital to us. The evolutionary process gave us feeling before thinking. Solving the emotion puzzle originates with quelling fear and the related motivation to defend ourselves. Because of this, *Fear Factor* isn't just a TV show; it's the essence of a sound emotional business strategy, as reflected by the old, but true, adage that "trust is the emotion of business."

Further breakthroughs in brain science are occurring at an increasingly faster pace, making it difficult to come to a close on the information contained in this book. It is an exciting time for new developments in consumer and employee insights. On an almost daily basis, I find news stories that affirm the guidance I've sought to provide in this book.

One day it's *The Wall Street Journal* reporting about *f*MRI scans that show different neurological reactions to strong and weak brands (Helliker). Another day it's the A.P. wire services detailing a study that shows women get paternal clues in men's faces ("Women") or *The New York Times* reporting on research indicating that men are better than woman at detecting an angry face in a crowd (Bakalar).

Within days of each other just this past week, *The Economist* made "Happiness (and how to measure it) its cover story and *Strategy + Business* named Fisher & Shapiro's *Beyond Reason: Using Emotions as You Negotiate* as one of the best new books.

But the most significant recent news story in terms of what Sensory Logic does to help companies measure and manage emotions came to me via the BBC News. This story further validates Charles Darwin's original work on facial coding—and in particular, the universality of facial expressions—because it is a dramatic study by a team of Israeli scientists who found that the facial expressions of family members align closely. In particular, their research found support for Darwin's belief that facial expressions are innate. In analyzing the expressions of 21 volunteers, some of whom who had been blind from birth along with those of their relatives, the scientists discovered that facial expressions were strikingly alike.

The revelation that facial expressions are inherited and have an evolutionary basis furthers the hunt. The next step? Looking for the genes that influence facial expression.

Meanwhile, armed with the emotional knowledge provided in this book readers can begin to see and identify the intellectual alibis that are present everywhere. Read faces and, by and large, it's possible to know where people stand. Changing peoples' beliefs is hard work: selling them on what they already believe and feel is far easier. My advice is to connect emotionally and then provide rational support. After all, the "facts" are malleable but our gut instincts are unyielding.

works cited

Ackerman, Diane. *A Natural History of the Senses*. New York: Vintage Books, 1990.

American Optometric Association.

"An Assessment of American Education." *Harris Education Research Council*. New York City. 1991.

Ander, Willard N., and Neil Z. Stern. *Winning at Retail: Developing a Sustained Model for Retail Success*. Hoboken: John Wiley & Sons, 2004.

Anderson, Eric, and Duncan Simester. "Mind Your Pricing Cues." *Harvard Business Review* September (2003).

Anderson, Rolph, Joseph Hair and Allen Bush. *Professional Sales Management*. New York: Wiley, 1992.

Applebaum, Alec. "The Constant Customer." *Gallup Management Journal* June 17 (2001).

Arvey, Richard D., and James E. Campion. "The Employment Interview: A Summary and Review of Recent Literature." *Personnel Psychology* 35 (1982): 281-322.

Atkin, Douglas. *The Culting of Brands*. New York: Portfolio, 2004.

Baig, Edward C. "Why Are Tech Gizmos So Hard to Figure Out?" *USA Today* 2 November 2005: B1-2.

Baker, Dan, Cathy Greenberg and Collins Hemingway. *What Happy Companies Know*. Upper Saddle River, NJ: Pearson Education, 2006.

Baldwin, Timothy, and J. Kevin Ford. "Transfer to Training." *Personnel Psychology* (1997): 50.

Bakalar, Nicholas. "Men Are Better Than Women at Ferreting Out That Angry Face in a Crowd." *The New York Times*. 13 June 2006 <http://www.nytimes.com/2006/06/13/health/psychology/13face.html>.

"Bandwidth of the Human Eye." *Medgadget.com*. 28 July 2006 <http://www.medgadget.com/archives/2006/07/the_bandwidth_o.html>.

Banich, Marie T. *Cognitive Neuroscience and Neuropsychology*. Boston: Houghton Mifflin, 2004.

Bardhan, Ashok Deo, and Cynthia Kroll. "The New Wave of Outsourcing." *Fisher Central Report #1103*. UC Berkeley 2 November 2003.

Barletta, Martha. *Marketing to Women*. Chicago: Dearborn, 2003.

Bates, Brian, and John Cleese. *The Human Face*. London: DK, 2001.

Begley, Sharon. "How Do You Keep the Public Shopping? Just Make People Sad." *The Wall Street Journal* 19 March 2004.

Bennis, Warren, and Patricia Ward Biederman. *Organizing Genius: the Secrets of Creative Collaboration*. Reading, MA: Addison-Wesley, 1997.

Berkowitz, Eric, Roger Kerin, Steven Hartley and William Rudelius. *Marketing*. Burr Ridge, IL: Irwin, 1994.

Bernbach, Bill. *Bill Bernbach Said*. New York: DDB Needham, 1989.

Bernthal, Karen. Interview with form recruitment agency staffer. October 2006.

"Best Business Books 2006." *Strategy+Business*. Winter 2006.

Bodenhausen, Galen, Lori Sheppard and Geoffrey Kramer. "Negative Affect and Social Judgment: the Differential Impact of Anger and Sadness." *European Journal of Social Psychology* 24 (1994): 45-62.

Boyatzis, Richard. "Resonant Leadership: Inspiring the Best in Us." Nationwide Insurance Leadership Council Presentation. 17 July 2006.

Breen, Bill. "The Seoul of Design." *Fast Company* December 2005: 90.

Brill, Peter, and Richard Worth. *The Four Levers of Corporate Change*. New York: AMACOM, 1997.

Broetzmann, Scott. "The Conventional Wisdom of Customer Care: Fact, Fiction or Management Myths." SOCAP Annual Conference. New York City. 11 October 2004.

Buckingham, Marcus, and Curt Coffman. *First, Break All the Rules*. New York: Simon & Schuster, 1999.

Byrne, John. "How Jack Welch Runs GE." *BusinessWeek* 8 June 1998.

Carey, Dennis C., and Dayton Ogden. *The Human Side of M & A: How CEOs Leverage the Most Important Asset in Deal Making.* New York: Oxford University Press, 2004.

Carleton, Robert, Kim Klein and Claude S. Lineberry. *Achieving Post-Merger Success.* San Francisco, CA: Pfeiffer, 2004.

Carr, Clay. "Choice." *Chance and Organizational Change: Practical Insights from Evolution for Business Leaders and Thinkers.* New York: AMACOM, 1997.

Catepillar Inc. Caterpillar Inc.'s "Cat U" Named Best Overall Corporate University. 29 Dec 2006 <http://www.cat.com/cda/components/fullArticle?ids=207849>.

Center for American Progress. "Outsourcing Statistics in Perspective." April 2007. <http://www.americanprogress.org>.

Childre, Loc Lew, and Bruce Cryer. *From Chaos to Coherence: the Power to Change Performance.* Boulder Creek, CO: Planetary Publications, 2000.

Chitwood, Roy. *World Class Selling.* Minneapolis: Best Sellers Publishing, 1996.

Clancy, Heather. "E-Tail Therapy." *Entrepreneur* January 2005.

Coe, John. *The Fundamentals of Business-to-Business Sales and Marketing.* New York: McGraw-Hill, 2003.

Collins, Jim. *Good to Great.* New York: HarperCollins, 2001.

Compton, Rebecca J. "The Interface Between Emotion and Attention." *Behavioral and Cognitive Neuroscience Review* 2.2 (2003): 115-129.

Conniff, Richard. *The Ape in the Corner Office: Understanding the Workplace Beast in All of Us.* New York: Crown Business, 2005.

Cooper, Robert, and Elko Kleinschmidt. *New Products: the Key Factors in Success.* Chicago: AMA, 1990.

Cornelius, Randolph R. *The Science of Emotion.* Upper Saddle River, NJ: Prentice Hall, 1996.

Crawford, Bob. "By the Board." *QSR Magazine* January 2006: 17-18.

Cummins, H. J. "Generations Collide." *The Minneapolis Star-Tribune* 27 November 2005.

Darwin, Charles. *The Expression of the Emotions in Man and Animals.* Oxford: Oxford UP, 1998.

Davenport, Thomas H., and John C. Beck. *The Attention Economy.* Boston: Harvard Business School Press, 2001.

Davis, Ann, Joseph Pereira and William M. Bulkeley. "Silent Signals." *The Wall Street Journal* 15 August 2002: A1, A6.

Davis, Kevin. *Getting into Your Customer's Head.* New York: Random House, 1996.

Daykin, Tom. "Big Goes Small." *The Minneapolis Star-Tribune* 5 August 2006: D1, D4.

De Koning, Guido M.J. "Evaluating Employee Performance." *Gallup Management Journal* 9 December (2004).

De Koning, Guido M.J. "Building Your 'Bench Strength.'" *Gallup Management Journal* 10 March (2005).

Desatnick, Robert L., and Denis H. Detzel. *Managing to Keep the Customer.* San Francisco: Josey-Bass, 1993.

Drucker, Peter F. "What Executives Should Remember." *Harvard Business Review* February (2006):145-152.

du Plessis, Erik. *The Advertised Mind.* Sterling, VA: Millward Brown, 2005.

Dunbar, Robin. *Grooming Gossip and the Evolution of Language.* London: Faber and Faber, 1996.

Dunham, Richard. "Read His Lips—and Smirk." *BusinessWeek.com* 19 October 2004.

Dychtwald, Ken, Tamara Erickson and Bob Morison. "It's Time to Retire Retirement." *Harvard Business Review* March (2004).

Ekman, Paul. *Emotions Revealed.* New York: Times Books, 2003.

Ekman, Paul. *Telling Lies.* New York: W. W. Norton, 1992.

Elliott, Stuart. "Advertiser-Agency Relationships Turn a Bit Brighter." *The New York Times* 6 November 2006: 8.

Ellison, Sarah. "P & G Chief's Turnaround Recipe: Find Out What Women Want." *The Wall Street Journal* 1 June 2005: A1.

"Face Expressions 'Hereditary'." *BBC.* 25 October 2006 <http://news.bbc.co.uk/1/hi/health/6055430.stm>.

"Feeling Good Matters in the Workplace." *Gallup Management Journal* 12 January (2006).

Feldman, Michael. "What' Ya Know?" *National Public Radio* 24 July 2004.

Fishman, Charles. "'But Wait, You Promised…'" *Fast Company* April 2001.

Florida, Richard. *The Rise of the Creative Class*. New York: Basic Books, 2002.

Forelle, Charles, and James Bandler. "The Perfect Payday." *The Wall Street Journal* 18 March 2006: A1, A5.

Frijda, Nico, Peter Kuipers and Elisabeth ter Schure. "Relations Among Emotions, Appraisal, and Emotional Action Readiness." *Journal of Personality and Social Psychology* 57 (1989): 212-228.

Frost, Peter. "Jumping Ship Statistic." *Toxic Emotions at Work*. Boston: Harvard Business School Press, 2003.

Garfield, Bob. *And Now a Few Words from Me*. New York: McGraw-Hill, 2003.

Gates, Bill. "A Robot in Every Home." *Scientific American* January 2007: 58-65.

Gerber, Robin. "Why Can't Women Be Leaders, Too?" *Gallup Management Journal* 13 October (2005).

Gitomer, Jeffrey. *Customer Satisfaction Is Worthless*. Austin, TX: Bard Press, 1998.

Gitomer, Jeffrey. *The Sales Bible*. New York: Wiley, 2003.

Gladwell, Malcolm. *Blink: the Power of Thinking without Thinking*. New York: Little, Brown & Company, 2005.

Gladwell, Malcolm. "The Naked Face." *The New Yorker* 5, August (2002): 38-49.

Gobé, Marc. *Emotional Branding*. New York: Allworth Press, 2001.

Goldberg, Carey. "Empathy May Begin at the Neurons." *The International Herald Tribune* 15 December 2005.

Goleman, Daniel. *Emotional Intelligence*. New York: Bantam Books, 1995.

Goleman, Daniel. *Working With Emotional Intelligence*. New York: Bantam Books, 2000.

Goleman, Daniel, Richard Boyatzis and Annie McKee. *Primal Leadership: Learning to Lead with Emotional Intelligence*. Boston: Harvard Business School Press, 2002.

Grantham, Charles, and Judith Carr. *Consumer Evolution*. New York: John Wiley & Sons, 2002.

Greenleaf, Robert K., Hamilton Beazley, Julie Beggs and Larry C. Spears. *The Servant-Leader Within*. Mahwah, NJ: Paulist Press, 2003.

"Happiness (and How to Measure It)." *The Economist* 23 December 2006.

Hawkins, Jeff, and Sandra Blakeslee. *On Intelligence*. New York: Times Books, 2004.

Heide, Christen P. "Dartnell's 30th Sales Force Compensation Survey." Chicago: Dartnell Corporation, 1998.

Heil, Gary, Tom Parker and Rick Tate. *Leadership and the Customer Revolution*. New York: Van Nostrand Reinhold, 1995.

Helliker, Kevin. "This Is Your Brain on a Strong Brand: MRIs Show Even Insurers Can Excite." *The Wall Street Journal*. 28 November 2006 <http://online.wsj.com/article_print/SB116468747325534284.html>.

Hitchcock, David. "Asian Values and the United States: How Much Conflict?" *Center for Strategic and International Studies.* November, 1994.

Hine, Thomas. *The Total Package*. Boston: Little, Brown & Company, 1995.

Howard, Pierce J. *The Owner's Manual for the Brain*. Atlanta: Bard, 2000.

Howard, Theresa. "Marketers Aim for 'Engaged' Consumers." *USA Today* 20 July 2006.

HR Focus 82.8 (August 2005).

The Human Face. Dir. James Erskine. Perf. John Cleese. 2001. VHS. BBC Video.

Huntington, Samuel. *The Clash of Civilizations and the Remaking of the World Order*. New York: Touchstone, 1997.

Hymowitz, Carol. "Women Swell Ranks as Middle Managers, But Are Scarce at Top." *The Wall Street Journal* 24 July 2006: B1.

Jarrett, Michael. "The Seven Myths of Change Management." *Business Strategy Review* 14 (2003).

Jeffrey, Scott. "The Effect of Tangible Rewards on Perceived Organizational Support." Waterloo, Ontario: University of Waterloo.

Jones, Del. "Besides Being Lonely at the Top, It Can Be 'Disengaging' as Well." *USA Today* 21 June 2005.

Jones, Del. "When You're Smiling, Are You Seething Inside?" *USA Today* 12 April 2004.

Kaplan, Allison. "These Days, the Store of Your Dreams May Be in Somebody's Basement." *The St. Paul Pioneer Press* 13 October 2006: E1, 13.

Kahneman, Daniel. "What Were They Thinking?" *Gallup Management Journal* 13 January (2005).

Kahneman, Daniel. "Are You Happy Now?" *Gallup Management Journal* 10 February (2005).

Khurana, Rakesh. *Searching for a Corporate Savior*. Princeton, NJ: Princeton UP, 2002.

Klein, Stefan. *The Science of Happiness*. New York: Marlowe & Company, 2002.

Kotkin, Joel. "Main Street 2020: Retail's Future in the Age of E-Commerce." Gensler Associates & La Jolla Institute Joint Report, 1999.

Kotler, Philip. "Atmospherics as a Marketing Tool." *Journal of Retailing* 49.4 (1973-1974): 48-61.

Kotler, Philip. *Marketing Management*. Englewood Cliffs, NJ: Prentice Hall, 1994.

Kouzes, James, and Barry Posner, eds. "A Prescription for Leading in Cynical Times." *Ivey Business Journal* July/August (2004).

Labaton, Stephen. "S.E.C. to Require More Disclosure on Executive Pay." *The New York Times* 18 January 2006: A1, C2.

Lakoff, George, and Mark Johnson. *Metaphors We Live By*. Chicago: University of Chicago Press, 2003.

Lauer, Harvey. *Quirk's*. July/August (2005).

Lawrence, Paul R., and Nitin Nohria. *Driven: How Human Nature Shapes Our Choices*. San Francisco: Jossey-Bass, 2002.

LeDoux, Joseph. "Emotion, Memory and the Brain." *Scientific American* June 1994: 50-57.

LeDoux, Joseph. "Management Wisdom from a Neuroscientist." *Gallup Management Journal* 11 December (2003).

LeDoux, Joseph. "Management Wisdom from a Neuroscience." Gallup Management Journal December (2003).

Lehrer, Jonah. "The Reinvention of the Self." *Seed* February/March 2006.

Leitch, Will. "Group Thinker: You Can Make a Living From Focus Groups—If You Tell Them What They Want to Hear." *New York*. 16 June 2004.

Lerner, Jennifer S., Deborah A. Small and George Loewenstein. "Heart Strings and Purse Strings." *Psychological Science* 15.5 (2004).

"Live from DMA06." Direct Marketing Association (DMA). 18 October 2006 <http://directmag.com>.

Loewenstein, George, and Jennifer Lerner. "The Role of Affect in Decision Making." *Handbook of Affective Science*. Eds. R. Davidson, K. Scherer and H. Goldsmith. New York: Oxford University Press, 2003.

MacIntyre, John. "Prime Numbers." *Profit* 24.4 (2005): 13.

Mackie, Diane, and Leila Worth. "Processing Deficits and the Mediation of Positive Affect in Persuasion." *Journal of Personality and Social Psychology* 57 (1989): 27-40.

Madique, Modesto, and Billie Jo Zirger. "A Study of Success and Failure in Product Innovation." *IEEE Transaction on Engineering Management* November (1998): 192-203.

Mahrabian, Albert. *Silent Messages*. Belmont, CA: Wadsworth, 1981.

Manning, Brian. "Measure Engagement, Not Satisfaction." iMediaconnection.com. 13 July 2006. <http://www.imediaconnection.com/content/10381.asp>.

Marcus, George. E. *The Sentimental Citizen*. University Park, PA: Pennsylvania State University Press, 2002.

Marriott, Michel. "Amanda Says, 'You Don't Sound Like Mommy.'" *The New York Times* 25 August 2005: C9.

Mateja, Jim. "Ford Helping Heftier People Fasten Their (Longer) Seat Belts." *The Chicago Tribune* 4 July 2006: (S3) 1, 6.

McEwen, William J. "Why Satisfaction Isn't Satisfying." *Gallup Management Journal* November (2004).

McGregor, Jena. "Face-Off." *Fast Company* October 2004: 36.

McNeill, Daniel. *The Face: a Natural History*. Boston: Little, Brown and Company, 1998.

Miller, James P. "A Hint of Restraint." *The Chicago Tribune* 2 July 2006: (S5) 1, 2.

Minneapolis/St. Paul Business Journal 5 August (2005).

Morris, John, et al. "The Power of Affect: Predicting Intention." *Journal of Advertising Research* May/June (2002).

"Most Execs Overpaid, Fund Managers Say." *The Chicago Tribune* 2 July 2006: (S5) 1, 4.

Mullet, Gary. "Data Abuse." *Quirk's* February (2003).

Nelson, Emily, and Sarah Ellison. "In a Shift, Marketers Beef Up Ad Spending Inside Stores." *The Wall Street Journal* 21 September 2005.

Nicholson, Nigel. "How Hardwired Is Human Behavior?" *Harvard Business Review* July-August (1998).

Norman, Donald. *Emotional Design*. New York: Basic Books, 2004.

O'Brien, Timothy. "Spinning Frenzy: P.R.'s Bad Press." *The New York Times* 13 February 2005.

O'Donnell, Jayne. "How Recruiters Catch a Rascal." *USA Today* 26 August 2004: 3B.

Ortony, Andrew, Donald A. Norman and William Revelle. "Effective Functioning: A Three Level Model of Affect, Motivation, Cognition, and Behavior." Unpublished paper provided to author, 2004.

Ortony, Andrew, Gerald R. Clore and Allan Collins. *The Cognitive Structure of Emotions*. Cambridge, UK: Cambridge UP, 1988.

O'Shaughnessy, John. *The Marketing Power of Emotion*. New York: Oxford University Press, 2003.

Owen, Nikki, and Andy Miller. "The Five Most Dangerous Issues Facing Sales Directors Today, and How to Guarantee a Permanent Improvement in Sales Results." Trainique LTD and Think Training Inc. 2004.

Peters, Tom. *Re-Imagine*. London: DK, 2003.

Phillips, Kevin. *American Theocracy*. New York: Viking, 2006.

Pine, Joseph II. "Generating Demand Through Marketing Experiences." Personal Lecture Notes. Carlson School of Management, University of Minnesota. 29 October 2004.

Pine, Joseph II, and James H. Gilmore. *The Experience Economy*. Boston: Harvard Business School Press, 1999.

Pine, Joseph II, and James H. Gilmore. "Welcome to the Experience Economy." *Harvard Business Review* July (1998).

Pink, Daniel. *A Whole New Mind*. New York: Riverhead, 2005.

Pinker, Stephen. *The Blank Slate*. New York: Penguin, 2003.

Plutchik, Robert. *The Emotions*. New York: University Press of America, 1990.

Pooler, Jim. *Why We Shop: Emotional Rewards and Retail Strategies*. Westport, CT: Praeger Publishers, 2003.

Postma, Paul. *The Ultimate Marketing Machine*. Amsterdam: Het Spectrum, 2005.

"Poor Interpersonal Skills Doom Many New Hires." *Expansion Management* November 2005.

"The Professor of Truth." *Oprah Magazine* January 2002: 167.

Quaid, Libby. "Beer Sales Pop." *The St. Paul Pioneer Press* 19 August 2006: C1.

Rackham, Neil. *Major Account Sales Strategy*. New York: McGraw-Hill, 1989.

Raghunathan, Rajagopal, and Michel Pham. "All Negative Moods Are Not Equal: Motivational Influences of Anxiety and Sadness on Decision Making." *Organizational Behavior and Human Decision Processes* 79 (1999): 56-77.

Rapaille, Clotaire. *The Culture Code*. New York: Broadway Books, 2006.

Ravindran, Pratap. "Mergers and Machismo – Are Take Over Chiefs Acting Rationally?" *Business Line* 14 June 2005.

Rawe, Julie. "Why Your Boss May Start Sweating the Small Stuff." *Time* 20 March 2006: 42.

Reichheld, Frederick. "The One Number You Need to Grow." *Harvard Business Review* December (2003).

Reilly, Tom. *Value Added Selling*. New York: McGraw-Hill, 2002.

Reis, Laura, and Al Reis. *The Origin of Brands*. New York: Collins, 2004.

Rigby, Darrell K., Frederick Reichheld and Chris Dawson. "Winning Customer Loyalty Is the Key to a Winning CRM Strategy." *Ivey Business Journal* March/April (2003).

Roseman, Ira, Ann Antoniou, and Paul Jose. "Appraisal Determinants of Emotion: Constructing a More Accurate and Comprehensive Theory." *Cognition and Emotion* 10.3 (1996): 247-277.

Sack, Michael. "Sex, Lies and the Internet." *Quirk's* January (2003).

Schermerhorn, John R., James G. Hunt and Richard N. Osborn. *Organizational Behavior*. 7th edition. New York: Wiley, 1999.

Schmitt, Bernd H. *Experiential Marketing*. New York: Free Press, 1999.

Schwartz, Tony. "How Do You Feel?" *Fast Company* June 2000.

"Secrets of the Male Shopper." *BusinessWeek* 4 September 2006.

Seligman, Martin E. *Authentic Happiness*. New York: Free Press, 2002.

Sharpe, Rochelle. "As Leaders, Women Rule." *BusinessWeek* 20 November 2000.

Shin, Annys. "What Customers Say and How They Say It." *The Washington Post* 18 October 2006.

Silverstein, Michael J., and Neil Fiske. *Trading Up: Why Consumers Want New Luxury Goods – and How Companies Create Them.* New York: Penguin, 2005.

Slywotzky, Adrian, and David J. Morrison. *The Profit Zone.* New York: Three Rivers Press, 2002.

Smith, Craig, and Phoebe Ellsworth. "Patterns of Cognitive Appraisal in Emotion." *Journal of Personality and Social Psychology* 48 (1985): 813-838.

Spillman, Mollie. "Cracking the Engagement Code." *iMediaconnection.com.* 26 July 2006 <http://www.imediaconnection.com/content/10518.asp>.

Steel, Jon. *Truth, Lies & Advertising.* New York: John Wiley & Sons, 1998.

Stevens, Mark. *Your Marketing Sucks.* New York: Three Rivers Press, 2005.

Stock, Howard J. "Getting Emotional About Sales." *Bank Investment Consultant* January (2005): 32-33.

Straits, Don. "Employer Hot Buttons." 2006 <http://careerbuilder.com>. Path: Advice & Resources; Career Advice; Employer Hot Buttons.

Sullivan, Luke. *Hey Whipple, Squeeze This.* New York: John Wiley & Sons, 1998.

Sutherland, Max, and Alice K. Sylvester. *Advertising and the Mind of the Consumer.* Sidney Australia: Allen & Unwin, 2000.

Sway, RoxAnna. "DDI's State of the Industry Report." Atlanta, Georgia 14 October 2005.

Thottam, Jyoti. "Happiness Variance. Thank God It's Monday." *Time* 17 January 2005.

Tiedens, Larissa, and Susan Linton. "Judgment Under Emotional Certainty and Uncertainty: The Effects of Specific Emotions on Information Processing." *Journal of Personality and Social Psychology* 81 (2001): 973-988.

Tierney, John. "Political Points: Of Smiles and Sneers." *The New York Times* 18 July 2004.

Toffler, Alvin. *Future Shock.* New York: Bantam, 1970.

Torday, Daniel. "How to Read Your Wife's Face." *Esquire* April 2003: 90.

Underhill, Paco. *Why We Buy.* New York: Simon & Schuster, 1999.

Wahrman, Harlan, Tom Fusso and Rich Serrins. "Behavioral Economics & Consumer Market Research." LIMRA Marketing Research Conference on Behavioral Economics, May 2003.

Wartik, Nancy. "Hard Wired for Prejudiced? Experts Examine Human Response to Outsiders." *The New York Times* 20 April 2004.

Welch, Jack. *Straight from the Gut.* New York: Warner Books, 2001.

Wellman, David. "Wal-Mart Is Not About Price." *Frozen Food Age* 50.6 (2002).

What the Bleep Do We Know? Dir. William Arntz, Marke Vincente and Betsy Chasse. Perf. Marlee Matlin. 2004. DVD. Lord of the Wind Films.

White, Erin. "For Relevance, Firms Revamp Worker Reviews." *The Wall Street Journal* 17 July 2006: B1, B5.

Wolfe, David, and Robert E. Snyder. *Ageless Marketing.* Chicago: Dearborn, 2003.

"Women Get Paternal Clues In Men's Faces." *WCCO.* 11 May 2006 <http://wcco.com/national/topstories_story_130125914.html>.

"Workers Have Strong Emotional Connection to Their Work Experience, But It's Mostly Negative New Study Finds." *Business Wire* 28 January 2003.

"Workforce Performance Is Top HR Priority." International Association for Human Resource Information Management & Knowledge Fusion. *TD* July (2005): 16.

World Almanac & Book of Facts 2005. New York: World Almanac Books, 2005.

Wundt, Wilhelm. *Outlines of Psychology.* Bristol, UK: Thoemmes Continuum, 1998 edition (1897).

Wright, Robert. *The Moral Animal.* New York: Vintage, 1995.

Zajonc, Robert. "Preferences Need No Inferences." *American Psychologist* February (1980).

Zaltman, Gerald. *How Customers Think.* Boston: Harvard Business Press, 2003.

Zaltman, Gerald. "Metaphorically Speaking," *Marketing Research* 8.2 (1996).

Zaslow, Jeffrey. "Happiness Inc." *The Wall Street Journal* 18 March 2006.

Zeitlin, David M., and Richard A. Westwood. "Measuring Emotional Response." *Journal of Advertising Research* October/November (1986): 34-44.

Zimmermann, Manfred. "Neurophysiology of Sensory System." In *Fundamentals of Sensory Physiology*, ed. Robert F. Schmidt. New York: Springer-Verlag, 1986.

index

credits and permissions

COVER

Jeffrey Coolidge/Iconica/Getty Images

INTRODUCTION

Pg 1, StockXCHNG/Bartlomiej Fulanty; **Pg 2**, Cover of *Blink* by Malcolm Gladwell provided by Little, Brown and Co. (©2005); **Pg 4**, StockXCHNG/Allen Pope; **Pg 5**, StockXCHNG/Florian Martin; **Pg 7**, StockXCHNG/Paul Williamson; **Pg 9**, Provided by Whirlpool Corporation; **Pg 10**, StockXCHNG/Steve Knight

CHAPTER 1

Pg 13, istock photo; **Pg 20**, Courtesy of *Defending the Caveman*; **Pg 23**, Library of Congress, Prints & Photographs Division, NYWT&S Collection, [Reproduction Number: LC-USZ62-126207]; **Pg 24**, StockXCHNG/Irvin Shahid; **Pg 27** (Figure 1.3), StockXCHNG/Anna H.G.; **Pg 29**, StockXCHNG/Hannah Boettcher; **Pg 30**, Provided by Princeton University; **Pg 32**, StockXCHNG/Luciano Tirabassi

CHAPTER 2

Pg 39, StockXCHNG; **Pg 40**, StockXCHNG/Sanja Gjenero; **Pg 41**, Stock/XCHNG/John Evans; **Pg 44**, StockXCHNG/Katherine de Vera; **Pg 48**, StockXCHNG/Emilia Stasiak; **Pg 57**, StockXCHNG/Henry Smaal; **Pg 60**, Courtesy of Reallear, LLC; **Pg 67**, StockXCHNG/Joshua Petyt

CHAPTER 3

Pg 71, StockXCHNG/Charles Sotello; **Pg 73**, StockXCHNG/Tim Van Damme; **Pg 74**, StockXCHNG/Martin K.; **Pg 80**, StockXCHNG/Benjamin Earwicker; **Pg 82**, StockXCHNG/Boris Gaasbeek; **Pg 88**, (a) StockXCHNG/Maurice Beer, (b) StockXCHNG/Stuart Bell; **Pg 89**, Courtesy of Dogfish Head Brewery

CHAPTER 4

Pg 90, istock photo; **Pg 93**, Stock XCHNG/Marcin Bertowski; **Pg 97** (Figure 4.2), StockXCHNG/Mike Johnson; **Pg 100**, StockXCHNG/Brian S.; **Pg 101** (Figure 4.4), Center for Strategic and International Studies, *Asian Values and the United States: How Much Conflict*, Hitchcock, David I., 1994, pg. 54; **Pg 105**, StockXCHNG/Tom De Bruin; **Pg 110** (Figure 4.10), Book by StockXCHNG/Robert Aichinger, model by StockXCHNG/Afonso Lima; **Pg 111**, Courtesy of Pinnacle Foods; **Pg 116**, StockXCHNG/Leo Cinezi

CHAPTER 5

Pg 123, StockXCHNG/Patrick Nejhuis; **Pg 125**, StockXCHNG/Michele Lukowski; **Pg 126**, StockXCHNG/Michal Zacharzowski; **Pg 128 (a)**, StockXCHNG/ Brian S.; **Pg 128 (b)**, Courtesy of IKEA UK; **Pg 130** (Figure 5.1), Courtesy of BMW USA; **Pg 131** (Figure 5.2), Courtesy of MGA Entertainment; **Pg 132 (a)**, Courtesy of Whirlpool Corporation; **Pg 132 (b)**, StockXCHNG/Edward Wahab; **Pg 135**, Courtesy of ING; **Pg 137**, (a) StockXCHNG/Jess Rafin, (b) StockXCHNG/Rurik Tullio; **Pg 141**, Stock/XCHNG/Audrey Johnson

CHAPTER 6

Pg 149, StockXCHNG/Evgenij Fursai; **Pg 150**, StockXCHNG/Arjun Chennu; **Pg 152**, StockXCHNG/Carlos Zaragosa; **Pg 154**, StockXCHNG/Richard Simpson; **Pg 155**, StockXCHNG/Davide Gulielmo; **Pg 166**, StockXCHNG/Sanja Gjenero; **Pg 170**, StockXCHNG/Cecilia Alegro; **Pg 172**, StockXCHNG/Diego Midrano; **Pg 175**, StockXCHNG/Sanja Gjenero

CHAPTER 7

Pg 181, StockXCHNG/Mark Brennan; **Pg 183**, StockXCHNG/Cathy Kaplan; **Pg 185**, StockXCHNG/Maryann Cummings; **Pg 187**, StockXCHNG/John Moore; **Pg 195** (Figure 7.5), From *Major Account Sales Strategy* by Neil Rackham, used with permission of Hutwaite (©1989); **Pg 195** (Figure 7.6), **(a)** StockXCHNG/Ramon Gonzales, **(b)** StockXCHNG/Christy Thompson; **Pg 197**, Courtesy of The SCOOTER Store; **Pg 199**, StockXCHNG/J.W.M. Pap; **Pg 200**, Melodi T.; **Pg 201** (Figure 7.8), From *Major Account Sales Strategy* by Neil Rackham, used with permission of Hutwaite (©1989); **Pg 205**, StockXCHNG/Tory Byrne; **Pg 206** (Figure 7.10), Reproduced with the permission of Nikki Owen, author of *The Five Most Dangerous Trends Facing Sales Directors Today*; **Pg 207** (Figure 7.11), From *Major Account Sales Strategy* by Neil Rackham, used with permission of Hutwaite (©1989)

CHAPTER 8

Pg 216, StockXCHNG/Martin Luckner; **Pg 220**, StockXCHNG/Santiago Cornejo; **Pg 222**, StockXCHNG/Rodolfo Clix; **Pg 223**, StockXCHNG/Michele Lukowski; **Pg 226**, StockXCHNG/Andreas Van de Berg; **Pg 227**, StockXCHNG/Phil Feer; **Pg 229**, StockXCHNG/Elena Buetler; **Pg 230**, StockXCHNG/Eduardo Oride; **Pg 231**, StockXCHNG/Constantin Kammerer

CHAPTER 9

Pg 234, istock photo; **Pg 235**, istock photo; **Pg 237**, StockXCHNG/Mike Esprit; **Pg 241**, Cover of *Straight from the Gut* by Jack Welch care of Little, Brown and Co.; **Pg 248**, StockXCHNG/Constantin Kammerer; **Pg 250**, StockXCHNG/Simon Stratford; **Pg 251**, StockXCHNG/With kind permission of www.tomtown.net / Eveline Holland; **Pg 254**, StockXCHNG/Kristen Price; **Pg 258**, StockXCHNG/Constantin Kammerer; **Pg 260**, StockXCHNG/Constantin Kammerer, StockXCHNG/Kathryn Mcallum and StockXCHNG/Carl Dwyer

CHAPTER 10

Pg 265, StockXCHNG/Niclas Ericsson; **Pg 268**, StockXCHNG/Constantin Krammerer; **Pg 269**, StockXCHNG/Elena Buetler; **Pg 270**, StockXCHNG/Balogh Cron; **Pg 273**, StockXCHNG/Ahmed Al-Shukaili; **Pg 278 (a)** StockXCHNG/unknown, **(b)** StockXCHNG/Constantin Krammerer, **(c)** StockXCHNG/Isaac Joo

*All other images are property of Sensory Logic, Inc. or StockXCHNG.

acknowledgements

When I started on this book two years ago, I never expected it would be this much work. Many drafts later, I owe a tremendous debt of gratitude to all of the people who have compelled me to keep revising so that the book could best achieve its potential.

Three people in particular deserve my heartfelt thanks. The first is my dear friend, Joe Rich, whose insights, humor and profound caring helped me get to the human dimension of the business issues discussed here. Conversations with Joe aided me greatly in developing the content. Second is my fiancée, Karen Bernthal, who not only read and re-read chapters, offering wise advice, but she also had patience as weekends and evenings went into this project. The third person is Andrew Langdell, who helped hone my prose and whose creative wit can be found in the visuals that so enhance this book. *Emotionomics* wouldn't exist without his talents and effort.

Readers and editors have emerged from numerous parts of my life. They include: Judy Bell, Arlene Carroll, Jeff Christiansen, Joe Dylla, Eldon Hill, Holly Johnson, Jennifer Manion, Jack Murphy, Kim Saxton, Paul Schuster and Kathy Seamon.

Thanks also goes to my book designer, Jay Monroe of Soulo Communications, and to Milt Adams of Beaver's Pond Press for having the vision and generosity of spirit to create a viable alternative to how the publishing industry is normally run. Without Milt, this book wouldn't have been possible.

Finally, I appreciate the valuable input of staffers not already cited: people like Dominique DuCharme, Luke Elstad, Rhonda Farran, Nik Hengel, Todd Kringlie, Kim Wanten and others who have kept Sensory Logic moving along while I was distracted by getting this book finished.

To one and all, thank you.

St. Paul, MN
December 2006

about the author

Photo by David Brewster

Dan Hill, Ph.D., is President of Sensory Logic and a recognized authority on the role of emotions in consumer and employee behavior. His blue-chip clients have included Target, Toyota, GlaxoSmithKline, Allstate, and Kellogg among many others. Dan has been featured in *The Wall Street Journal*, *The New York Times*, *China Forbes*, *Business 2.0* and *Fast Company* and has appeared on Discover and NPR's Marketplace. A popular speaker internationally, Dan has presented to corporations, conferences, associations and universities and can be reached at dhill@sensorylogic.com.

To learn more about Sensory Logic, a scientific research-based consultancy that also trains CEOs, salespeople, lawyers and others on emotional expression and rapport, go to:

www.sensorylogic.com